THE
McSWEENEY'S
ANTHOLOGY
of
CONTEMPORARY
LITERATURE

THE McSWEENEY'S ANTHOLOGY

of

CONTEMPORARY LITERATURE

Seventy-Fourth Edition

McSWEENEY'S • *San Francisco* • *California*

LUNCH BOX ART: Art Spiegelman.

COVER ART: *The Song of the Shirt* (ca. 1849), by John T. Peele (1822–1897).

*This project is supported in part by the National Endowment for the Arts.
To find out more about how National Endowment for the Arts grants
impact individuals and communities, visit www.arts.gov.*

Printed in China.

INTRODUCTION

by CLAIRE BOYLE

THIS ANTHOLOGY, WHICH HELPS celebrate the twenty-fifth anniversary of *McSweeney's Quarterly Concern*, gathers some of the best stories we've published in the last ten years. We've put out a few anthologies like this before. They've been non-exhaustive, somewhat arbitrarily timed, and separated by yawning years of silence between them. This most recent ten-year stretch of dormancy is by far the longest.

I mention all this ramshackleness only to illustrate our ambivalence when it comes to anthologizing the work we publish. It feels so authoritative, so final. The reality, of course, is that these are only *our* top stories. Yours very well may be different. In fact, they almost certainly are.

That's something that has always startled and delighted me: so often, upon releasing an issue, I'm *sure* one particular story will be the standout, but instead we'll hear fourteen different readers name fourteen different stories as their favorite in the collection. It's a good reminder, generally, about the subjectivity of fiction—or, for that matter, of people, or ideas, or anything good and worth our time.

Dave once told me, not long after I started editing the magazine, that there should be something in each issue for everyone. This idea was so liberating: not everything had to appeal to everyone—how could it?—but instead we had succeeded if each reader who encountered the issue found in it something (a story, a description, a character) that resonated with them. Like Arnold Schoenberg said, "If it is art, it is not for all, and if it is for all, it is not art."

Despite this, or maybe due to it, we find it a meaningful project to put these anthologies together. Issues of the *Quarterly* come and go so quickly—every three months when the ship is really sailing—that to step back occasionally and reflect on all this work, all that these authors have shared with us, is a special opportunity.

While pulling these fourteen stories from my time editing *McSweeney's Quarterly Concern*, which spanned issues 49 through 69, I reflected on what characterizes the stories we've been attracted to over the years. I think, overall, we've tended to look for work that uncovers strangeness in the world and handles it with vulnerability. It's this kind of writing—both venturesome and deeply felt—that's able to catch you most off-guard, and ultimately, when done right, break your heart. We look for work that is not purely in the head. Work that cuts to the quick, without ego or showiness. Work that plays with language in surprising and honest ways.

More than anything, though, the work that has excited us has looked immensely different from story to story: it's hyperrealistic in one piece and surreal in the next. Slapstick here and somber there. It spans fifty pages or just a paragraph. You can find these qualities of a good story in any form, in any genre, from any writer.

Perhaps, if we were to revisit these issues in another ten years, we'd choose a whole new batch of stories. These sixteen are just a representation of all we've loved and felt so honored to publish. Each one has stuck with us, and we're so glad to get to share them with you, here under one roof.

SKINNED

by LESLEY NNEKA ARIMAH

(This story, from McSweeney's 53, *was the winner of
the 2019 Caine Prize for African Writing and a winner
of the 2019 National Magazine Award in Fiction.)*

THE UNCLOTHED WOMAN HAD a neatly trimmed bush, waxed to resemble a setting sun. The clothed women sneered as she laid out makeup and lotion samples, touting their benefits. "Soft, smooth skin, as you can see," she said, winking—trying, and failing, to make a joke of her nakedness. Chidinma smiled in encouragement, nodding and examining everything Ejem pulled out of the box. Having invited Ejem to present her wares, she would be getting a free product out of this even if none of her guests made a purchase.

Ejem finished her sales pitch with a line about how a woman's skin is her most important feature and she has to take care of it like a treasured accessory. The covered women tittered and smoothed their tastefully patterned wife-cloth over their limbs. They wore them simply, draped and belted into long, graceful dresses, allowing the fabric to speak for itself. They eyed Ejem's nakedness with gleeful pity.

"I just couldn't be uncovered at your age. That's a thing for the younger set, don't you think?"

"I have a friend who's looking for a wife; maybe I can introduce you. He's not picky."

Ejem rolled her eyes, less out of annoyance than to keep tears at bay. Was this going to happen every time? She looked to Chidinma for help.

"Well, I for one am here for lotions, not to discuss covered versus uncovered, so I'd like this one." Chidinma held up the most expensive cream. Ejem made a show of ringing it up, and the other women were embarrassed into making purchases of their own. They stopped speaking to Ejem directly and began to treat her as if she were a woman of the osu caste. They addressed product questions to the air or to Chidinma, and listened but did not acknowledge Ejem when she replied. Ejem might have protested, as would have Chidinma, but they needed the sales party to end before Chidinma's husband returned. It was the only stipulation Chidinma had made when she'd agreed to host. It was, in fact, the only stipulation of their friendship. *Don't advertise your availability to my husband.* Chidinma always tried to make a joking compliment of it—"You haven't had any kids yet, so your body is still amazing"—but there was always something strained there, growing more strained over the years as Ejem remained unclaimed.

The woman who had first addressed Chidinma instead of Ejem, whom Ejem had begun to think of as the ringleader, noticed them glancing at the clock, gave a sly smile, and requested that each and every product be explained to her. Ejem tried, she really did, whipping through the product texts with speed, but the clock sped just as quickly and eventually Chidinma stopped helping her, subdued by inevitable embarrassment. Before long, Chidinma's husband returned from work.

Chance was all right, as husbands went. He oversaw the management of a few branches of a popular bank, a job that allowed them to live comfortably in their large house with an osu woman to spare Chidinma serious housework. He could even be considered somewhat progressive; after all, he had permitted his wife's continued association with her unclothed friend, and he wasn't the sort to harass an osu woman in his employ. True, he insisted on a formal greeting, but after Chidinma had bowed to him she raised herself to her tiptoes for a kiss and Chance indulged her, fisting his hands in the wife-cloth at the small of her back.

But he was still a man, and when he turned to greet the women his eyes caught on Ejem and stayed there, taking in the brown discs of her areolae, the cropped design of hair between her legs, whatever parts of her went unhidden in her seated position. No one said anything, the utter impropriety of an unclaimed woman being in the house of a married man almost too delicious a social faux pas to interrupt. But as Chidinma grew visibly distressed, the ringleader called the room to order and the women rose to leave, bowing their heads to Chance, giving Chidinma's hands encouraging little squeezes. No doubt the tale would make the rounds—"the way he *stared* at her"— and Chidinma wouldn't be able to escape it for a while. The women walked by Ejem without a word, the message clear: Ejem was beneath them.

Chidinma tried to distract her husband by asking about his day. Chance continued to stare at Ejem while he answered. Ejem wanted to move faster, to get out as quick as she could, but she was conscious of every sway of her breasts, every brush of her thighs as she hurried. Chance spoke to Ejem only as she was leaving, a goodbye she returned with a small curtsy. Chidinma walked her to the door.

"Ejem, we should take a break from each other, I think," she said with a pained air of finality, signaling that this break wasn't likely to be a temporary one.

"Why?"

"You know why."

"You're going to have to say it, Chidinma."

"Fine. This whole thing, this friendship, was fine when we were both uncovered girls doing whatever, but covered women can't have uncovered friends. I thought it was nonsense at first, but it's true. I'm sorry."

"You've been covered for thirteen years and this has never been a problem."

"And I thought by this time you'd be covered too. You came so close with that one fellow, but you've never really tried. It's unseemly."

"He's only seen me this once since you made it clear—"

"Once was enough. Get covered. Get claimed. Take yourself off the market. Until then, I'm sorry, but no."

Chidinma went back inside the house before Ejem could respond. And what could she say anyway? *I'm not sure I ever want to be claimed?* Chidinma would think her mad.

Ejem positioned her box to better cover her breasts and walked to the bus stop. Chidinma hadn't offered her a ride home, even though she knew how much Ejem hated public transportation— the staring as she lay the absorbent little towel square on her seat, the paranoia of imagining every other second what to do if her menstrual cup leaked.

At the stop, a group of young men waited. They stopped talking when they saw Ejem, then resumed, their conversation now centered on her.

"How old you think she is?"

"Dude, old."

"I don't know, man. Let's see her breasts. She should put that box down."

They waited and Ejem ignored them, keeping as much of herself as possible shielded with the box and the cosmetic company's branded tote.

"That's why she's unclaimed. Rudeness. Who's gonna want to claim that?"

They continued in that vein until the bus arrived. Even though the men were to board first, they motioned her ahead, a politeness that masked their desire for a better view. She scanned the passengers for other uncovered women—solidarity and all that—and was relieved to spot one. The relief quickly evaporated. The woman was beautiful, which would have stung on its own, but she was young, too, smooth-skinned and firm. Ejem stopped existing for the group of young men. They swarmed the woman, commenting loudly on the indentation of her waist, the solid curve of her arm.

The young woman took it all in stride, scrolling a finger down the pages of her book.

Ejem felt at once grateful and slighted, remembering how it had been in her youth, before her waist had thickened and her ass drooped. She'd never been the sort to wear nakedness boldly, but she'd at least felt that she was pleasant to look at.

The bus took on more passengers and was three-quarters full when an osu woman boarded. Ejem caught herself doing a double take before averting her gaze. It wasn't against the law; it just wasn't done, since the osu had their own transport, and the other passengers looked away as well. Embarrassed. Annoyed. Even the bus driver kept his eyes forward as the woman counted out her fare. And when she finally appeared in the center aisle, no one made the polite shift all passengers on public transportation know, that nonverbal invitation to take a neighboring seat. So even though there were several spots available, the osu woman remained standing. Better that than climb her naked body over another to sit down. It was the type of subtle social correction, Ejem thought, that would cause a person to behave better in the future.

But as the ride progressed, the osu woman squeezing to let by passengers who didn't even acknowledge her, Ejem softened. She was so close to becoming an unseen woman herself, unanchored from the life and the people she knew, rendered invisible. It was only by the grace of birth that she wasn't osu, her mother had said to her the very last time they spoke. "At least you have a choice, Ejem. So choose wisely." She hadn't, had walked away from a man and his proposal and the protection it offered. Her parents had cut her off then, furious and confounded that she'd bucked tradition. She couldn't explain, not even to herself, why she'd looked at the cloth he proffered and seen a weight that would smother her.

At her stop, Ejem disembarked, box held to her chest. With the exception of a few cursory glances, no one paid attention to her. It was one of the reasons she liked the city, everybody's inclination to mind their own business. She picked up the pace when she spotted the burgundy awning of her apartment building. In the elevator, an older male tenant examined her out of the corner of his eye. Ejem backed up until he would have had to turn around to continue looking. One could never tell if a man was linked or not, and she hated being inspected by men who'd already claimed wives.

In her apartment she took a long, deep breath, the type she didn't dare take in public lest she draw unwanted attention. Only then did she allow herself to contemplate the loss of Chidinma's friendship, and weep.

When they were girls, still under their fathers' covering, she and Chidinma had become fast friends. They were both new to their school and their covers were so similar in pattern they were almost interchangeable. Ejem remembered their girlhood fondly, the protection of their fathers' cloth, the seemingly absolute security of it. She had cried when, at fifteen, her mother had come into her bedroom and, stroking her hair, told Ejem that it was time to remove her cloth. The only people who could get away with keeping their daughters covered for long were the wealthy, who often managed it until the girls could secure wife-cloth. But Ejem's father had grown up a poor man in a village where girls were disrobed as early as possible, some even at age ten, and it was beyond time as far as he was concerned. He knew what happened to the families of girls who stayed covered beyond their station, with the exception of girls bearing such deformities that they were permitted "community cloth" made from donated scraps.

But if a girl like Ejem continued to be clothed, the town council would levy a tax that would double again and again until her father could not pay it. Then his girl would be disrobed in public, and her family shamed. No, he couldn't bear the humiliation. Things would happen on his terms.

The day Ejem was disrobed was also the day her father stopped interacting with her, avoiding the impropriety of a grown man talking to a naked girl. Ejem hadn't wanted to go to school or market or anywhere out of the house where people could see her. Chidinma, still under her father-cloth, told her (horrified, well-off) parents that she, too, felt ready to disrobe so that she and Ejem could face the world together, two naked foundlings.

Chidinma's parents had tried to spin it as piousness, a daughter disrobed earlier than she had to be because she was so dedicated to tradition. But it'd had the stink of fanaticism and they'd lost many friends, something for which, Chidinma confided, her parents had never forgiven her.

A part of Ejem had always believed they'd be claimed at the same time, but then Chidinma had secured a wife-cloth at twenty, with Ejem as her chief maid. And then Chidinma gave birth to a boy, then two girls, who would remain covered their entire lives if Chidinma had anything to say about it. And through it all, Ejem remained uncovered, unclaimed, drifting until the likelihood passed her by.

She downed a mug of wine in one huge gulp, then another, before sifting through yesterday's mail. She opened the envelope she'd been avoiding: the notice of her upcoming lease renewal, complete with a bump in monthly rent. With the money she'd earned today, she had enough to cover the next two months. But the raised rent put everything in jeopardy, and Chidinma's abandonment meant Ejem could no longer sell to her wealthy set. If she couldn't secure income some other way, a move to a smaller town would soon be a necessity.

When she'd first leased the apartment, Ejem had been working at the corporate headquarters of an architecture firm. Though her nakedness drew some attention, there were other unclaimed women, and Ejem, being very good at what she did, advanced. Just shy of a decade later, she was over thirty, the only woman in upper management, and still uncovered.

Three months ago, Ejem was delivering a presentation to a prospective client. As usual, she was the only woman in the room. The client paid no attention to her PowerPoint, focusing instead on what he considered to be the impropriety of an unclaimed woman distracting from business matters. Ejem was used to this and tried to steer the conversation back to the budget. When the man ignored her, none of her coworkers bothered to censure him, choosing instead to snicker into their paperwork. She walked out of the room.

Ejem had never gone to human resources before; she'd always sucked it up. The HR manager, a covered woman who was well into her fifties, listened to her with a bored expression, then, with a pointed look at Ejem's exposed breasts, said, "You can't seriously expect a group of men to pay attention to pie charts or whatever when there is an available woman in the room. Maybe if you were covered this wouldn't happen. Until you are, we can no longer put you in front of clients."

Ejem walked out of the building and never returned. She locked herself away at home until Chidinma came knocking with a bottle of vodka, her youngest girl on her hip, and a flyer for home-based work selling makeup.

Now that lifeline was gone, and it would be only a matter of time until Ejem exhausted her savings. She switched on the TV, and flipped channels until she reached an uncovered young woman relating the news. The woman reported on a building fire in Onitsha and Ejem prepared dinner with the broadcast playing in the background, chopping vegetables for stir-fry until she registered the phrase "unclaimed women" repeated several times. She turned up the volume.

The newscaster had been joined by an older man with a paternal air, who gave more details.

"The building was rumored to be a haven of sorts for unclaimed women, who lived there, evading their responsibilities as cloth makers. Authorities halted firefighters from putting out the blaze, hoping to encourage these lost women to return to proper life. At least three bodies were discovered in the ashes. Their identities have yet to be confirmed."

That was the other reason Ejem wanted to remain in the metro area. Small towns were less tolerant of unclaimed women, some going so far as to outlaw their presence unless they were menials of the osu caste. They had a certain freedom, Ejem thought—these osu women who performed domestic tasks, the osu men who labored in the mines or constructed the buildings she'd once designed— though her envy was checked by the knowledge that it was a freedom born of irrelevance. The only place for unclaimed women, however, as far as most were concerned, was the giant factories, where they would weave cloth for women more fortunate than they.

The town's mayor appeared at a press conference.

"This is a decent town with decent people. If folks want to walk around uncovered and unclaimed, they need to go somewhere else. I'm sorry about the property loss and the folks who couldn't get out, but this is a family town. We have one of the world's finest factories bordering us. They could have gone there." The screen flipped back to the newsman, who nodded sagely, his expression somehow affirming the enforcement of moral values even as it deplored the loss of life.

Ejem battled a bubble of panic. How long before her finances forced her out into the hinterlands, where she would have to join the cloth makers? She needed a job and she needed it fast.

What sorts of jobs could one do naked? Ejem was too old for anything entry-level, where she'd be surrounded day after day by twentysomethings who would be claimed quickly. Instead, she looked for jobs where her nudity would be less of an issue. She lasted at a nursing home for five weeks, until a visiting relative objected to her presence. At the coffee shop she made it two and a half hours until she had to hide in the back to avoid a former coworker. She quit the next day. Everywhere she went heightened how sheltered she'd been at her corporate job. The farther from the center of town she searched, the more people stared at her openly, asking outright why she wasn't covered when they saw that she didn't bear the mark of an osu woman. Every once in a while Ejem encountered osu women forced outside by errands, branded by shaved heads with scarification scored above one ear. Other pedestrians avoided them as though they were poles or mailboxes or other such sidewalk paraphernalia. But Ejem saw them.

As her search became more desperate, every slight took a knife's edge, so that Ejem found herself bothered even by the young girls still covered in their father-cloth who snickered at her, unaware or not caring that they, too, would soon be stripped of protection. The worst were the pitying *Oh, honey* looks, the whispered assurances from older covered women that someone would eventually claim her.

After a while, she found work giving massages at a spa. She enjoyed being where everyone was disrobed; the artificial equality was a balm. Her second week on the job, a woman walked in covered with one of the finest wife-cloths Ejem had ever seen. She ordered the deluxe package, consisting of every single service the spa offered.

"And may I have your husband's account number?"

"*My* account number," the woman emphasized, sliding her card across the counter.

The desk girl glared at the card, glared at the woman, then left to get the manager. Everyone in the waiting room stared.

The manager, a woman close to Ejem's age, sailed in, her haughty manner turning deferential and apologetic as soon as she caught sight of the client. "I'm so sorry. The girl is new, still in father-cloth. Please excuse her." The finely clothed one remained silent. "We will, of course, offer you a significant discount on your services today. Maria is ready to start on your massage right away."

"No," the woman said firmly. "I want her to do it." Ejem, who'd been pretending to straighten products on the shelves, turned to see the woman pointing at her.

Soon she was in one of the treatment rooms, helping the woman to disrobe, feeling the texture of the cloth, wanting to rub it against her cheek. She left to hang it and encountered the manager, who dragged her down the hall and spoke in a harsh whisper.

"Do you know who that is? That is Odinaka, *the* Odinaka. If she leaves here less than pleased, you will be fired. I hope I'm clear."

Ejem nodded, returning to the massage room in a nervous

daze. Odinaka was one of a handful of independently wealthy women who flouted convention without consequences. She was unclaimed, but covered herself anyway, and not in modest cloth, either, but in fine, bold fabric that invited attention and scrutiny. She owned almost half the cloth factories across the globe. This unthinkable rebellion drew criticism, but her wealth ensured that it remained just that: words but no action.

Odinaka sat on the massage table, swinging her legs. At Ejem's direction, she lay on her stomach while Ejem warmed oil between her hands. She coated Odinaka's ankles before sliding up to her calves, warming the tissue with her palms. She asked a few casual questions, trying to gauge whether she was a talker or preferred her massages silent. She needn't have worried. Not only did Odinaka give verbose replies, she had questions for Ejem herself. Before long, she had pried from Ejem the story of how she'd come to be here, easing muscle tensions instead of pursuing a promising career as an architect.

"It doesn't seem fair, does it, that you have to remain uncovered?"

Ejem continued with the massage, unsure how to reply to such seditious sentiments.

"You know, you and I are very similar," Odinaka continued.

Ejem studied the woman's firm body, toned and slim from years of exercise. She considered the other ways in which they were different, not least that Odinaka had never had to worry about a bill in her life. She laughed.

"You are very kind, but we're nothing alike, though we may be of the same age," she responded, as lightly as she could, tilting the ending into a question. Odinaka ignored it, turning over to face her.

"I mean it; we are both ambitious women trying to make our way unclaimed in male-dominated fields."

Except, Ejem didn't say, *you are completely free in a way I am not, as covered as you wish to be.*

"Covering myself would be illegal—" she started.

"Illegal-smeagle. When you have as much money as I do, you exist above every law. Now, wouldn't you like to be covered too?"

Odinaka was her savior. She whisked Ejem away from her old apartment, helping her pay the fee to break her lease, and moved her into a building she owned in one of the city's nicest neighborhoods.

Ejem's quarters, a two-bedroom apartment complete with a generously sized kitchen, had the freshness of a deep clean, like it had been long vacant, or had gone through a recent purge, stripped of the scent and personality of its previous occupant. The unit had a direct intercom to the osu women who took care of the place. Ejem was to make cleaning requests as needed, or requests for groceries that later appeared in her fridge. When Ejem mentioned the distance from the apartment to her job, Odinaka revealed that she didn't have to work if she didn't want to, and it was an easy choice not to return to the spa. The free time enabled her to better get to know the other women in the building.

There was Delilah, who seemed like a miniature Odinaka in dress and mannerisms, but in possession of only half as much confidence. Doreen, a woman close to forty, became Ejem's favorite. She owned a bookstore—one that did well as far as bookstores went—and she had the air of someone who knew exactly who she was and liked it. She eschewed the option to self-clothe.

"Let them stare," Doreen would declare after a few glasses of wine. "This body is a work of art." She would lift her breasts with her hands, sending Ejem and the other women into tipsy giggles.

The remaining women—Morayo, Mukaso, and Maryam— were polite but distant, performing enough social niceties to sidestep any allegations of rudeness, but only just. Ejem and Doreen called them the three M's or, after a few drinks, "Mmm, no," for their recalcitrance. They sometimes joined in Odinaka's near-nightly cocktail hour, but within a few weeks the cadre solidified into Odinaka, Delilah, Doreen, and Ejem.

With this group of women, there were no snide remarks about Ejem's nakedness, no disingenuous offers to introduce her to a man—any man—who could maybe look past her flaws. Odinaka talked about her vast business, Doreen about her small one, and they teased each other with terrible advice neither would ever take. Ejem talked some about the career she'd left behind, but didn't have much to add. And for the first time, her shyness was just shyness, not evidence of why she remained unclaimed, nor an invitation to be battered with advice on how she could improve herself.

Besides, Odinaka talked enough for everyone, interrupting often and dominating every topic. Ejem didn't mind, because of all of them, Odinaka had had the most interesting life, one of unrelenting luxury since birth. She'd inherited the weaving company from her father when he retired, almost a decade ago, which had caused an uproar. But if one of the wealthiest dynasties wanted a woman at the helm, it was a luxury they could purchase. And if that woman indulged in covering herself and collecting and caring for other unclaimed women, who had the power to stop her?

"I imagine creating a world," Odinaka often said, "where disrobing is something a woman does only by choice."

On Ejem's first night in the building, Odinaka had brought a length of cloth to her, a gift, she said, that Ejem could wear whenever she wanted. Ejem had stared at the fabric for hours. Even in the confines of the building, in her own unit, she didn't have the courage to put it on. At Odinaka's cocktail hour, Doreen would sit next to her and declare, "It's us against these bashful fuckers, Ejem," setting off an evening of gentle ribbing at everyone's expense.

"You really go to your store like that?" Ejem asked Doreen one afternoon. "Why don't you cover yourself? No one will say anything if they know you're one of Odinaka's women, right?" She was trying to convince herself that she, too, could don the cloth and go out in public without fear.

Doreen stopped perusing invoices to give Ejem all her attention. "Look, we have to live with this. I was disrobed at age ten. Do you know what it feels like to be exposed so young? I hid for almost a decade before I found myself, my pride. No one will ever again make me feel uncomfortable in my own skin. I plan to remain unclaimed and uncovered for as long as I live, and no one can say a damn thing about it. Odinaka rebels in her own way, and I in mine. I don't yearn for the safety of cloth. If the law requires me to be naked, I will be naked. And I will be goddamned if they make me feel uncomfortable for their law."

The weeks of welcome, of feeling free to be her own person, took hold and, one night, when Ejem joined the other women in Odinaka's apartment, she did so covered, the cloth draped over her in a girl's ties, the only way she knew how. Doreen was the first one to congratulate her, and when she hugged Ejem, she whispered, "Rebel in your own way," but her smile was a little sad.

Odinaka crowed in delight, "Another one! We should have a party."

She mobilized quickly, dispensing orders to her osu women via intercom. Ejem had yet to see any of the osu at work, but whenever she returned to her quarters from Odinaka's or Doreen's, her bed was made, the bathroom mirror cleared of flecks, the scabs of toothpaste scrubbed from the sink, and the rooms themselves held an indefinable feeling of having only just been vacated.

In less than the hour it took Ejem and the other residents to get themselves ready for the party, Odinaka's quarters had become packed. Men and women, all clothed except Doreen, mingled and chatted. Doreen held court on the settee, sipping wine and bestowing coy smiles.

Ejem tried to join in, but even with the self-cloth, she couldn't help feeling like the uncovered woman she'd been her entire adult life. Odinaka tried to draw Ejem into her circle of conversation, but after Ejem managed only a few stilted rejoinders, she edged away, sparing herself further embarrassment. Ejem ended up in a corner watching the festivities.

She was not aware that she herself was being watched until a man she'd seen bowing theatrically to Odinaka leaned against the wall next to her.

"So, you're the newest one, huh?"

"I suppose I am."

"You seem reasonable enough. Why are you unclaimed?"

Ejem tensed, wary.

"What's that supposed to mean, 'reasonable'?"

He ignored the question.

"Do you know I have been trying to claim that woman ever since she was a girl?" He nodded toward Odinaka. "Our union would have been legendary. The greatest cloth weaver with the greatest cotton grower. What do you think?"

Ejem shrugged. It was really none of her business.

"Instead she's busy collecting debris."

Stunned by his rudeness, Ejem turned away, but he only laughed and called to someone across the room. Suddenly, every laugh seemed directed at her, every smile a smirk at her expense. She felt herself regressing into the girl who'd needed Chidinma's tight grip in hers before she could walk with her head high. She ducked out, intending to return to her quarters.

She ran into Delilah, who held a carved box under her arm, a prized family heirloom Ejem recognized from their many gatherings. It was one of the few objects Odinaka envied, as she could not secure one herself, unable to determine the origin of the antique. She was forever demanding that Delilah bring it out to be admired, though Delilah refused to let Odinaka have it examined or appraised, perfectly content to let her treasure remain a mystery.

Ejem didn't particularly like Delilah. She might have been a mini Odinaka, but unlike Odinaka, Delilah was pretentious and wore her fine breeding on her sleeve. Ejem's distress was visible enough that Delilah paused, glancing between her and the door that muted the soiree.

"Is everything okay?" she asked.

Ejem nodded, but a tight nod that said it was not. She watched Delilah's concern war with the promise of fun on the other side of the door. Delilah's movements, a particular twist in her shoulders, the way she clenched her fist, an angled tilt of her head, suddenly brought to Ejem's mind the osu woman on the bus. Something must have crossed her face because Delilah lifted a furtive, self-conscious hand to pat her hair into place—right where an identifying scar would have been if a government midwife had scored it into her head when she was six months old, and then refreshed it on return visits every two years until she turned eighteen. That practice was the extent of Ejem's osu knowledge. Her people lived side by side with the osu and they knew nothing of each other.

Looking at Delilah's box, it occurred to Ejem that an osu girl—if she were clever enough, audacious enough, in possession of impossibly thick hair—could take her most prized possession—say, a fine carved box that had been in the family for many generations—and sneak away in the middle of the night. She could travel farther than she had ever been in her life, to a city where no one knew her. And because she was clever, she could slip seamlessly into the world of the people she knew so well because she'd had to serve them all her life.

Before the thought could take hold, the uncertainty in Delilah's face was replaced by an artificial sweetness, and she patted Ejem's shoulder, saying, "Rest well, then," before escaping into the party.

Ejem was awoken at dawn by the last of the revelers leaving. She stayed in her apartment till eight, then took advantage of Odinaka's open-door policy to enter her benefactor's apartment. If she hadn't been there herself, she would never have believed it had been filled with partiers the night before. In three hours, someone, or several someones, had transformed the wreckage of fifty guests—Ejem remembered at least two spilled wineglasses and a short man who'd insisted on making a speech from an end table—back into the clean, modern lines preferred by one of the wealthiest women in the world. A woman who apparently collected debris, like her. She wasn't exactly sure what she wanted to say to Odinaka—she couldn't childishly complain that one of the guests had insulted her—but she felt injured and sought some small soothing.

She found Odinaka lounging in her bed, covers pulled to her waist.

"Did you enjoy yourself, Ejem? I saw you talking to Aju. He just left, you know." She wiggled her brows.

Well. Ejem couldn't exactly condemn him now. "We had an interesting conversation," she said instead.

"'Interesting,' she says. I know he can be difficult. Never mind what he said."

Odinaka pressed the intercom and requested a breakfast tray, then began to recap the night, laughing at this and that event she didn't realize Ejem hadn't been there to see.

After ten minutes, she pressed the intercom again. "Where is my tray?" she demanded, a near shout.

Catching Ejem's expression, she rolled her eyes.

"Don't you start as well."

Ejem opened her mouth to defend the osu women, but shut it just as quickly, embarrassed not only by the unattractive revolutionary bent of what she'd almost said, but also because it felt so much like a defense of herself.

"You are just like Doreen," Odinaka continued. "Look, I employ an army of those women. They have a job and they need to do it. You remember how that goes, right?" Odinaka turned on the television. A commercial advertised a family getaway that included passes to a textile museum where the

children could learn how cloth was made. Ejem recalled a documentary she'd seen in school that showed the dismal dorms to
which unclaimed women were relegated, the rationed food, the
abuse from guards, the "protection" that was anything but. It
had been meant to instill fear of ending up in such a place, and
it had worked.

When the program returned, Odinaka turned up the volume
until it was clear to Ejem she had been dismissed.

Ejem decided that her first foray in her new cloth would be to visit
Doreen in her shop. Doreen would know just what to say to ease
the restless hurt brewing inside her. She may even know enough
of Delilah's history to put Ejem's runaway suspicions to rest.
Doreen had invited her to visit the bookstore many times—"You
can't stay in here forever. Come. See what I've done. See what an
unclaimed woman can build on her own."

Wearing self-cloth in the safety of Odinaka's building was one
thing. Ejem dawdled in front of the mirror, studying the softness
of her stomach, the firm legs she'd always been proud of, the droop
of her breasts. She picked up the cloth and held it in front of her.
Much better. She secured it in a simple style, mimicking as best
as she could the draping and belting of the sophisticated women
she'd encountered.

For the first time in her adult life, no one stared at her. When
she gathered the courage to make eye contact with a man on the
sidewalk and he inclined his head respectfully, she almost tripped
in shock. It was no fluke. Everyone—men and women—treated
her differently, most ignoring her as yet another body on the
street. But when they did acknowledge her, their reactions were

friendly. Ejem felt the protective hunch of her shoulders smooth itself out, as though permission had been granted to relax. She walked with a bounce in her step, every part of her that bounced along with it shielded by the cloth. Bound up in fabric, she was the freest she'd ever felt.

Ejem was so happy that when she saw a familiar face, she smiled and waved before she remembered that the bearer of the face had disowned their friendship some months ago. Chidinma gave a hesitant wave in return before she approached Ejem, smiling.

"You're covered! You're claimed! Turn around; let me see. Your wife-cloth is so fine. I'm upset you didn't invite me to the claiming ceremony."

The words were friendly but the tone was strained, their last exchange still echoing in the air.

"There wasn't a ceremony. There was nothing to invite you to."

Chidinma's smile faded. "You don't have to lie. I know I was awful to you; I'm sorry."

"No, really, there wasn't." Ejem leaned closer, yearning to confide, to restore their former intimacy. "It's self-cloth. I covered myself."

It took Chidinma a moment to absorb this. Then she bristled, pulling back any lingering affection. Her smile went waxy and polite.

"You must be very happy with your husband."

"Chidinma, I don't have a husband. I'm covering myself."

Chidinma's look turned so vicious that Ejem stepped back, bumping into a man who excused himself.

"Are you, now? A self-cloth, is it? Someone from a good family like yours? I don't believe it." Unlike Ejem, Chidinma didn't lower her voice, earning startled glances from passersby. Ejem shushed her.

"Oh, are you ashamed now? Did something you're not entirely proud of?"

When Ejem turned to leave, Chidinma snatched her by the cloth. Now she whispered, "You think you're covered, but you're still naked. No amount of expensive 'self-cloth'—how ridiculous!—will change that."

It was a spiteful and malicious thing to say, meant to hurt, and it did. Ejem tried to pull her cloth from her old friend's fist, but Chidinma didn't let go. She continued, her voice cracking with tears.

"You don't get to be covered without giving something up; you don't get to do that. It's not fair. After everything I did for you, it's not fair."

Chidinma cried openly now and Ejem used the opportunity of her weakened grip to twist away, near tears herself.

It had been easy, Ejem thought, in the opulence of Odinaka's house, to forget that they were breaking laws. Easy, too, to clink glasses night after night. What had some woman given up so that Ejem could have this cloth? Was she a weaver by choice or indentured, deemed past her prime and burdened to earn the care of the state? The fabric felt itchy now, as though woven from rough wire.

Ejem hurried back the way she had come, to the safety of Odinaka's building. On the verge of panic, she fumbled with the keys to her apartment and let herself in. Once inside, she leaned against the door and slid to the floor, head to knees, catching her breath. She felt... something, that made her look around, and that's when she saw the osu woman standing in the corner. Her skin was light, almost blending into the dusky beige of the wall, her scar a gristly, keloided mass on the side of her head. She appeared to be Ejem's age or older. She held a bottle of cleaning solution and a rag. She was naked.

It was clear by the hunch of her shoulders and the wary look in her eye that it was not a nakedness she enjoyed. How long had it been since Ejem had carried that very look on her own face? How long since she'd felt shame so deep she'd nearly drowned in it?

The day she'd lost her father-cloth, she'd pleaded with her father, fought him as he'd attempted to rip the fabric away. Her mother had cried to her to bear it with some dignity, but Ejem had gone mindless. When her father had finally taken all of the cloth, uncurling her fingers to snatch even the frayed strip she'd held on to, Ejem had curled into herself, making a cover of her appendages. Each day since had been a management of this panic, swallowing it deep in her belly where it wouldn't erupt.

The osu woman nodded to Ejem, then slipped through a panel in the wall and disappeared. The panel slid back into place soundlessly, and when Ejem went to the wall she could feel no seam. She clawed at it, bending and breaking her nails, trying to force a way in. Finding no entry from her side, she pounded and called out, seeking a welcome.

THE APARTMENT

by T. C. BOYLE

(This story, from McSweeney's 56, *was selected for*
The Best American Short Stories 2020.*)*

WHO WAS TO KNOW? She might have outlived most of her contemporaries, but she was so slight and small, almost a dwarf, really, her eyesight compromised and her hearing fading, and if she lived a year or two more, it would have been by the grace of God alone. Yes, she was lively enough, even at ninety, wobbling down the street on her bicycle like some atrophied schoolgirl and twice a week donning her épée mask and fencing with her shadow in the salon of her second-floor apartment,

overlooking rue Gambetta on the one side and rue Saint-Estève
on the other, but his own mother had been lively, too, and she'd
gone to bed on the night of her seventy-second birthday and
never opened her eyes again. No, no: the odds were in his favor.
Definitely. Definitely in his favor.

He turned forty-seven the year he first approached her, 1965,
which meant that at that point he'd been married to Marie-
Thérèse for some twenty years, years that had been happy enough
for the most part—and more than that, usual. He liked the usual.
The usual kept you on an even keel and offered up few surprises.
And this was the important thing here, the thing he always liked
to stress when the subject came up: he was not a gambling man.
Before he'd made any of the major decisions in his life—asking
for his wife's hand all those years ago, applying for the course of
study that would lead to his law degree, making an offer on the
apartment they'd lived in since their marriage—he'd studied all
the angles with a cold, computational eye. The fact was, he had
few vices beyond a fondness for sweets and a tendency to indulge
his daughters, Sophie and Élise, sixteen and fourteen, respectively,
that year (or maybe they were seventeen and fifteen—he never
could quite keep that straight; as he liked to say, "If you're very,
very fortunate, your children will be twelve months older each
year"). He didn't smoke or drink, habits he'd given up three years
earlier after a strenuous talk with his doctor. And he wasn't covet-
ous, or not particularly. Other men might drive sleek sports cars,
lease yachts, and keep mistresses, but none of that interested him.

The only problem—the sole problem in his life at that point—
was the apartment. It was just too small to contain his blossoming
daughters and the eternally thumping music radiating from their
bedroom day and night, simplistic music, moronic, even—the

Beatles, the Animals, the Kinks, the very names indicative of their juvenility—and if he wanted a bigger apartment, grander, more spacious, *quieter*, who could blame him? An apartment that was a five-minute walk from his office, an apartment that was a cathedral of early-morning light? An apartment surrounded by shops, cafés, and first-class restaurants? It was, as they say, a no-brainer.

He put together a proposal and sent Madame C. a note wondering if he might see her, at her convenience, about a matter of mutual interest. Whether she would respond or not, he couldn't say, but it wasn't as if he were some interloper—he knew her as an acquaintance and neighbor, as did just about everyone else in Arles, and he must have stopped with her in the street half a dozen times in the past year to discuss the weather, the machinations of de Gaulle and Pompidou, and the absurdity of sending a rocket into space when life here, on terra firma, was so clearly in need of *immediate attention*. A week went by before he heard back from her. He'd come home from work that day to an empty apartment—Marie-Thérèse was out shopping and the girls were at rehearsal for a school play, but the radio in their room was all too present, and regurgitating rock and roll at full volume ("We gotta get out of this place," the singer insisted, in English, over and over) until he angrily snapped it off—and he was just settling down in his armchair with the newspaper when he noticed her letter on the sideboard.

"Cher monsieur," she wrote in the firm, decisive hand she'd learned as a schoolgirl in the previous century, "I must confess to being intrigued. Shall we meet here at my residence at 4 p.m. Thursday?"

*　*　*

In addition to the contract he'd drawn up in advance—he was an optimist, always an optimist—he brought with him a bouquet of spring flowers and a box of chocolate truffles, which he presented somberly to her when she met him at the door. "How kind of you," she murmured, taking the flowers in one all-but-translucent hand and the box of chocolates in the other and ushering him through the entrance hall and into the salon, and whether by calculation or not she left him standing there in that grand room with its high ceilings, Persian carpets, and dense mahogany furniture while she went into the kitchen to put the flowers in a vase.

There was a Bösendorfer piano in one corner, with a great spreading palm—or was it a cycad?—in a ceramic pot beside it, and that, as much as anything, swept him away. To think of sinking into the sofa after work and listening to Bach or Mozart or Debussy instead of the Animals or whoever they were. And so what if no one in the family knew how to play or had ever evidenced even the slightest degree of musical talent—they could take lessons. He himself could take lessons, and why not? He wasn't dead yet. And before long the girls would be away at university and then married, with homes of their own, and it would be just Marie-Thérèse and him—and maybe a cat. He could see himself seated on the piano bench, the cat asleep in his lap and Debussy's *Images* flowing from his fingertips like a new kind of language.

"Well, don't these look pretty?" the old lady sang out, edging into the room to arrange the vase on the coffee table, which he now saw was set for two, with a blue-and-rose Sèvres teapot, matching cups and saucers, cloth napkins bound in silver rings, and a platter of macarons.

He sat in the armchair across from her as she poured out two cups of tea, watching for any signs of palsy or Parkinson's—but no, she was steady enough—and then they were both busy with their spoons, the sugar and the cream, until she broke the silence. "You have a proposition for me, is that it?" she asked. "And"—here a sly look came into the flickering remnants of her eyes—"I'll bet you five francs I know what it is. I'm clairvoyant, monsieur, didn't you know that?"

He couldn't think of anything to say to this, so he just smiled.

"You want to make me an offer on the apartment, *en viager*—isn't that right?"

If he was surprised, he tried not to show it. He'd been prepared to condescend to her, as with any elderly person—politely, of course, generously, looking out for her best interests as well as his own—but she'd caught him up short. "Well, yes," he said. "That's it exactly. A reverse annuity."

He set down his cup. The apartment was absolutely silent, as if no one else lived in the building, and what about a maid—didn't she have a maid? "The fact is, Marie-Thérèse and I—my wife, that is—have been thinking of moving for some time now." He let out a little laugh. "Especially with my daughters growing into young women and the apartment getting smaller by the day, if you know what I mean, and while there are plenty of places on the market, there's really hardly anything like this—and it's so close to my office..."

"And since my grandson passed on, you figure the old woman has no one to leave the place to, and even if she doesn't need the money, why wouldn't she take it anyway? It's better than getting nothing and leaving the place for the government to appropriate, isn't that right?"

"Yes," he said, "that was my thinking."

As far as he knew—and he'd put in his research on the subject—she had no heirs. She'd been a bride once, and a mother, too, and she'd lived within these four walls and paced these creaking floorboards for an astonishing sixty-nine years, ever since she'd returned from her honeymoon, in 1896, and moved in here with her husband, a man of means, who had owned the department store on the ground floor and had given her a life of ease. Anything she wanted was at her fingertips. She hosted musical parties, vacationed in the Alps, skied, bicycled, hunted and fished, lived through the German occupation and the resumption of the republic without noticing all that much difference in her daily affairs, but of course no one gets through life unscathed. Her only child, a daughter, had died of pneumonia in 1934, after which she and her husband had assumed guardianship of their grandson, until first her husband died unexpectedly (after eating a dish of fresh-picked cherries that had been dusted with copper sulfate and inadequately rinsed), and then her grandson, whom she'd seen through medical school and who had continued to live with her as her sole companion and emotional support. He was only thirty-six when he was killed in an auto accident on a deserted road, not two years ago. It was Marie-Thérèse who'd seen the notice in the paper; otherwise he might have missed it altogether. They sent a condolence card, though neither of them attended the funeral, which, given the deceased's condition, would have been a closed-casket affair in any case. Still, that was the beginning of it, the first glimmer of the idea, and whether he was being insensitive or not ("ghoulish," was the way Marie-Thérèse put it), he couldn't say. Or no, he could say: he was just being practical.

"What are you offering?" the old woman asked, focusing narrowly on him now as if to be certain he was still there.

"Fair market value, of course. I want the best for you—and for me and my family too. Here," he said, handing her a sheet of paper on which he'd drawn up figures for comparable apartments in the neighborhood. "I was thinking perhaps twenty-two hundred francs a month?"

She barely glanced at the paper. "Twenty-five," she said.

It took him a moment, doing a quick mental calculation, to realize that even if she lived ten more years he'd be getting the place for half of what it was worth, and that didn't factor in appreciation either. "Agreed," he said.

"And you won't interfere?"

"No."

"What if I decide to paint the walls pink?" She laughed, a sudden strangled laugh that tailed off into a fit of coughing. She was a smoker, that much he knew (and had taken into account on the debit side of the ledger). Yes, she could ride a bicycle at ninety, an amazing feat, but she'd also been blackening her lungs for seventy years or more. He watched her dab at her eyes with a tissue, then grin to show her teeth—yes, she still had them. Unless they were dentures.

"And the ceiling chartreuse?" she went on, extending the joke. "And, and—move the bathtub into the salon, right there where you're perched in my armchair looking so pleased with yourself?"

He shook his head. "You'll live here as you always have, no strings attached."

She sat back in her chair, a tight smile compressing her lips. "You're really throwing the dice, aren't you?"

He shrugged. "Twenty-five hundred a month," he repeated. "It's a fair offer."

"You're betting I'll die—and sooner rather than later."

"Not at all. I wish you nothing but health and prosperity. Besides, I'm not a betting man."

"You know what *I'm* doing?" she asked, hunching forward so he could see the balding patch on the crown of her head and the slim tracery of bones exposed at the collar of her dress, where, apparently, she'd been unable to reach back and fasten the zipper.

"No, what?" he said, grinning, patronizing her, though his stomach sank because he was sure she was going to say she was backing out of the deal, that she'd had a better offer, that she'd been toying with him all along.

"I'm throwing the dice too."

After he left that day, she felt as if she'd been lifted up into the clouds. She cleared away the tea things in a burst of energy, then marched around the apartment, going from room to room and back again, twice, three times, four, pumping her arms for the sake of her circulation and letting her eyes roam over the precious familiar things that meant more to her than anything else in the world, and not just the framed photos and paintings, but the ceramic snowman Frédéric had made in grammar school and the mounted butterflies her husband had collected when they first married. She'd been blessed, suddenly and unexpectedly blessed, and if she could have kicked up her heels, she would have—she wasn't going to a nursing home like so many other women she'd known, all of them lost now to death or the straitjacket of old age. No, she was staying right here. For the duration. In celebration, she unwrapped the box of chocolates, poured herself a glass of wine, and sat smoking by the window, looking out on the street and the parade of pedestrians that was the best show on earth, better than any television, better than *La comédie humaine*—no, it *was La comédie humaine*. And there were no pages to turn and no commercials either.

She watched a woman in a ridiculous hat go into the shop across the street and immediately come back out again as if she'd forgotten something, then press her face to the glass and wave till the shopgirl appeared in the window and reached for an equally ridiculous hat on the mannequin there, and here came a boy on a motor scooter with a girl clinging to him from behind and the sudden shadow of a black Renault sliced in front of them till the goat's bleat of the boy's horn rose up in protest and the car swerved at the last minute. Almost an accident, and wouldn't that have been terrible? Another boy dead, like her Frédéric, and a girl too. It was everywhere, death, wasn't it? You didn't have to go out and look for it—it was right there, always, lurking just below the surface. And that was part of the *comédie* too.

But enough morbidity—this was a celebration, wasn't it? Twenty-five hundred francs! Truly, this man had come to her like an angel from heaven—and what's more he'd never even hesitated when she countered his offer. Like everyone else, he assumed she was better off than she was, that money meant nothing to her and she could take or leave any offer no matter how extravagant, but in fact, if you excluded the value of the apartment, she had practically nothing, her savings having dissipated in paying for Frédéric's education and his clothes and his car and his medical degree—Frédéric, lost to her now and forever. She got by, barely, by paring her expenses and the reduced needs that come with having lived so long. It wasn't as if she needed theater tickets anymore. Or concert tickets either. She never went anywhere, except to church on Sundays, and that didn't cost anything more than what she put in the collection box, which was between her and God.

After Frédéric's death she'd reduced the maid's schedule to two days a week rather than the six she'd have preferred, but that was going to change now. And if she wanted a prime cut of meat at the butcher's or *l'écrevisse* or even *le homard* at the fishmonger's, she would just go ahead and order it and never mind what it cost. Bless the man, she thought, bless him. Best of all, even beyond the money, was the wager itself. If she'd been lost after Frédéric had been taken from her, now she was found. Now—suddenly, wonderfully—purpose had come back into her life. Gazing out the window at the bustle of the street below, bringing the cigarette to her lips just often enough to keep it glowing, she was as happy as she'd been in weeks, months, even, and all at once she was thinking about the time she and her husband had gone to Monte Carlo, the one time in all their life together. She remembered sitting there at the roulette table in a black velvet evening gown, Fernand glowing beside her in his tuxedo, the croupier spinning the wheel, and the bright, shining silver ball dropping into the slot for her number—twenty-two black; she would never forget it—and in the next moment using his little rake to push all those gay, glittering chips in her direction.

He went to visit her at the end of the first month after the contract went into effect, feeling generous and expansive, wondering how she was getting on. He'd heard a rumor that she'd been ill, having caught the cold that was going around town that spring, which, of course, would have been all the more severe in someone of

her age with her compromised immune system, not to mention
smoker's cough. A steady rain had been falling all day, and it was
a bit of a juggling act for him to balance his umbrella and the
paper-wrapped parcels he was bringing her: a bottle of Armagnac,
another box of chocolates (two pounds, assorted), and a carton of
the Gauloises he'd seen her smoking on his last visit. This time
a girl met him at the door—a woman, that is, of fifty or so, with
sucked-in cheeks, badly dyed hair, and listless eyes. There was a
moment of hesitation until he realized that this must be the maid
he'd wondered about and then a further moment during which
he reflected on the fact that he was, in a sense, paying her wages.
"Is madame in?" he inquired.

She didn't ask his name or business, but simply nodded and
held out her arms for the gifts, which he handed over as if they
were a bribe, and then led him into the salon, which as far as
he could see remained unchanged, no pink walls or chartreuse
ceiling, and no bathtub, either. He stood there awhile, revel-
ing in the details—the room was perfect, really, just as it was,
though Marie-Thérèse, who'd yet to see the place from the inside,
would want to do at least some redecorating, because she was a
woman, and women were never satisfied till they'd put their own
stamp on things—and then there was a noise behind him and he
turned round to see the maid pushing the old woman down the
hall in a wheelchair. *A wheelchair!* He couldn't suppress a rush
of joy, though he composed his features in a suitably concerned
expression and said, "Madame, how good to see you again," and
he was about to go on, about to say, *You're looking well*, but that
was hardly appropriate under the circumstances.

The old woman was grinning up at him. "It's just a cold,"
she said, "so don't get your hopes up." He saw that the presents

he'd brought were arranged in her lap, still wrapped in tissue paper. "And I wouldn't have caught a cold at all, you know, if someone"—and here she glanced up at the maid—"hadn't carried it home to me. Isn't that right, Martine? Unless I picked it up by dipping my hand in the font last Sunday morning at church. You think that's it, Martine? Do you? You think that's likely?"

The maid had wheeled her up to the coffee table, where she set the gifts down, one by one, and began unwrapping them, beginning with the Armagnac. "Ah," she exclaimed when she'd torn off the paper, "perfect, just what a woman needs when she has a head cold. Fetch us two glasses, will you, Martine?"

He wanted to protest—he didn't drink anymore and didn't miss it either (or maybe he did, just a little)—but it was easier to let the old woman take the bottle by the neck and pour them each a dose, and when she raised her glass to him and cried, "Bonne santé!" and drained it in a single swallow, he had no choice but to follow suit. It burned going down, but it clarified things for him. She was in a wheelchair. She had a head cold, which, no doubt, was merely the first stage of an infection that would invariably spread to her lungs, mutate into pneumonia, and kill her sooner rather than later. It wasn't a mercenary thought, just realistic, that was all, and when she poured a second glass, he joined her again, and when she unwrapped the chocolates and set the box on the table before him, he found himself lifting one morsel after another to his lips, and if he'd ever tasted anything so exquisite in his life, he couldn't remember it, especially now that the Armagnac had reawakened his palate. He'd never liked Gauloises—they were too harsh—preferring filtered American cigarettes, but he found himself accepting one anyway, drawing deeply, and enjoying the faint crepitation of the nicotine working its way through his bloodstream. He exhaled in the rarefied air of the apartment that was soon to be his, and though he'd intended to stay only a few minutes, he was still there when the church bells tolled the hour.

What did they talk about? Her health, at least at first. Did he realize she'd never been sick more than a day or two in her entire life? He didn't, and he found the news unsettling, disappointing, even. "Oh," she said, "I've had little colds and sniffles like this before—and once, when my husband and I were in Spain, an episode of the trots, but nothing major. Do you know something?"

Flying high on the cognac, the sugar, the nicotine, he just grinned at her.

"Not only am I hardly ever ill, but I make a point of keeping all of my blood inside my body at all times—don't you think that's a good principle to live by?"

And here he found himself straddling a chasm, the flush and healthy on one side, the aged, crabbed, and doomed on the other, and he said, "We can't all be so lucky."

She was silent a moment, just staring into his eyes, a faint grin pressed to her lips. He could hear the maid off in the distance somewhere, a sound of running water, the faint clink of cutlery— the apartment really was magnificent, huge, cavernous, and you could hear a pin drop. It was a defining moment, and Madame C. held on to it. "Precisely," she said finally, took the cigarette from her lips, and let out a little laugh, a giggle, actually, girlish and pure.

Three days later, when the sun was shining in all its power again and everything was sparkling as if the world had been created anew, he was hurrying down the street on an errand, a furtive cigarette cupped in one palm—yes, yes, he knew, and he wouldn't lie to his doctor next time he saw him, or maybe he would, but there was really no harm in having a cigarette every once in a while, or a drink either—when a figure picked itself out of the crowd ahead and wheeled toward him on a bicycle, knees slowly pumping, back straight and arms braced, and it wasn't until she'd passed by, so close he could have touched her, that he realized who it was.

For the first eighty-odd years of her existence, time had seemed to accelerate, day by day, year by year, as if life were a bicycle race, a kind of Tour de France that was all downhill, even the curves, but in the years after she'd signed the contract, things slowed to a crawl. Each day was a replica of the last, and nothing ever happened beyond the odd squabble with Martine and the visits from Monsieur R. At first he'd come every week or two, his arms laden with gifts—liquor, sweets, cigarettes, foie gras, quiche, even a fondue once, replete with crusts of bread, marbled beef, and *crépitements de porc*—but eventually the visits grew fewer and further between. Which was a pity, really, because she'd come to relish the look of confusion and disappointment on his face when he found her in such good spirits, matching him chocolate for chocolate, drink for drink, and cigarette for cigarette. "Don't think for a minute you're fooling me, monsieur," she would say to him as they sat at the coffee table laden with delicacies, and Martine bustled back and forth from the salon to the kitchen and sometimes even took a seat with them and dug in herself. "You're a sly one, aren't you?"

He would shrug elaborately, laugh, and throw up his hands as if to say, *Yes, you see through me, but you can't blame a man for trying, can you?*

She would smile back at him. She'd found herself growing fond of him, in the way you'd grow fond of a cat that comes up periodically to rub itself against your leg—and then hands you twenty-five hundred francs. Each and every month. He wasn't much to look at, really: average in height, weight, and coloring—average, in fact, in every way, from the man-in-the-street look on his face to his side-part and negligible mustache. Nothing like Fernand, who'd been one of the handsomest men of his generation, even into his early seventies, when, in absolutely perfect health and the liveliest of moods, he'd insisted on a second portion of fresh-picked cherries at a *ferme-auberge* in Saint-Rémy.

She'd gotten sick herself, but she really didn't care for cherries all that much and had eaten a handful at most. Fernand, though, had been greedy for them, feeding them into his mouth one after another, spitting the pits into his cupped palm and arranging them neatly on the saucer in front of him as if they were jewels, pausing only to lift the coffee cup to his lips or read her the odd tidbit from the morning paper, joking all the while. *Joking*, and the poison in him even then. He spent the next six weeks in agony, his skin drawn and yellow, the whites of his eyes the color of orange peels and his voice dying in his throat, till everything went dark. It was so hard to understand—it wasn't an enemy's bullet that killed him, wasn't an avalanche on the ski slopes or the failure of an overworked heart or even the slow advance of cancer, but cherries, little round fruits the size of marbles, nature's bounty. That had been wrong, deeply wrong, and she'd questioned God over it through all these years, but he had never responded.

When she turned one hundred, people began to take notice. The newspaper printed a story, listing her among the other centenarians in Provence, none of whom she knew, and why would she? She was photographed in her salon, grinning like a gargoyle. Someone from the mayor's office sent her a commendation, and people stopped her in the street to congratulate her as if she'd won the lottery, which, in a sense, she supposed she had. She really didn't want to make a fuss over it, but Martine, despite having fractured her wrist in a fall, insisted on throwing a party to commemorate "the milestone" she'd reached.

"I don't want a party," she said.

"Nonsense. Of course you do."

"Too much noise," she said. "Too many busybodies." Then a thought came to her and she paused. "Will he be there?"

"Who?"

"Monsieur R."

"Well, I can ask him—would you like that?"

"Yes," she said, gazing down on the street below, "I think I'd like that very much."

He came with his wife, a woman with bitter, shining eyes she'd met twice before but whose name she couldn't for the life of her remember, beyond "Madame," that is. He brought a gift, which she accepted without enthusiasm, his gifts having become increasingly less elaborate as time wore on, and his hopes of debilitating her ran up against the insuperable obstacle of her health. In this instance, he came forward like a petitioner to where she was seated on the piano stool preparatory to treating her guests to a meditative rendition of "Au clair de la lune," bent formally to kiss her cheek, and handed her a bottle of indifferent wine from a vineyard she'd never heard of. "Congratulations," he said, and though she'd heard him perfectly well, she said, "What?" so that he had to repeat himself, and then she said, "What?" again, just to hear him shout it out.

There were thirty or more people gathered in the salon, neighbors mostly, but also the priest from the local church, a pair of nuns she vaguely recognized, a photographer, a newspaperman, and the mayor (an infant with the bald head of a newborn who'd come to be photographed with her so that his administration, which hadn't even come into existence till three years ago, could take credit for her longevity). They all looked up at the commotion and then away again, as if embarrassed for Monsieur R., and there wasn't a person in the room who didn't know of the gamble he'd taken.

"Thank you," she said. "You can't imagine how much your good wishes mean to me—more even than the mayor's." And then, to the wife, who was looking positively tragic behind a layer of powder that didn't begin to hide the creases under her eyes, "And don't you fret, madame. Be patient. All this"—she waved a hand to take in the room, the windows, and the sunstruck vista beyond—"will be yours in just, oh, what shall we say, ten or fifteen years?"

If Marie-Thérèse had never been one to nag, she began to nag now. "Twenty-five hundred francs," she would interject whenever there was a pause in their conversation, no matter the subject or the hour of the day or night, "*twenty-five hundred francs*. Don't you think I could use that money? Look at my winter coat—do you see this coat I'm forced to wear? And what of your daughters, what about them? Don't you imagine they could use something extra?"

Both their daughters were out of the house now, Sophie married and living in Paris with a daughter of her own and Élise in graduate school, studying art restoration in Florence, for which he footed the bill (tuition, books, clothing, living expenses, as well as a room in a pension on via dei Calzaiuoli, which he'd never laid eyes on and most likely never would). The apartment seemed spacious without them, and lonely—that, too, because he missed them both terribly—and without the irritation of their rock and roll it seemed more spacious still. If there'd been a time when he'd needed Madame C.'s apartment—needed, rather than hungered for—that time had passed. As Marie-Thérèse reminded him every day.

It would be madness to try to break the contract at this point—he'd already invested some three hundred thousand francs, and the old lady could drop dead at any minute—but he did go to her one afternoon not long after the birthday celebration to see if he might persuade her to lower the monthly payment to the twenty-two hundred he'd initially proposed or perhaps even two thousand. That would certainly be easier on him—he had his own retirement to think about at this point—and it would mollify his wife, as least for the time being.

Madame C. greeted him in the salon, as usual. It was a cold day in early March, rain at the windows and a chill pervading the apartment. She was seated in her favorite armchair, beside an electric heater, an afghan spread over her knees and a pair of cats he'd never seen before asleep in her lap. He brought her only cigarettes this time, though the maid had let slip that madame didn't smoke more than two or three a day and that the last several cartons he'd given her were gathering dust in the kitchen cupboard. No matter. He took the seat across from her and immediately lit up himself, expecting her to follow suit, but she only gazed at him calmly, waiting to hear what he had to say.

He began with the weather—wasn't it dreary and would spring never arrive?—and then, stalling till the right moment presented itself, he commented on the cats. They were new, weren't they?

"Don't you worry, monsieur," she said, "they do their business in the pan under the bathroom sink. They're very well behaved and they wouldn't dream of pissing on the walls and stinking up your apartment. Isn't that right?" she cooed, bending her face to them, her ghostly hands gliding over their backs and bellies as if to bless them.

"Oh, I'm not worried at all, I assure you—I like cats, though Marie-Thérèse is allergic to them, but there is one little matter I wanted to take up with you, if you have a moment, that is."

She laughed then. "A moment? I have all the time in the world."

He began in a roundabout way, talking of his daughters, his wife, his own apartment, and his changed circumstances. "And really, the biggest factor is that I need to start putting something away for my retirement," he said, giving her a meaningful look.

"Retirement? But you can't even be sixty yet?"

He said something lame in response, which he couldn't remember when he tried to reconstruct the conversation afterward, something like *It's never too soon to begin*, which only made her laugh.

"You're telling me," she said, leaning forward in the chair. "Thanks to you, I'm all set." She paused, studying him closely. "But you're not here to try to renegotiate, are you?"

"It would mean so much to me," he said. "And my wife too." And then, absurdly, he added, "She needs a new winter coat."

She was silent a moment. "You brought me an inferior bottle of wine on my birthday," she said finally.

"I'm sorry about that. I thought you would like it."

"Going on the cheap is never appealing."

"Yes, but with my daughter in graduate school and some recent reverses we've experienced at the office, I'm just not able"—he grinned, as if to remind her they were on the same team—"to give you all you deserve. Which is why I ask you to reconsider the terms—"

She'd already held up the palm of one hand to forestall him. The cats shifted in her lap, the near one opening its jaws in a yawn that displayed the white needles of its teeth. "We all make bargains in this life," she said, setting the cats down on the carpet beside her. "Sometimes we win," she said, "and sometimes we lose."

When she turned 110, she was introduced to the term *super-centenarian*, the meaning of which the newspaper helpfully provided—that is, one who is a decade or more older than a mere centenarian, who, if you searched all of France (or Europe, America, the world), were a dime a dozen these days. Her eyes were too far gone to read anymore, but Martine, who'd recently turned seventy herself, put on her glasses and read the article aloud to her. She learned that the chances of reaching that threshold were one in seven million, which meant that for her to be alive still, 6,999,999 had died, which was a kind of holocaust in itself. And how did that make her feel? Exhausted. But indomitable too. And she still had possession of her apartment and still received her contractual payment of twenty-five hundred francs a month.

One of the cats—Tybalt—had died of old age, and Martine wasn't what she once was, but for her part Madame C. still sat at the window and watched the life of the streets pulse around her as it always had and always would, and if she couldn't bicycle anymore, well, that was one of the concessions a supercentenarian just had to make to the grand order of things.

Monsieur R. didn't come around much anymore, and when he did, she didn't always recognize him. Her mind was supple still even if her body wasn't (rheumatism, decelerating heartbeat, a persistent ache in the soles of her feet), but he was so changed even Martine couldn't place him at first. He was stooped, he shuffled his feet, his hair was like cotton batting, and for some unfathomable reason he'd grown a beard like Père Noël. She had to ask him to come very close so she could make him out (what her eyes gave her now was no better than the image on an old black-and-white television screen caught between stations), and when he did, and when she reached out to feel his ears and his nose and look into his eyes, she would burst into laughter. "It's not between you and me anymore, monsieur," she would say. "I've got a new wager now."

And he would lift his eyebrows so she could see the exhaustion in his eyes, all part of the routine, the comedy, they were bound up in. "Oh?" he would say. "With whom?"

Martine hovered. The pack of the cigarettes he always brought with him lay on the table before him, and a smoldering butt—his, not hers—rested in the depths of the ashtray. "You can't guess?"

"No, I can't imagine."

"Methuselah, that's who," she would say, and break into a laugh that was just another variant on the cough that was with her now from morning till night. "I'm going for the record, didn't you know that?"

*   *   *

The record keepers—the earthly record keepers from the Guinness Brewery, that is, who were in their own way more authoritative than God, and more precise too—came to her shortly after her 113th birthday to inform her that Florence Knapp, of the State of Pennsylvania in the United States of America, had died at 114, making her the world's oldest living person. The apartment was full of people. The salon buzzed. There were lights brighter than the sun, cameras that moved and swiveled like enormous insects with electric red eyes, and here was a man as blandly handsome as a grade-A apple, thrusting a microphone at her. "How does it feel?" he asked, and when she didn't respond, asked again. Finally, after a long pause during which the entire TV-viewing audience must have taken her for a dotard, she grinned and said, "Like going to the dentist."

Marie-Thérèse, who'd been slowed by a degenerative disk in her lower back that made walking painful, came clumping into the kitchen one bleak February morning in the last dwindling decade of the century—and where had the years gone?—to slap the news-paper down on the table before him. "You see this?" she demanded, and he pushed aside his slice of buttered toast (the only thing he was able to keep down lately) to fumble for his reading glasses, which he thought he had misplaced until he discovered them hanging from the lanyard around his neck. Marie-Thérèse's finger tapped at the photograph dominating the front page. It took him a moment to realize it was a close-up of Madame C., seated before a birthday cake the size of a truck tire, the candles atop it ablaze, as if this, finally, were her funeral pyre, but no such luck.

Whole years had gone by during which he'd daily envisioned her death—plotted it, even. He dreamed of poisoning her wine, pushing her down the stairs, sitting in her bird-shell lap and crushing her like an egg, all eighty-eight pounds of her, but, of course, because he was civilized, he never acted on his fantasies. In truth, he'd lost contact with her over the course of the years, accepting her for what she was—a fact of nature, like the sun that rose in the morning and the moon that rose at night—and he was doing his best to ignore all mention of her. She'd made him the butt of a joke, and a cruel joke at that. He'd attended her 110th birthday, and then the one four years later, after she'd become the world's oldest living human, but Marie-Thérèse had been furious (about that and practically everything else in their lives), and both his daughters had informed him he was making a public spectacle of himself, and so, finally, he'd declared himself *hors de combat*.

Besides which, he had problems of his own, problems that went far deeper than where he was going to lay his head at night—the doctor had found a spot on his lung and that spot had morphed into cancer. The treatments, radiation and chemo-therapy both, had sheared every hair from his body and left him feeling weak and otherworldly. So when Marie-Thérèse thrust the paper at him and he saw the old lady grinning her imperturbable grin under the banner headline WORLD'S OLDEST LIVING PERSON TURNS 120, he felt nothing. Or practically nothing.

"I wish she would die," Marie-Thérèse hissed.

He wanted to concur, wanted to hiss right back at her, *So do I*, but all he could do was laugh—yes, the joke was on him, wasn't it?—until the laugh became a rasping, harsh cough that went on and on till his lips were bright with blood.

Two days later, he was dead.

*   *   *

At first she hadn't the faintest idea what Martine was talking about ("Dead? Who's dead?"), but eventually, after a painstaking disquisition that took her step by step through certain key events of the past thirty years, she was given to understand that her benefactor had been laid to rest—or, actually, incinerated at the crematorium, an end result she was determined to avoid for herself. She was going to be buried properly, like a good Catholic. And an angel—her guardian angel, who had seen her this far— was going to be there at her side to take her to heaven in a golden chariot. Let the flesh rot, dust to dust; her spirit was going to soar.

"So he's dead, is he?" she said in the general direction of Martine. She was all but blind now, but she could see everything in her mind's eye—Martine, as she'd been five years ago, hunched and crabbed, an old woman herself—and then she saw Monsieur R. as he had been all those years before, when he'd first come to her to place his bet. Suddenly she was laughing. "He made his bet; now he has to lie in it," she said, and Martine said, "Whatever are you talking about? And what's so funny—he's dead, didn't you hear me?"

Very faintly, as if from a distance, she heard herself say, "But his twenty-five hundred francs a month are still alive, aren't they?"

"I don't—I mean, I hadn't really thought about it."

"*En viager*. I'm still alive, aren't I? Well, aren't I?"

Martine didn't answer. The world had been reduced. But it was there still, solid, tangible, as real as the fur of the cat—whichever cat—that happened to be asleep in her lap, asleep, and purring.

BRIGIT

by EMMA HOOPER

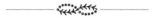

(This story appeared in McSweeney's 67.*)*

IRELAND, FIFTH CENTURY

THERE WAS ONCE A man who loved his wife very much, so much, for a while, but then he forgot. He was a busy man, a busy guy, he had business to do with ships, with being sure the right number of ships were coming in and also that the right number of ships were going out, and, as if that weren't enough, he also had to be sure the ships coming in had the right stuff on them, the right cargo, and ditto the ones going out.

And also keep a handle on things like disease and rats and all that.

It was a lot.

It was, at times, overwhelming, like the sea over the side, like the foam spilling over and onto everything, everything covered, everything wet. He liked it, his job, and was good at it, usually, mostly, but at times it was a lot. At times, like that morning, say, when the ships that were meant to have sheep on them headed out with mead and turnips on them instead, and the ships that were meant to come in with pepper, turmeric, and cardamom on them hadn't turned up at all, except for one that didn't, anyway, have any spice on it, just a whole load of rats that ran out at him, spilled out like water all around him when he opened the hatch, to check, to do his job. At times like that he forgot, for a while, that he had a wife and that he loved her.

He also had children but we won't worry about that for now.

Anyway, he wasn't a lazy man, or didn't think of himself as a lazy man, how could you be lazy and have a job like that, maintain a job like that? He wasn't lazy, he was just busy, which is the opposite of lazy, really.

This is what he told me, basically. After stepping, dripping, soaking wet, into my office. The floor was wooden, because everything was wooden, because we were in the church, and all the buildings in town, including the church, were made of wood because it rained so much that no one ever worried about what a bit of fire could do to a place like that. The wood did get waterlogged, true, eventually. It drooped with the weight of wet a little more each year, until our ceilings were patting us lightly on the head like gentle parents. Then we'd know it was time to take those boards out and throw them into the swamps, swamps the exact same consistency as rotten wood, and put new boards in.

The floors, however, being inside, sheltered, lasted longer. But not if people came and dripped all over them. Not if people like this man didn't even have the decency to remove their coats and boots and hats, and gloves, too, if being truly polite, at the door.

Anyway, I didn't hold it against him. To be fair it was also freezing in there, always.

So, I said. You have a wife?

Yes, he said. Exactly. Exactly.

I'd seen men like him before. Loads and loads and loads. First loving their wives, then their ships or market stalls or sheep or books or whatever, then getting confused because a ship is not, actually, a woman, a person, then coming to me. They came here, they dripped on my floor.

So, I asked. What about it? Even though I knew the answer.

Well, he said, looking at his hands.

Yes? I said.

Well, he said, the thing is...

Uh-huh? I said.

He looked at his hands again. They were clasped in front of him, right on top of left, he didn't seem comfortable. He tried putting them the other way around, left on top of right. She, he said.

Yeah?

She doesn't love me anymore, he said.

Oh, I said. Is that so?

His wife was a true beauty. Not like any other woman. You think you've seen plenty of women, sure, sure, heck, you even are one, maybe, and no offense to you or to the others, but the truth must be stated, he told me, that his wife was the Most Beautiful Girl in the World. He had seen (and Seen, you know) women from All Over the Place, and still, this one, this one girl, woman, actually, she outdid them all. In some ways, he said. In some ways she did.

The funny thing was, she hadn't always been so beautiful. When they first met she had been, of course. They'd met at the bit of harbor where you can get slightly less-fresh fish quite cheap. Not that she worked there, no, no! She was just prudently checking their offerings, sussing them out, seeing if they would be up to snuff for the mother and nine brothers and six sisters at home that she, and only she, had to provide for. Then, there, she'd been gorgeous. A bit grimy, sure, but a real knockout nevertheless.

Look, the man had said to her. Marry me and I'll buy that fish for you. I'll buy *three* fish for you.

Yeah? she'd said, and had looked up to him, for she was so petite and fine and he was so tall and strong. How about five?

Four, he'd said.

She'd taken a moment, considered his stature, his decent but not ostentatious clothes, the impressively clean hand he was holding out to her. Then she'd looked back to the fish, not too bad, not too many flies, yet. And then she'd said, Yeah, okay, sure. After you buy them, though, right?

And he'd taken her up in his firm but tender embrace and had kissed her a thousand times right there and then and said, Sure, of course. And then he had called the monger over and, in front of all the other customers and the monger, he had bought her *six* fish.

And all was good for a while? I said, while at the same time laying down some rags to soak up the puddles by his feet.

Yeah, he said. All was great for a while. Mind-blowing, even.

For a while, all was better than you can imagine. His house filled with laughter and light, and, he said, and I apologize for saying this in front of you, a nun, but also sex. It had been dark before, you know, he said. I didn't know it, but it had been dark; I had been. But then, suddenly, I, I wasn't.

He stopped then, looked around himself. Looked at me.

I'm not a nun, I said.

Oh, he said.

I pushed an old upside-down potato box toward him. Sit, I said. You've been here awhile now, you might as well sit.

He sat.

There was one time, he said.

I pushed another box out. I sat. Yeah? I said.

There was one time, he said, when work had been especially demanding, and, well, I don't want to waste your time.

*   *   *

And he did look a bit sad then, genuinely. He was looking down at his hands in his lap like a boy in school who still quietly misses his mother. No, I said, go on, tell me, tell me about that time.

Well, he said, fidgeting his fingers against one another, it's nothing, really, really. There was one time, just, when work had been especially hard, no one listening to him, rats everywhere, when he was trying to do a lot, too much, all at the same time, shouting at some haulers who were bringing in their ship to the wrong mooring and also directing a shipment of sheep out, and also trying to get the attention of his boss, the harbormaster, to see if they could, finally, maybe, have that chat about a bit of a bump in pay, now that he had four kids at home, it had been that time when he had been doing too much and hadn't seen the puddle of sheep shit and had stepped in it exactly as he was twisting round toward the harbormaster and had, because of that, because of all that, slipped.

He had landed in the shit. All of him. Face, even. Everything.

Everyone had laughed. The haulers, the sailors, the mongers. Even the harbormaster, who never looked his way, looked his way, and, with the rest of them, laughed.

And there he'd been, on the ground, in the shit, nothing happening like it was supposed to, there he'd been, and then, all of a sudden, there she had been too. His wife, who, it turned out, did work at the unfresh-fish stall, but only sometimes, who had seen and had pushed through the low-level cloud of sheep to get to him and had come to him and had looked at him and not laughed and had held out her hand and helped him up, back to standing. She had held his shitty hand.

*   *   *

The man sat there on the potato box and closed his eyes, just for a second.

Anyway, he said. Then we had five more kids and she got busy and stopped cooking so much and didn't look so hot there, for a while. And I was busy at the dock still, more, even, because the harbormaster, in the end, *had* agreed to give me that raise I damn well deserved, so long as I also agreed to work an extra two hours in the morning and one at night, the eel and keel shifts, we call them, because the eels are only out first thing before the sun and because the keel is, well, the bottom.

So...

So they didn't talk so much anymore then, he and his wife. Or laugh or hold hands or, you know, sex and all that. She went away. Like, not actually, but you know. She turned into a gray ghost, his wife, he told me. Basically only worried about the kids and the still-okay-fish job and the house and when I got home, he said, finally home, after all that eel and keel and all the rest, where was she with my dinner? With holding my hand and so on? She wasn't there. Like, she was there, unless she was with the day-old fish and clams, etc., but not really, not fully, she wasn't there *with me.* And, when she was, because sometimes she was, true, like, sometimes she still said, Yeah, sure, we can do that, just wait until I get these four kids down and tell the other ones to go walk round the house twelve times, sure, even then, she wasn't really there, she wasn't having fun; she was gone.

Not so hot, I said. For you, I mean.

No, no, no, said the man, not that. Not just that. She wasn't beautiful anymore. Not beautiful. From the inside out, I mean. You know?

Yeah, okay, I said. Then, because it had started raining harder and I could see the ceiling above us groaning its way, slowly, down, in, and I knew I had to use these potato boxes to make a stack to hold it up, for now, at least, until I could afford new boards, hopefully from the money he'd give me soon, and also because it was almost noon and I was hungry, I said,

Sure, beautiful. Or not beautiful. From the inside.

And then he didn't say anything, so I said, But then...

But then, he said, one day, she wasn't so gray. One day I woke up, almost late for work as usual, what with those early shifts, and there she was, combing the children with one hand and mashing the gruel with the other and she was *humming*.

No.

Yes.

Yes, she was humming to herself and even kind of smiling a bit and she was wearing the dress one of the babies had eaten the top two buttons off of so it fell open like a perfectly filleted fish and showed her collarbones, both of them, and she was humming and smiling and her skin was downright rosy. Her cheeks and that. Glowing.

And then, because she hadn't looked at him yet, he said, because, despite all this glowing, etc., she still hadn't seen him, not properly, anyway, he'd said,

Hope the gruel's not cold this time, eh?

Like, as a joke, he'd said it. But when he did, something, maybe his voice, maybe not, maybe a small fly or something, something else, made her wince and frown and turn away, turn gray again. The dog next to her—oh, they also had some dogs, the man liked dogs, he was a Dog Man, had always pictured himself surrounded by loving dogs when he got older—winced, too, and shuffled itself under the table.

So he, the man, decided to skip the gruel and leave. He was late, after all.

She started wearing that one dress more and more. She didn't have to, she had two dresses, but she did. He noticed. And combing not just the children's and the dogs' hair, but her own too. And pushing away from him at night, sleeping tucked tight against the wall, the curve of her hip under the nightdress so perfect and so far away.

So one day, well, today, actually, I was thinking about that, he said. About the dress and the collarbones and the hair and the nights and that one time when I'd fallen down, long ago but not so long ago, really, and I decided that, even though I only get twenty-five minutes for lunch and usually spend them alone, at the very end of Long Dock, eating my cold potato while staring out to sea, this time, I decided, I would walk over to the really-just-fine-fish stall to, well, just to see her; to say hello, to maybe stand together, again, for a little while. Eighteen minutes or so, once you factor in travel time.

*　*　*

He paused. Fiddled with a bit of twine that was sticking out of the side of his crate.

Sounds nice, I said.

I thought so, he said.

But, I said.

But, he said. I don't want to talk about it.

Hm, I said.

Well, he said. Anyway… Well…

Well?

Well, she wasn't alone, okay? That's the thing. That's, that's the thing, anyway. She wasn't alone, with the fish and clams and the not-so-fuzzy eels. There was a new kid there. He was working at the stall with her. Some new kid, younger than me, even, working there alongside her, and when one of the eels in the pile she was stacking slid down and would otherwise have landed in the misc. fish bits barrel he caught it, just in time, I saw him, he caught it, and handed it back to her and she took it and she looked at him and she smiled. And he smiled, and she smiled. And for a moment, one breath, neither of them did anything else, they just looked, and smiled, and looked and smiled and smiled and smiled.

She hasn't smiled that kind of smile at me for years, he said. Maybe not any kind of smile, if I'm honest. But especially not that kind. So I just stood there. I just watched. And she was so beautiful, and so was he, not in a weird way, you know what I mean; I mean his goddamn face was happy. Beautiful with happiness.

They both were.

And I watched them, he said,

and I watched,

and the potato sank in my stomach, cold and heavy,

and he, the boy, leaned over, down toward her, he leaned down and,

and I turned around and left.

I went and sat on the end of Long Dock. I watched the gray sea. And then I came here.

You'd already eaten it, your potato? You had time?

I ate it en route. On my way to the stall. I was starving, said the man.

My stomach and my roof both groaned. Well, I said. What do you want me to do about it?

You're a witch, right? he said.

No, I said. Not exactly. I'm a—

Yes, yes, exactly, he said. So, it's simple. A pretty basic request, nothing much. I want a potion, he said. Please don't tell anyone, don't tell them I've been here or told you all this or asked you, but, please: I want you to make her love me again.

Just that? I said.

Just that, he said. He looked down, away from me, and fiddled with his crate twine.

You're sure? I said.

I'm sure, he said.

It can be potent, I said. It can be very powerful.

I know, he said.

You're sure? I said.

Yes, yes, he said. I'm sure.

Well. I said. How strong do you want it?

I want it as strong as possible, he said. Insuperable. Overwhelming.

Like the sea over the side of a ship, I said.

Drenched, he said. Drowned.

Really?

Really.

Really?

Really, really, really.

I sighed. My roof sighed. You brought something of hers? I asked. A bit of cloth, a button, a hair?

I have this, he said, reaching into his pocket and digging out an old comb that was missing two-thirds of its teeth. I took it, he said, so that she couldn't... Well, I took it, he said. He handed it to me. It was light in my hand and stank. Okay, I said. If you're sure.

I'm sure, he said.

I sent him out behind the church to find a five-leaf clover. I knew there was one there, but only one. I knew it would take him ages. Also it was raining pretty hard by then, so that would slow him down a bit too. He sprang out the door, eager, almost sweet, and I watched him go and sighed again. Better not to think about it. Better just to carry on, a ball set in motion, etc., etc. Better to just do, at this point.

I shut the door behind him to keep out at least some of the wet and stacked up the crates to hold the roof. I ate some old bread for lunch and swept up the crumbs and set them beside the crack in the floor where the mice lived. Then I lit the fire and got to work.

By the time he got back, the room was so smoky I had to ask to be sure it was him.

It's me, he said.

Who? I said.

Me, he said. The man with the wife, it's me. I felt his hand reach through the smoke and touch my shoulder.

You've got it? I said.

I've got it, he said. I think I've got it.

We waited a couple minutes with the door open so the smoke could drift out a bit. When it was clear enough to see, I turned around to face him. He was soaked, his hair flattened like a drowned cat. It made him look smaller. Are you sure? I asked, muffled by the rag I had tied around my face to protect against the smoke.

Yes, he said. Look, five leaves, look, one, two, three, four—

No, I said, taking the plant. Are you sure, still sure, about the potion?

Yes, he said, and a drip fell from his nose onto the floor between us.

Okay, I said. I dropped the clover into my pocket and reached around to untie my rag. It's ready, then. It's finished, I said, unmuffled.

       *   *   *

Like all of them, he was surprised it was he who had to drink it, not her, but, like all of them, he drank it, all of it.

Only a sip, I said. One very small sip every day for a year. This is important, I said. There should be enough for a year.

And, still, like all of them, he drank it all, all at once, gone.

There, he said. Job done.

There, I thought. Job done.

He paid me twenty coins and five old fish.

Thank you, he said. He wasn't crying but his hair was still dripping everywhere so it looked like he was.

Well, I said. You really shouldn't—

Thank you, thank you, he said. Then he turned and left.

That night, they said, he and his wife made love with such passion and enthusiasm and noise that their children ran out of the house to the neighbors, terrified, and their dogs howled and howled.

The next morning, they said, the man went to work, of course he did, he still had to work, but he was happy on his walk, he was smiling. And, there, maybe a hundred steps behind, his wife followed, her heart beating so loud the dogs mistook it for a giant's footsteps and stayed in, whimpering, tucked under blankets with the babies. She looked... said the neighbors. She looked... thirsty. Parched.

The next morning, they said, the man had work on the docks and the ships, like he always did. In particular he had work on one specific ship, like he sometimes did, that was heading out at crack of eel to get a split in the cross-timber looked at. It was headed to the works yard a couple miles down the coast. The split wasn't a big deal, they said, was a small enough thing, but one that, left untended, could grow, would grow, into a real problem. So this ship was setting out before it got busy on the water, before the way was clogged with goats and guts and all the other things shipping in and out, and the man was going with it to be sure the repairmen didn't strip the ship's good iron nails this time. The harbormaster owned a percentage of this ship and didn't want it stripped again, so the man went along to keep watch, to be sure.

If they'd asked me if I knew he'd be going out on-boat so soon, I would have said no. I would have said, *Don't be stupid, of course I didn't know. How could I have known?*

But no one asked me anything. They never do.

So the man stood on the aft deck of the ship. He watched the docks and shore fade as his boat pushed out toward the pale, early horizon.

His wife, they tell one another, arrived just in time to see him floating away.

He says he didn't see her, they say. Don't you think he would have seen her? they say. Well, anyway, they say. We saw her, and,
and
she looked so...
thirsty.

✻   ✻   ✻

She reached a hand out toward him. She was fully dressed, though with two buttons missing. She reached out toward the ship, toward him, as the first light of day cut the water from the sky. And then she stepped in. And then stepped farther in. And then farther. And then farther.

We called out to her, they say. But we can't swim. Who among us can swim? So we called out, but the morning surf was loud and she wasn't listening, anyway. She didn't look as though she heard anything, any of it.

And then, they say, she took one more step and the water slipped over her head and she was gone. It was almost beautiful, they say. Probably the most beautiful she had ever been, really. And that was all. That was that.

Then they sigh.

They sigh, and say,

Poor man.

So many kids and all on his own now, they say. Poor man. He'll have to give away his dogs now, they say. Poor man, poor man.

THE WOMAN IN THE CLOSET

by MIMI LOK

(This story, from McSweeney's 57*, was a finalist for the 2020 National Magazine Award in Fiction.)*

AUGUST

IN THE SPACE OF a few hours, Granny Ng was made an official member of the village. She was given her own blue tent, just like the others had—over a hundred of them dotted the southeastern side of Hong Kong Park like giant petals from outer space. That's how they'd once seemed to her, in the days when she still lived with her son and daughter-in-law. Back then, she would take her morning stroll around the turtle pond with Maru, her daughter-in-law's shih tzu. She'd occasionally look over to that strange blue sight, and whenever she saw people moving among the tents, she would turn away, embarrassed that she'd been staring. She had never given much thought to why people lived that way. Then one morning a middle-aged woman with a sleek black bob and a pink tracksuit stopped her at the turtle pond. The woman said she'd noticed her walking her dog there in the mornings, and asked if she was all right. She had her hand on Granny Ng's arm and a concerned, hopeful look on her face. Granny Ng had to admit she was feeling hungry, having had only a few crackers for breakfast. The woman—she introduced herself as Kitty—seemed well-spoken and polite, so Granny Ng was surprised when, after answering a few questions about her home life, her new acquaintance led her toward the mass of blue tents. They stopped at an awning at the southern perimeter of the tents, where a short, silver-bearded man was stirring a pot of soup on a camp stove.

"Uncle Chow, this is Granny Ng," said Kitty. "Her son and daughter-in-law want to kick her out of her apartment and put her in an old people's home at the end of the month. She doesn't want to go."

Granny felt her cheeks warm with embarrassment. The silver-bearded man tasted a spoonful of the soup and nodded slowly, though it wasn't clear if it was to himself or to Kitty. He turned abruptly, wiped his hands on the front of his overalls, and invited Granny Ng to sit on one of the plastic children's stools dotted around the outdoor kitchen.

"Granny, take the weight off your feet. Kitty, give her some of this soup, will you?" He brought over another stool and sat facing her. "Well, Granny, I'm sorry to hear your son doesn't want to take care of you. This kind of thing is getting more and more common these days."

Granny Ng blinked at the bowl of beef soup in her hands and nodded.

"But the fact is that you still have somewhere to stay, true? None of the people here can say the same."

Kitty looked concerned. "Tell him, Granny Ng. Tell Uncle Chow what you told me."

The soup smelled so good to Granny Ng. She hadn't had beef soup in years; her son and daughter-in-law were recent converts to Taoism, and had taken a three-year vow of vegetarianism. She brought the bowl to her lips, then hesitated. It was too hot to drink just like that, but she didn't want to be rude. Then again, she'd burned her tongue several times that week to avoid her daughter-in-law hitting her for eating too slowly. She peered around hopefully for a spoon.

"Granny, please allow me to speak for you," said Kitty. She squatted on the ground next to Granny Ng and looked imploringly at the silver-bearded man. "It's terrible in there, Uncle Chow. The staff beat the old people and steal their valuables. They hide their letters and have to be bribed in order to hand them over. On visiting days, they put on a big show of caring for the residents so the children don't get concerned, but as soon as they leave, it all starts again. We can't let this poor granny end up in a place like that, can we? We can't let her go from bad to worse."

Uncle Chow scratched his beard. "Which old people's home is this?"

"Does it matter?" Kitty sighed. Then she lowered her head, as if admitting defeat. "My mother was in that home."

Uncle Chow considered Granny Ng as she blew on her soup. "How are you, Granny? Are you enjoying the soup?"

"It's delicious," she said, blowing harder on the soup. It was still too hot to taste. "The best I've ever had."

"Uncle Chow here used to be a cook," said Kitty. "He worked for some of the best hotels in the city."

"Oh? How did you end up here?" asked Granny Ng.

When Uncle Chow smiled, she could see how densely packed his teeth were, like a dolphin's. She imagined him pulling out one of his silver whiskers and flossing with it.

"Luck," he replied.

"Luck?" said Granny Ng. "You think you're lucky?"

"I didn't say what kind of luck, Granny. Now drink up your soup. It should be cool enough now."

Uncle Chow and Kitty pitched a tent for Granny Ng close to the center of the settlement. Although it wasn't something she usually did, Kitty accompanied Granny Ng to the small apartment she shared with her son and daughter-in-law and helped her gather some belongings into a duffel bag. It was clear that Granny Ng hadn't packed a bag in some time; Kitty had to keep telling her to put things back, or explain that some things, like the rice cooker and the ironing board, were not practical to bring. Before they left, Granny Ng wrote a note for her son and taped it to the refrigerator door:

Dear Son,
I have received a call from a relative who is very sick, and I must visit her at once. I don't know how long I'll be gone. Please don't worry about me. I'll be in touch.
    Please take care of yourself,
    Your mother

Don't call the police, Son, she thought. And don't worry about me. Once things were more settled, she would write again. She thought he wouldn't approve of her making her own arrangements in this way, and might even feel as if he'd let her down. But she felt it was the right decision; in the long run, her daughter-in-law would be happier, which meant that her son would have a chance of being happier.

That first week, Kitty was a constant presence, bringing visitors like Rocky, a construction worker. He fitted Granny Ng's tent with mesh sheets that he assured her would protect her from cold, bugs, and damp. Rocky's wife gave her acupressure massages for her aching back, while a young woman called Miss Kwan came by to donate a pair of gloves.

Uncle Chow explained how the village worked: the time-table for communal meals, the mail system, the procedures for submitting suggestions and complaints, and so on. Meanwhile, Kitty showed her where to go for drinking water and the washing facilities. Her favorite spots were the public bathrooms near the British Council, which tended to be the cleanest, but she warned her not to go there after dark. She showed her places around town where she could collect cans and bottles for recycling, the best underpasses from which to hawk goods without being bothered by police, and the best flyovers from which to beg, or, as they liked to call it, "ask for donations."

At first, Granny Ng did not sleep well in her new environment. She didn't mind the ground, which was not much harder than her previous bed, or the smallness of the space, though it would have been nice to have been able to stand up instead of crawling and stooping all the time. It was the noises, which seemed to go on all night till the morning: fellow tent dwellers chatting and cooking, voices and songs from their radios, teenagers' yells and screams floating over from the other side of the park. Also, traffic seemed never to stop, the roar of engines and horns constant through the night; she wondered where these people were driving to under cover of darkness, and when they planned to catch up on the sleep they were losing. In the mornings she found she was stiffer than usual, and it took about half an hour of stretching and walking about before she felt normal again.

Granny Ng learned that people had come to the tent village for different reasons. Some had lost their homes during the last financial crisis. Many of the men in their late forties and fifties were construction workers who'd been laid off and couldn't find steady work.

Miss Kwan was one of the newer residents. She'd lost her sales job at a securities firm three months ago and had been able to keep the news from her parents, who had emigrated to Canada several years ago. However, she had an old classmate in the city with whom she had a standing lunch date on the last Thursday of each month. For the past three months, Miss Kwan had put on her old work suit and walked over to the other side of the park, where her friend, who managed a cosmetics store, waited on a bench by the koi pond. She and her friend took turns treating each other. Miss Kwan had to save for three weeks in order to buy two rice box lunches from their favorite restaurant. She never finished the lunch box, claiming that she was full, or that she was trying to lose weight, but the truth was that she was keeping half of it for her evening meal. Afterward, she would return to her tent, slip her work suit into its plastic cover, and put it carefully away until the next time.

Granny Ng got the scoop on her neighbors from Kitty, who happily volunteered details of their life stories, but was vague when it came to Uncle Chow.

"He lost his job at a hotel—a good one, I think—but no one really knows the details. Now he makes a bit here and there by repairing electrical items—radios, lamps, clocks, that kind of thing. We're not even sure how long he's been here. Find the oldest, longest-standing resident and they'll tell you Uncle Chow was already here and running things when they arrived."

Granny Ng found it odd that Kitty knew so little about her friend. Then again, after several weeks of confidences, she had not yet told Granny Ng her own story of coming to live in the tent village. She had once mentioned a husband, but Granny Ng sensed her reluctance to elaborate. And while she tried to ignore the casual gossip from some of her fellow villagers—the husband was a drinker, a gambler, a wife-beater—she couldn't help but invest in a version of Kitty's past, one filled with adversity, suffering, and courage. This led to a newfound appreciation of her friend's cheerful efficiency and eagerness to help, which at first, she had to admit, she had rather taken for granted, and at times had even found a little intrusive. Whatever the case, it seemed to Granny Ng that Kitty was content here, and this inspired in her the possibility that she could be too.

Despite her circumstances, Granny Ng was quite good at keeping herself clean and presentable. She bathed and did laundry in public washrooms, and even looked respectable enough to occasionally pass through shining hotel lobbies and use their bathrooms. She was careful to avoid going to the same hotels too often, and to bring only one or two garments to wash each time. Once, noticing the suspicious gaze of a bathroom attendant, she said she'd spilled something on herself in the restaurant and wanted to get the stain out. But maintaining a neat appearance wasn't always helpful, as people found it difficult to believe that the old woman sitting on the pedestrian flyover really needed to beg. Some of them would say, "Come on, Granny, you've had your fun. Now stop slumming it and go home to your family. They'll be worried about you." She ignored the comments and held out her bowl, feeling it was less shameful to beg from strangers than from family.

OCTOBER

Granny Ng had been living in the tent village for forty-two days when the city officials removed her, and about twenty other new-comers, from the park. When Uncle Chow asked them, "Why? What trouble were they causing?" the officials told him they'd been given fresh orders to prevent the spreading of the tent village. Granny Ng assumed there was some kind of understanding between the officials and the old-timer tent dwellers, since they had been left alone. As the officials stood over Granny Ng, watching Rocky help her pack up her tent and belongings, they seemed genuinely sorry, even a little embarrassed. Kitty and Uncle Chow gave her small packets and tins of food, and suggestions about where she could try setting up next. Kitty looked as if she might cry. "I'm so sorry you can't stay, Granny Ng. I feel like I've let you down." Granny Ng patted her on the shoulder and continued packing up her tent. She folded it slowly, and with much care. It may be just a sheet of cloth held up by poles, she thought, but even a millimeter of fabric can provide a small feeling of security.

Granny Ng took Kitty's suggestion and tried another tent village, in a park about ten miles west. Kitty had taken her to the bus station and pointed to the name of the stop where she had to get off, making her repeat it three times. She saw her off with a cube of green bean cake wrapped in wax paper, and a flask of hot tea.

This new tent village was much smaller, with perhaps ten or twelve tents. They called themselves an association, and everything was shared. There was no chief, but the resident who seemed to speak the most was a gaunt, wiry man called Mr. To. He explained to Granny Ng that as long as you paid one hundred HKD a month, you could share their rice, cooking gas, and water. This association had managed to get some farming land donated to them by a homeless coalition.

"We started growing vegetables on it about a year ago," said Mr. To. "The land had previously been used for growing pomegranates. It took us months to clear the roots by hand."

"I can help," said Granny Ng. "I know a little about gardening."

"Ah, no, Granny," said Mr. To. "It's too much for you. The men have to cycle for almost an hour to get there. Besides, the first crops have just been harvested. We'll sell the vegetables in the park in the next few days. I think we'll make about one thousand HKD."

Granny Ng nodded.

"You're probably better off collecting recyclables or asking for donations," said Mr. To.

Granny Ng said, "I understand," but really she envied the men. How satisfying it must be to make something that could be sold to appreciative customers. If she couldn't help the association with farming, she could perhaps do other things. She had always been good with her hands, and as a young girl had assisted her father in his studio. He had been a carpenter by trade, but he had also made beautiful wood carvings that he sold to a small number of clients. She had loved to watch him work. During her final year of primary school, she decided to carve a set of six animals, each the size of a child's fist. When after a week it became clear that they would barely resemble their real-life counterparts, she decided to turn them into mythical creatures of her own devising. The pig, for example, would have the stripes of a tiger. The bird, whose legs were too thick, would have horse legs. She worked on them every day after school for almost two months. The most difficult one to get right was a creature with the body of a leopard and the head of an elephant; this one alone took two weeks. She finally presented the set to her father on his birthday; his chuckling delight she remembered more clearly than any words of praise he may have uttered. Several days later, when he saw her sorting through blocks of wood for another project, he said, "Daughter, your high school entrance exams are just two months away. I think you should spend your time studying." Granny Ng couldn't recall anything she had made since then. Still, throughout her life she occasionally wondered if, had she not become a wife and mother, or if she'd been born in a different time, she might have followed in her father's footsteps.

She went around the park collecting branches and nubs of wood. Then she borrowed a selection of tools from the communal kitchen and workshop—a saw, a cutting knife, and several chisels—and set to work. She worked with great concentration, determined that from these coarse pieces of wood a delicately contoured animal would be conjured. She spent almost an entire day on the project, and by dusk, when she had to return the tools, she was disappointed that she'd managed to achieve only a crudely shaped figure. Her fellow villagers showed little surprise. A few said, "Good effort, Granny," before retiring to their tents. Disheartened, Granny Ng joined some of the others the next day in collecting cans and bottles for recycling.

DECEMBER

Granny Ng managed to stay in the village for little over a month before city officials came and cleared out the newcomers. She went to another park, where she stayed for twenty-six days before being moved again. She began worrying about the cooler weather that was coming. Upon leaving the last tent village, she was given the name of another park up in the New Territories. A few minutes into the bus ride, Granny Ng fell into a light sleep. When she awoke, she was alarmed to find herself traveling along an open highway with fields and hills on either side, sparsely dotted with low-rise houses. At the next stop, she went up to the driver and showed him the piece of paper with the name of the park written on it.

"Don't worry, Granny," said the driver. "You've still got about six more stops."

"When did we leave Hong Kong Island?"

He shrugged. "About twenty miles back."

Granny Ng returned to her seat. She gazed out of the window at the quiet, unfamiliar landscape: the expanse of sky and the dense green peaks that loomed in the distance. She had not traveled so far from home in years, and in those extra twenty miles she felt as if she were suddenly in another country. Panicked, she pressed the bell and hurried off the bus at the next stop, pausing only to thank the driver. She set down her duffel bag on the side of the highway and watched the bus disappear into the pinkish-blue horizon.

She had to get to the other side. Something told her that whatever she needed was situated there. But even though it seemed relatively quiet at this time, she was afraid to step onto the tarmac in case a vehicle appeared out of nowhere and knocked her flat.

A sudden breeze, and Granny Ng hugged herself against the chill. She picked up her duffel bag and started walking along the highway, squinting at the sunset. After a quarter of an hour, she came to an underpass marked by a sign: TIN HAU GARDEN. An arrow pointed to the other side of the highway. It was several degrees cooler in the underpass, which was dim and smelled of damp leaves and urine. She hurried past a peeling mural of children flying kites on a hill, and up a sloping path that brought her onto the other side of the road. Another sign for Tin Hau Garden pointed to a narrow, overgrown path, which eventually opened onto a small patch of green. A stone bird fountain stood in the middle of it, full of mashed leaves and dirty water. Next to it was an iron bench with a memorial plaque on the back. Granny Ng avoided reading it. It made her uncomfortable, this monument after death. She wondered about the person it was dedicated to, how they would feel knowing there was a big, uncomfortable bench built in their name. She decided it was useless and in the way—too hard to sit on, let alone sleep on. Not that I would ever sleep on a bench, she thought.

Granny Ng decided to set up her sleeping arrangements while there was still some light. A thick line of bushes near the highway seemed to be a good choice—enough cover from passing cars and people, and an escape route of sorts in case she needed it (who could tell if unruly teenagers had claimed this spot for their drinking and goodness knows what else?). Pulling back some branches and hunching a little, she edged herself in. She beat back some more branches to make enough room to lay down a narrow piece of tarp and unfurl her ground mat and sleeping bag. She hooked the loops of the tent cover onto overhanging branches. There was just enough room to sit up straight and to lie down. Now that she had made her nest, she felt reluctant to leave it, reassured by the cover it gave her. She pulled a flashlight from her duffel bag and laid it down beside her hip. She also pulled out a clock radio and a plastic bag containing a roll of toilet paper and set them down beside the flashlight. Then she arranged a picnic of her evening meal: a tangerine, some slices of SPAM, and a flask of green tea.

Granny Ng's greatest fear had once been that the older she got, the more likely it was that she would be forgotten. Her second greatest fear was of being a burden, though that was sometimes the only guarantee of being remembered. But now, munching on the tangerine, she decided it would be ideal to depart from this life with no trace. How nice, she thought, to lie down on a patch of earth and simply be absorbed in rapid degrees throughout the night, and by morning you'd be gone. How efficient. Passersby would not have to deal with the inconvenience of a body, and would only delight in finding use for the objects inside the tent: the sleeping bag, the clock radio, the tube of toothpaste, the three sweaters and two pairs of comfortable shoes, the Swiss Army knife, the roll of toilet paper, the flashlight, the tin bowl, the pair of silver chopsticks, and the three tins of SPAM.

Granny Ng spent the following morning contemplating the house on the other side of the highway. It was low and cream-colored, with a dark-glass door. It intrigued her that a family would want to live in the middle of a field with no other houses in sight, and a restless, noisy highway right in front. She decided to watch the house and wait for a glimpse of this family. She imagined a young, successful couple ushering their children, a boy and a girl, out of the house each morning and onto a school bus. Perhaps they had a dog. Her daughter-in-law had kept poor Maru cooped up in a cage in the kitchen, and Granny Ng, unable to bear its mournful whining, had taken it upon herself to walk it around the park every morning. But this family, she thought: they have so much space, they could keep a dog of any size and it would be happy.

Granny Ng watched the house all morning, but no one appeared. She had to get up every half hour or so and walk about to warm herself up and stretch her legs. She had been hungry since waking up, but made herself wait until noon before she ate. She had two and a half tins of SPAM left; with rice, they could last her a few more days, but on their own, she didn't know. She took small bites, washing down the saltiness with small sips from her flask of tea, which had now grown tepid and slimy. The food put a weight in her stomach but made her feel colder than before.

She watched the house for the rest of the afternoon, and still no one appeared. Eventually, she climbed into her sleeping bag and tried to nap for a while. A horn from a passing truck woke her. She drew back the tent covering and saw the sky was darkening, streaked with smoky grays and blues. A little while later, at around seven o'clock, she saw a young, small-faced man approach the front door. A salesman? But no; he rummaged in his trouser pocket, fished out a key, and let himself in.

Over the next three days, Granny Ng watched the house and the young man, who emerged each morning in a tie and a short-sleeved shirt, munching on an apple. On the fourth day, she made her move.

The gate to the side of the house unlatched lightly, and she stepped into a flat garden with a pear tree at the edge. She pulled up a patio chair under an open window, stood on the chair, and climbed in, slowly lowering herself backward into a sink. As she brought her left leg toward the floor, she was distracted by her plastic flip-flop sliding off her foot; turning to look at it, she lost her balance, caught the edge of the sink for balance, and banged her elbow, cursing.

She leaned back against the sink and took a moment to rub her elbow, then her lower back and thighs. She felt as if she had stones lodged in her joints. As the blood started returning to her limbs, she realized that, for the first time in weeks, she didn't feel cold.

The room smelled of warm dust and lemons. Plastic detergent bottles lined a single shelf above a chrome washer-dryer. She eyed her distorted reflection in the door: her face stretched like a balloon, her short, greasy hair a smear of black ink. She gathered up her flip-flops and glanced at the wall clock: 8:05 a.m.

Granny Ng stepped out into a long corridor, her toes nudging the edge of the tatami runner that stretched to the end. In the quiet, her breathing sounded amplified and coarse. She listened for the scrape of a chair, a cough. All she heard was a low hum of electricity. Still, she stood paralyzed with doubt. Maybe she wasn't so original after all. Maybe someone else had got there first.

She considered the closed doors along the corridor, and opened the first one on her right. Bathroom. Empty. The next door revealed a thermostat. The opposite door opened onto an office. Next to that was a closet full of towels and bedding. The last door opened onto the master bedroom. No one there. She sighed with relief, then chuckled at her faintheartedness. The end of the corridor revealed an open kitchen on the left and a living room on the right. The kitchen was spacious, with a preparation counter in the middle and shiny orange pots and pans hanging from a metal rafter above it. In the living room there was a large, thin television mounted on the wall and a brown L-shaped sofa facing it. The sparseness of her surroundings stirred in her feelings of awe and unease. The objects around her seemed to exist within an impersonal kind of order, as if they had been arranged according to an instruction manual. The only suggestion that someone might actually reside here was the small collection of framed photographs on the living room side table. Granny Ng picked up a photograph of the young man. In the photograph he was wearing a graduation cap and gown. He had a small, pebble-smooth face, and eyes that looked ready to flinch.

"Ah, who's been bullying you, son?" she said softly. He looked like a nice boy, the kind who had good manners. A slight, uncertain smile rested on his pillowy lips. He reminded Granny Ng of the classical poet from the painting—what was its name? In it, the poet sits on a rock with cranes perched on branches around him. He is reciting a poem, which is inscribed in the upper-right corner of the painting. She had seen it throughout her life: as a young girl, she'd seen it in one of her father's art books in his studio; as a student, she'd seen it at the University Museum in Pok Fu Lam; and throughout the rest of her life she'd encountered the image on T-shirts, mugs, and posters in souvenir shops. But, as with many things now, she couldn't recall its name.

In another photograph, the young man was at a lake, wearing a baggy T-shirt with the letters NYU on it, standing next to an older man with the same pillowy mouth. With one hand, the older man held up a plump, chrome-colored fish the size of a small boy, and with the other hand he squeezed the young man's shoulder. They were smiling. No, the older man was smiling; the young man seemed to be squinting into the sun, or about to cry.

Granny Ng liked the look of the sofa, and thought it couldn't hurt to sit for just a moment. She sank into the cushions, and was startled by how soft and comfortable they were. She rubbed her cheek against the cool suede and let out a deep "Aaahhh…"

Then she became aware of a darkly sour odor. She pulled some strands of hair across her face and gingerly sniffed them, then her shirtsleeve. Although she'd tried to keep herself as clean as possible, the salty, earthy smells of the park and her lack of access to a bathroom these last few days had hindered this effort. She suddenly felt filthy, slick with dirt and sweat, and was seized with an urge to rid herself of it. She went into the bathroom, closed the toilet lid, removed her clothes, and folded them in a neat pile on top.

The shower was glorious. She'd forgotten how good it felt to stand under hot, steaming water. It was so soothing that she almost dozed off, and it was only the jabbing hunger in her stomach that jolted her and made her turn off the water. Squeezing a towel around herself, she frowned at the pile of clothes on the toilet seat. She gathered them in her arms and padded across the corridor into the office. This room had a futon sofa, a framed photograph of Mount Fuji, a desk with a computer on it, and a built-in closet with sliding wooden doors. Inside the closet she found some suits and coats hanging in filmy covers. Plastic boxes were stacked in threes, containing T-shirts, sweaters, and jogging pants. The jogging pants she picked out were too long—she had to fold up the ends three times—but the T-shirt fit nicely.

In the kitchen, she found garbage bags under the sink. She pulled one out and started filling it up. First she put in some clothes from the closet: two pairs of thick socks, a sweater, and two T-shirts. Then she went back to the kitchen and collected several tins of SPAM, dace in black beans, preserved vegetables, a few packets of ramen noodles, and a liter bottle of mineral water. She wrapped three eggs in a dishcloth. She thought about taking some soap and detergent to wash her clothes, then realized she could just come back and use the washer-dryer.

Okay, she told herself. You've got your supplies. Time to go. But still there was the jabbing in her stomach. She decided it couldn't hurt to make herself something to eat. I've got all day, after all, she reasoned. The prospect of hot food was too tempting to pass up. And while she was here, she might as well throw those dirty clothes into the washer.

Granny Ng cooked some ramen noodles in a saucepan, cracked an egg into it, and ate from a large bowl on the sofa in front of the TV. She was relishing the warmth of the soup too much to pay attention to the bright, flickering images on the screen. She fell asleep with the bowl in her lap and woke later in darkness with a shiver, then was seized by a mild panic, momentarily forgetting where she was and then suddenly feeling cold and heavy with tiredness. In the dark kitchen, the microwave clock glowed at her: 6:45 p.m. The young man came home at 7 p.m.

Granny Ng grabbed the saucepan and started scrubbing at the noodles that had stuck to the bottom. Then she rinsed off the bowl and the chopsticks, dried them, and put them back in their places. She wiped down the counters with a sponge and wiped them again with a paper towel to avoid leaving water marks.

It was 6:55 p.m. The sky was dark. The branches of the pear tree at the edge of the garden had retreated into shadow. Granny Ng headed to the back of the house, toward the laundry room, took the damp clothes out of the washer, and with some effort, managed to pull herself onto the sink counter. Then she remembered the garbage bag full of supplies.

"Stupid!" she whispered. She lowered herself back down and hurried into the bedroom. No bag. She went down the hall and searched the office, the kitchen, before finally spotting it at the foot of the sofa.

"Friday is good for me too."

Granny Ng froze at the sound of the young man's voice on the other side of the front door. Her hand hovered over the neck of the garbage bag and she carefully closed her fingers around it.

"Whatever you prefer. Excuse me; I'm just letting myself in."

Granny Ng grabbed the garbage bag, hurried back down the hall into the office, opened the closet door, crouched on the floor behind the plastic boxes, and slid the door shut, breathing in the sharp, acrid smell of mothballs in the dark.

With her cheek against the closet wall, Granny Ng heard the slam of the front door and the young man's wavering voice. "Sounds good. Great, great. Yes, I'll call you on Wednesday. Me too: very glad."

In the quiet that followed, she imagined the young man stopping on the doormat to slip off his tight office shoes and put them away. She couldn't remember if there was a shoe rack, or if she'd seen pairs of shoes lined up on the floor just inside the door. She thought of her son's cotton-socked toes wedged between the forks of his plastic slippers; a grown man of almost forty, and still his feet looked so childish.

She heard the microwave door open and shut, and a series of beeping sounds. He's heating up some takeout, she thought. He probably eats takeout every night. No wonder the kitchen looks so undisturbed. The radio came on, a show where people talked about jazz musicians. Then she heard slow, heavy footsteps coming down the corridor toward her. She startled at the sound of a door opening, then realized it was the bathroom door across the hall. A blast of water, quickly muted. More footsteps down the hall—his steps were very heavy... perhaps he was flat-footed?—then drawers sliding open and banging lightly against the coasters. The young man was humming something without an obvious melody. His voice was pleasantly soft and light. A high-pitched beep from the microwave echoed down the hall. A blast of water, then muted again. The young man had stepped into the steam of the bathroom, ignoring the food that was waiting for him.

Several hours passed before Granny Ng finally heard the door shut to the main bedroom. Over the course of the evening, she had listened to the young man's movements. He'd spent about twenty minutes munching on his dinner in front of his computer, before going into the living room and watching a movie. Then he'd returned to the office and started blowing into a musical instrument; it sounded like a small elephant braying. Whatever it was, she thought, it must have water in it, the way it wheezed and whistled.

In the closet, she'd found a stack of towels on the shelves and spread several of these on the floor behind the plastic storage boxes. Using the garbage bag she'd filled with supplies as a pillow, she had lain down for a few hours. After the first hour or so, she'd become quite stiff and cold from the floor, but apart from that it hadn't been so bad. Upon hearing the bedroom door close, Granny Ng decided it was finally safe to come out. She stepped out of the closet and stretched her arms and legs.

She decided she would tidy up and sneak out of there while the young man slept. She peered out of the window and saw that the highway was slick with wet. Thinking of her flimsy tent, she hoped it had been a light, brief rain. Her eyes had to strain to make out her spot in the bushes through the window in the dark.

Then it started to pour. Granny Ng sighed. There was nothing for it. She climbed back into the closet, despairing over the state her tent would be in by the morning.

That night, Granny Ng dreamed of her son. Perhaps it was the smell of the mothballs, so pungently antiseptic and reminiscent of the wardrobe in the apartment they'd shared. He appeared to her as a child, in what seemed to be less of a dream than a memory. She had just picked him up from his first day at school. While children had run past him into their mothers' embrace, he had stood hopelessly at the gate, his pale little legs knocking against each other uncertainly.

"I'm taking you for an ice cream, for being such a brave boy," she said. His hand was so small and soft in hers, it seemed that if she squeezed any harder she would crush it like a marshmallow. His fragility made her anxious, and often brought her to the brink of tears. It took all the restraint she could manage to refrain from coddling him.

In the café, she waited a few minutes for him to enjoy his lemon ice cream before asking, "So, was your first day really as bad as you thought it would be?"

Hesitation flickered across his face; he continued working on his ice cream with greater resolve.

"Is your teacher strict? Or kind?" Her own ice cream was melting in its bowl. "What about your classmates? Did you end up in the same class as your friend Ah Bo?" She regretted how her questions were spoiling his enjoyment of his treat, but she couldn't help probing, urged on by the belief that it was better for him to share these things with her.

He scraped the last of the ice cream onto his spoon and gazed upon it mournfully, as if he were bidding farewell to a dear friend. Then he turned to her with an anguished look and said, "Why must I go to school?"

She was not prepared for this question. "Why, because... because it's the law." She wished she had come up with a more persuasive answer, but it was the first thing that had come to mind. "Ah, and also, of course, because you must learn things, and become a smart boy, and grow up to be a useful young man. Do you want all the other boys to be better than you?"

She smiled hopefully at her son, appealing to his understanding, perhaps his pride, but he was staring at his empty bowl and dragging his spoon back and forth across it. He started tapping it against the bottom of the bowl, as if it were a spade hitting a treasure chest in the ground. The sound became loud enough that the other customers in the café started looking over at them.

"Son," she pleaded softly.

Her son continued hitting the spoon against the bowl. Tears welled in his eyes, and his cheeks were flushed with fearful determination. How had she produced such a sensitive, sullen child? she wondered. As a baby he had seemed so cheerful and full of good nature. She left some money on the table and surprised her son by roughly scooping him up by the armpits and carrying him out of the café, beyond the discreet stares of the other customers, only to return moments later to hand over the ice cream spoon to the waitress.

The next morning, Granny Ng waited for the slam of the front door, then hurried out of the closet and across the hall, sat on the toilet, and gave a long sigh of relief as she felt the burden she'd been carrying all night leave her body. She stretched her limbs, stiff and aching from sleeping on the cold floor. Then she climbed through the laundry room window with her garbage bag of supplies and crossed the highway toward the bushes. The air was fresh and cool after the night's rain, and the tarmac gleamed in the faint sunshine.

The bushes had been ripped open. The contents of her nest were strewn across the ground. The tent covering hung limp from a broken branch, and underneath lay the sleeping bag, bloated with damp like a giant slug. Granny Ng let herself cry, quietly and briefly. Then she noticed that just a few objects lay on the ground—her clothes, the chopsticks, the tin bowl, and the soaked roll of toilet paper. Her initial distress was replaced by a sense of consolation as she realized it had not been a pointless vandalism; whoever had come to ransack the nest in the night had found things they'd needed. She wondered if this was a skewed manifestation of her wish: to disappear in the night, leaving nothing but items of use. No one can accuse me now of taking up space, she thought, gathering up the discarded items. Not even the bushes or the worms in the ground. The feeling didn't last long, though. She knew she was fooling herself; the fact remained that her feet were still on this patch of grass and she had not really disappeared. Then, looking over at the young man's house, it occurred to her that although she could not pull off this impossible feat of disappearance, she might be able to come close to it.

She crossed back over the highway, unlatched the garden gate, pushed her garbage bag of supplies through the back window, and climbed in after it. She threw her rain-soaked clothes, sleeping bag, ground mat, and tent cover into the washing machine and went across the hall into the office. She opened the closet doors. The space looked smaller than it had earlier that morning, or the objects in it larger: big plastic storage boxes stacked three by three in the front, and a row of jackets, trousers, and coats in dry-cleaning bags hanging above them. She guessed that the young man was the kind of person who bought impulsively and accumulated too many of those sweatshirts with logos on the breast, or suits that were too mature for him. He probably bought these things out of boredom, or because a coworker or a girlfriend had encouraged him to.

At the back of the closet, behind the boxes and under the hanging clothes, she contemplated the space where she had slept the night before: roughly two feet wide and five feet long, about three and a half feet between the clothes and the floor. The young man had so much space, he didn't have enough to fill it.

Granny Ng couldn't help shaking her head at how much he probably took for granted. She had been raised with the belief that wastefulness was a dire offense; if you had space, you found useful things to occupy it. Her son and daughter-in-law, despite their flaws, knew the value of this, though perhaps too much—they had, after all, in the end decided that their space was of more use to them than she was. Granny Ng grimaced at this brief moment of self-pity and turned her attention to her next course of action.

She would make use of that small rectangle of space at the back of the closet, at least until the weather got warm and dry again. Then, she thought, perhaps she would try her luck in another tent village. But the idea of moving again immediately nauseated her.

No need to think about it now, she told herself. Just rest up here for a while and you'll feel more prepared to go out there again. Pushing the hanging clothes to one side, she looked upon her new home with a hopeful imagination. Once her ground mat and sleeping bag had dried, she would lay them down there in the corner, with extra towels for bedding, and make it quite cozy and comfortable. It would be like a smaller version of her first tent, with more insulation than any tent dweller could wish for. Her bag of clothes would sit at her feet, or she could use it as a pillow. Her flashlight had been taken, but what was this? A light cord hung from the ceiling on the left side of the closet. She pulled on it with a click, and the space was filled with a watery yellow glow. As long as the young man was not in the room, she could use this, but otherwise a flashlight would be much better. She would get a toilet roll from the bathroom and lay it next to her head in case she needed to blow her nose in the night. She could deposit her used bits of toilet paper in a plastic bag looped around the handle of one of the boxes. Yes, it would all come together nicely.

To pass the time as she waited for the washing cycle to finish, Granny Ng surveyed the office. She noticed that the computer keyboard had oily keys, and guessed that he spent a lot of time in front of that machine. A printer sat next to it with paper sticking out of its tray; it looked like it was sticking its tongue out at her. A black rectangular case leaned against the corner of the room. She opened it and saw a slim black instrument that had been dismantled and stored in several parts. So it's a clarinet, she thought, not a small elephant, ha ha.

She sat in the big, puffy office chair on wheels and scooted around the room for a bit until she started feeling dizzy and had to lie down on the white futon sofa. Another waste, she thought. How well I could use that sofa! She wondered about the picture of Mount Fuji on the wall—if it was somewhere the young man had been. She didn't recall seeing any photos of him in cold-weather clothes. Perhaps it was somewhere he wanted to visit one day, or perhaps he just thought it was pretty. She felt she could understand, as she used to cover her bedroom door with scenic pictures torn from out-of-date calendars: glassy lakes mirroring lush forests, clusters of banyan trees silhouetted by a crimson dusk, or cherry blossoms against a blue sky.

As she surveyed the rest of the house, she tried to imagine how a man of so few years could be successful enough to maintain as large and as comfortable a home as this. Perhaps he was one of those people who had a gift for computers, business, something like that, or perhaps he'd inherited some money.

Upon further investigation, she soon saw through the minimal, ordered appearance of the house. The blinds were full of dust. The metallic sheen of the kitchen cupboards opened to shelves haphazardly stacked with packets of food, crockery, and water bottles. She disapproved of the young man's choice of laundry detergent— too expensive, no brightening agent—and was dismayed to find there was no fabric softener on the shelves. She got on her hands and knees and straightened the thick tatami mat that ran askew along the length of the corridor. In the young man's bedroom, the dresser drawers contained a jumble of socks, underpants, and vests. His wardrobe was no better—clothes squashed together, ties tangled up—and a quick glance under his bed was enough to tell her it was a site of neglect. She was sure she could straighten the place out in a day or two, but she knew she couldn't do it without drawing attention to her efforts. So that day she contented herself with taking a damp cloth to the blinds and throwing out some moldy food from the refrigerator. Over the next few days, then weeks, she learned to take a deep breath before opening a drawer or a door, and to face the disorder within by moving just a few things here, a few things there.

JANUARY

Dear Son,

How have you been? I hope you and Daughter-in-law are both in good health. I am sorry if you've been worried about my well-being. I have found a nice place out of town, and I think I will stay here awhile. My accommodations are clean and warm, and there is a washer-dryer that makes things very convenient. It is nice here.

The kitchen is well equipped, although it was terribly disorganized when I first arrived. Pots were with plates, cups and bowls were with packets of food. It really was chaos. I straighten things out a bit here and there, because it is the least I can do for my host. He is a young man in his thirties. He has a full-time job, and is often tired when he gets home in the evening. A woman comes on Mondays and Thursdays to clean and run errands, but, frankly, she is useless. She gets paid for three hours each time, but she spends only one hour working and the rest of the time she spends on the phone or watching TV. It isn't an exaggeration to say that I do three times as much cleaning as she does. But as I have said, it is the least I can do for my host.

Do you want to hear something funny? The other day I heard the so-called cleaner talking on the phone. She is convinced that the young man has found himself a girlfriend, and that the girlfriend has taken it upon herself to tidy up the place! Meanwhile, the young man noticed how much better things have been organized lately, and he gave the cleaner a small raise and thanked her for all her hard work. What a shock that must have been for her! You can imagine how popular this imaginary girlfriend was with her.

Although I make light of it, I really would like to see him with a nice young woman. Lately there has been someone he talks to a lot on the phone, but she doesn't sound like she's right for him. He always sounds as if he's apologizing or trying to calm her down. She came here one evening after they'd been out for dinner. I could hear her voice all the way from the living room. She was complaining about a waitress she thought had been rude to her at the restaurant. "For such a high-class place, they hire really low-class staff" were her words. I thought she must be very beautiful for him to put up with such an ugly temperament. I was right. A week or so later, he put a framed picture of her in the office, next to his computer. She looks like a movie star: long hair, very pretty.

When the lazy cleaner isn't around, and the young man is at work or out on the weekends with his young woman, I have the whole place to myself. This is my favorite time. I usually try and find something to keep myself busy. Today I took down the curtains and washed and ironed them. Yesterday I collected the young man's socks and darned the ones that looked like they were starting to get holes in them. I don't mind it at all.

I relax by practicing tai chi in the garden. It's also been nice to catch up on some TV shows. Remember I used to follow that soap opera set in a countryside clinic? I stopped watching it for a few months, and now everything's different—new actors are playing old characters, people are married or divorced or dead. I can barely keep up; everything's changed so quickly. Fortunately, real life moves a little more slowly.

I wish you could see what a nice place this is.

Please take care of yourself,

Your mother

FEBRUARY

Granny Ng could not understand why the grass in the garden seemed not to have grown during the time she'd been there. She pressed her palms lightly against the blades; they felt real enough. The sparseness of the garden made it seem like something no one wanted to care for or devote any time or thought to, and this made her feel sad for it. She started imagining a row of orchids here, a fishpond there, a water feature there, and sometimes drew variations of these ideas on sheets of printer paper. It was a strangely liberating feeling; she hadn't drawn for years, and was amazed to find that her hands were still somewhat faithful to her imagination, and that she was capable still of rendering the images in her mind. Sometimes, when she tired of drawing gardens, she drew animals. Later, she attempted reproductions of famous paintings, but found that her memory often failed her in the details. She taped all of these drawings, finished or not, to the back and side walls of the closet, where they hung over her sleeping head like dreams in waiting.

Dear Son,

The weather is turning cooler. How have you been? The more I think about it, the more I find similarities between you and this young man. You are both tidy but not very clean. You both dislike bananas and enjoy music. He plays the clarinet. He plays it once in the morning after his shower, and once in the evening before bed. He never plays an entire tune. He usually plays scales, or practices the same part of a song over and over again, maybe fifteen or twenty times. It gives me a bit of a headache, to tell you the truth. You are more gifted musically. You played the flute very well. It's a shame you gave it up after high school.

But there are also differences. You are up and out of the apartment in less than forty-five minutes. He takes an hour and a half. At 6:30 a.m., the radio comes on in his bedroom and in the kitchen, a jazz station that plays very energetic music. He always walks to the bathroom singing or humming whatever song is playing that morning. If he's in a good mood, he'll sing loudly in the shower. That cheers me up. When I use the bathroom after him, it smells of cucumber and mint, and it is full of condensation. I have to turn on the extractor fan, open the window, and hang up the bath mat to dry.

Straight after his shower, he goes into the office, and he plays that clarinet for about ten or fifteen minutes. I can hardly bear it, not so much because of the noise but because I think surely he's going to catch a cold doing that. Of course, it's not my place to tell him what to do, but I don't understand why he can't wait till he's put some clothes on. Maybe once he's dressed for work, he's no longer in the mood to play.

Like you, he enjoys his coffee. The kitchen always smells of it after he leaves. He has a cup in the kitchen while he watches the breakfast news on TV, and then he pours the rest into a flask, which he takes to work. As he gathers up his things, he starts on an apple, and I can hear him crunching all the way from the end of the hall. I think a young man should have more than coffee and an apple in the mornings, but who knows—maybe he has a big, hearty lunch at work.

I hope you and Daughter-in-law are well. Remember not to work too hard, and be sure to eat lots of warming food as the weather gets cooler—lots of ginger and garlic, make some pork soup. Please give Maru my love.

Take care of yourself,
Your mother

Granny Ng confirmed that the young man often brought home takeout dinners or ate instant ramen in the evening. The morning apple seemed to be the only healthy thing he ate. She wanted to cook for him, encourage him to eat more, but the only feasible way of doing this was to use the cleaner as a cover. Every Monday and Thursday at eleven o'clock, the cleaner let herself in. Thursdays there was a white envelope of cash with "Mrs. Lee" written on the front, stuck to the door of the fridge. By two o'clock, the cleaner had left and the envelope was gone from the fridge door, and in its place was an instructive note: "Mr. Mok, Please remember to leave money for milk, eggs, and rice" or "Mr. Mok, Usual detergent out of stock, different brand costs extra 15 HKD. Please add amount to envelope."

After practicing the cleaner's handwriting, Granny left a note on the fridge door: "Mr. Mok, Curried vegetables and rice in fridge. Too much for family, please help eat. Cover dish with glass lid. Microwave 3 minutes." The next morning, Granny Ng was pleased to find a dirty plate in the dishwasher and no leftovers in the trash. After the second dish—"Fried snapper with scrambled egg and tomato. Splash a little water on egg and tomato. Microwave 1 minute"—she was surprised to find a Post-it note on the fridge door: "Dear Mrs. Lee, I enjoyed the food. Thank you, you are too kind."

Granny Ng felt a flush of happiness, then panic. She tore the note from the fridge door, crumpled it up, and threw it in the trash. Then, fearing he might find it in there and take offense, she fished it out, smoothed it open, and stuck it on the back wall of her closet next to her drawings. The young man made a habit of leaving a thank-you Post-it on the fridge each time a dish had been left for him, even when Granny Ng knew he hadn't enjoyed the food so much (the next morning she might find half of it in the trash, along with an empty ramen noodle packet). Granny Ng dutifully collected these thank-you notes and found a place for each one on the closet wall among her drawings. Gradually, they spread like vine leaves, and occasionally one would peel off in the night and she'd wake to find it resting on her forehead or cheek.

MARCH

Dear Son,

How have you been? I'm glad that everything has worked out for both of us. Things are going well here, and with the extra room you now have, you and Daughter-in-law can start thinking about having a baby. It's a shame your father isn't here to see you move into this phase of life.

Granny Ng put down the pen. She struggled to conjure her late husband's face in her mind. Absentmindedly, she stroked the thin silver band on her finger. It had lost its shine over the years and was now a foggy gray, bearing a closer resemblance to tin than to silver. She had never thought of selling it, not even at her most desperate; it had not occurred to her, just as it wouldn't have occurred to her to cut off a finger or an ear and think it would be worth anything to anybody.

She couldn't see her husband's face, but she could feel the flat, smooth plane of the back of his head against her palm. She had held it every day toward the end, helping him keep his head up as she spooned warm broth into his mouth. As a child, he had been affectionately nicknamed Flatheaded Boy by everyone in the village. She had never given much thought to this feature of his, and was surprised to think of it now. Over the years, her memories of him had appeared in increasingly broad strokes: his narrow, thoughtful face; his stubbornness; his pale, weakening body that smelled of old bread; her quiet despair at being left alone just a year after her son was born. She stroked the creases of her palm, and for a moment wondered if she had remembered correctly—that the flat back of the head was indeed her husband's, and not her infant son's.

Granny Ng heard the young man pacing about the room. She curled up tighter. She was waiting for him to curse, or slam a door, or break a glass. Although she knew it wasn't like him to lose his temper, still, she waited for the sound of something. But there was only the clink and groan of the ironing board being folded up, the static hiss of a machine coming to life. *Click. Click.*

Another evening alone at his computer. Occasionally the quiet was interrupted by a voice or an advertising jingle—an announcement that he'd won a million dollars, an invitation to join a fun party by dialing this number. Then sound effects—a rippling of cards, plastic chips clinking against one another, and the dealer's catchphrase, "The house always wins—but maybe not tonight!"

Granny Ng recognized the game. Her son had played online poker until his wife found out and forced him to transfer all of his money to their joint account. The sound effects continued for some time, and from the increasingly frequent exclamations from the dealer—"You're really cleaning up!"; "You've got the moves!"— Granny Ng surmised that he was on a winning streak. She felt happy for him, that he had some consolation for the disappointments of this evening. Earlier, while he was in the shower, she'd cracked open the closet door and seen that he'd carefully placed on the futon a shirt with the price tag still attached, a pair of pants, and a tube of hair gel. Granny Ng had heard him on the phone with the young woman a few days before, agreeing that he needed to give his hair "some personality." Still, it appeared that for some reason the young woman had decided she didn't want to spend the evening with him. Granny Ng had listened as he tried to sound understanding, saying that no, he hadn't gone to a lot of trouble for the evening. She'd listened as he called to cancel the restaurant reservation, as he washed the gel out of his hair in the bathroom sink, and as he shoved the plate of food Granny Ng had made for him into the microwave. But now he was winning money online, and amid the clamor of sound effects, she could hear him saying, "Yes! Yes!"

She was happy for him, although her happiness would have been greater were she not in such desperate need of the toilet. Her bladder, she felt, was the only thing about her age that betrayed her in this situation, the only inconvenience. In an effort to reduce the frequency of her urination, she had taken to drinking only two glasses of water a day. It seemed to have some effect during the daytime—she needed to use the toilet only twice—but after 7 p.m., when the young man returned and she had stowed herself away in the closet, the urge to urinate visited her two to three times before morning. This discovery she'd made the hard way: on one of her first nights there, she had brought with her into the closet an empty half-liter water bottle and a funnel, which served their purpose until she woke in the middle of night with both a bladder and a bottle that needed to be emptied. She'd had to open the closet door, tiptoe to the window, and trickle the contents of the bottle onto the lawn before she could use it again. After that, she brought a second half-liter bottle into the closet with her. In the mornings, after the young man left for work, Granny Ng went to the bathroom and disinfected the bottles and the funnel, filling them with diluted detergent and setting them in the bathtub for thirty minutes before rinsing them out.

Granny Ng clutched the empty bottle in the dark, hoping she could wait it out. Usually when the young man was at his computer in the evenings, she would time her toilet breaks with his; so far, this solution had worked without complications. But this evening, the young man was not doing his part.

The telephone started ringing from down the hall. The young man continued playing his game. Granny Ng silently pleaded with him, *Please, go to the phone. It might be that young woman! Maybe she's come to her senses and wants to tell you she's sorry! Please, answer the phone, if only to give her a piece of your mind!*

The dealer congratulated him again—"Expertly played!" A few more telephone rings, then silence. Granny Ng sank into despair, and her sympathetic feelings for the young man turned into sharp annoyance. Then she heard his chair roll across the floor, and the young man's footsteps as he left the room. Granny Ng seized the moment and quickly unscrewed the bottle cap.

Granny Ng had been holding on for so long that when the time came to urinate, she at first missed the top of the funnel and got the floor of the closet—*You should know better! How many times have you done this now!*—and had to mop up the wet patch with a towel from the shelf. Footsteps again; the chair squeaked under his weight. For the next few minutes Granny Ng heard little except the hum of the computer, the swish of cars passing on the freeway, and some occasional clicks. He's probably had enough of poker, she thought. She was glad he'd quit while he was ahead. Maybe he was reading the news now. She leaned her head against the wall and closed her eyes. She thought about the scrapbook where she used to keep her favorite news articles. These were often unusual or uplifting stories, such as the Japanese family vacationing in Kyoto who lost their beloved dog in an amusement park, returned heartbroken to Osaka, and a week later were amazed to find the dog sitting on their doorstep, having miraculously found its way home. In another article, a sixty-three-year-old British man who'd been blind his entire life claimed to have regained his sight after traveling to Italy and catching his first whiff of pizza.

Granny Ng had kept a special section in her scrapbook devoted to tales of reunited families. Her favorite stories concerned twins who'd been separated at a young age and, after twenty, thirty, forty years, had reunited under fantastically coincidental circumstances. She thought of the woman from Tokyo who had been honeymooning in Niagara Falls with her French husband. Lunching at their hotel restaurant overlooking the falls, the woman spilled wine on her blouse and went up to their room to change. Her husband stayed at their table, and after a few minutes finished his glass of wine and decided to visit the seafood buffet. Seeing his wife examine the oyster-shaped ice sculpture, he sneaked up behind her, grabbed her waist, and planted a kiss on her neck. He was alarmed by her screams, and couldn't understand why she was shouting at him in English. He was even more alarmed by the angry-looking blond man approaching them, demanding to know what he'd done to upset his wife. His confusion deepened when another woman who looked just like his wife joined in, asking in Japanese what was going on.

From this confusing encounter, the truth emerged: the two women were twin sisters who'd been separated at birth after their parents' divorce. One had been raised by their mother in Tokyo, the other by their father in Boston. The sisters were both architects, enjoyed ice skating, and had married a coworker, also both architects, and had both chosen to honeymoon in Niagara Falls. After the accidental reunion, the sisters called each other every day and visited each other twice a year. Their mother had died years before, but their father was still alive. When he met his long-lost daughter, it was the first time in his life that he'd wept in front of another person.

Another memorable story concerned a young married couple who were featured on a medical TV show in Germany. They wanted to get pregnant, so they took a screening test to rule out possibilities of genetic defects in their future child. This couple believed that they were the perfect match for each other. They had met at the same company (both were engineers), had the same taste in food and music, and even had the same allergies. The screening test showed them why they were such a perfect match:

more than a quarter of their genes were the same. They eventually discovered that both their mothers had lived in the same area in their youth, and had received sperm from the same donor to conceive a child. At the time, the procedure was very new and there were few donors available, so sperm banks used the same donors in the same area. Confronted with the knowledge that they were half siblings, and facing enormous societal pressure, the couple split up. However, six months later, rumors surfaced of the couple reuniting and running away to England.

The article had ended there, but Granny Ng had longed to know more. She wanted to know what had become of them, if they had succeeded in eluding their interfering families and friends. Perhaps they'd assumed new identities? Would that mean they wouldn't be able to get the same kind of work? Or maybe they had a sympathetic boss who helped connect them with another engineering firm in England? And what about children? Despite her concerns, Granny Ng liked to imagine they were living quietly and happily in their newfound anonymity. She wished she hadn't listened to Kitty, who had made her leave the scrapbook behind when she was helping her pack for the tent village. "Don't worry, Granny. You can collect more stories," she'd told her.

Granny Ng didn't know how long she'd been asleep. She came around to the faint smell of urine, and the sound of a woman gasping thirstily for air. A man's grunts and moans joined the woman's gasps, which got faster and throatier. A prickly warmth spread across Granny Ng's cheeks and she covered her ears, then stuck her fingers in them, after which she could hear only the thumping of her pulse. After a few minutes of this, she took her fingers out of her ears. There was no sound, not even the click of the computer mouse. She wondered if the young man had left the room, and then it came—his quiet, crushing moan, like a wounded animal in its death throes.

The next morning Granny Ng found that she'd woken up half an hour earlier than usual and that the closet reeked of urine. She stuffed some tissue paper into her nostrils and crossed her arms tightly as she waited for the young man to get up and out of the house. As she listened to the noises that had become so familiar by now—the jazz station on the radio, his singing, the blast of the shower, the clarinet squeakily climbing scales—each one felt like a minor affront, painfully drawing out the moments she had to spend next to the urine-caked towel.

At the slam of the front door, Granny Ng got up and filled a bucket with warm, soapy water, moved the plastic storage boxes and her sleeping bag out of the way, and started scrubbing the closet floor, becoming increasingly agitated with the effort. In just a few minutes she had grown uncomfortably hot and her back and elbows were aching.

For the rest of the day she tried to go about her routine, but found herself stopping in the middle of washing the dishes or wiping down a cabinet, and had the dreadful feeling that the experience did not wholly belong to her. These dishes were not hers, nor the cabinet, nor the cloth in her hand. No one even knew she was doing any of this.

"All this effort," she muttered, "and for what?" It took a great force of will to finish each chore, until finally she gave up. The tasks she had once been eager to do now felt like a punishment, a sentence.

The lazy cleaner was coming today. Just before eleven o'clock, when Granny Ng took her place inside the closet, she was surprised by her sudden violent feelings toward Mrs. Lee.

"I do your work, and then I hide myself in here while you laze about. What use are you on this earth?!"

Half an hour after Mrs. Lee's arrival, as Granny Ng was imagining the woman halfheartedly dragging a cloth across the kitchen counters and stealing snacks from the fridge, the phone rang. Granny Ng heard her speak quite animatedly for about five minutes to the person at the other end; her loud, grating laugh; then the sound of the front door slamming. After waiting awhile, Granny Ng came out of her hiding place and looked around. The cleaner had left a note on the fridge door for the young man: "Mr. Mok, My apologies. Must leave a few minutes early today. Son called home sick from school. Usual chores taken care of. Thank you."

It was unnecessary for her to leave the note—the young man would have no idea when she'd actually come and gone—but she liked to do things like this to appear more honest than she actually was. That was one of the many small, subtle deceits that seemed to be second nature to the woman. From the beginning, the notes had struck Granny Ng as arrogant and disrespectful, and she had made a point of disposing of them whenever the cleaner felt compelled to leave one. That day, though, she left Mrs. Lee's note on the fridge door and had a cup of tea on the sofa. Let him be deceived, she thought. I can't always be looking out for him.

She picked up the remote control and turned on the television. Immediately, the faces and voices made her feel a little better. During the course of the day, she watched a cooking program, a talk show, a travel show, a wildlife documentary, and a drama set in a police academy. She got up from the sofa only to use the toilet and get an apple from the kitchen. By the time she realized she'd forgotten to make any food for herself, it was too late; the young man was due to return any minute. Granny Ng went to sleep hungry, annoyed at how she'd let time slip away from her and feeling nauseated by all the TV she'd watched that day.

APRIL

It was not enough to live among the objects and habits of another person; she needed to sit down with someone over a cup of hot tea and bean cake. She tried to distract herself by reinvesting her attention in fixing things around the house: darning the young man's socks, washing the blinds and the windows, leaving him dinner twice a week. But still, she missed the company of friends.

She pulled a few maps down from the bookshelf and began looking for the location of her first tent village, where Kitty and Uncle Chow had taken her in. At the time she had not fully warmed to the experience of communal living, everyone in such close quarters and knowing one another's business. But now she looked back on that time with a regretful appreciation and longing.

It took her some time to work out a route from the young man's house to the tent village, and she was a little disheartened to find that it was farther than she'd imagined. It would take almost an hour and a half to get there by bus, and would involve three route changes. She was determined, however, to make the journey.

She decided she should go the next day. She had enough money for the bus fare; she had not spent any of what she'd made at the last tent village, from begging and collecting recyclables. The problem was figuring out what she should bring. She couldn't drop by both unannounced and empty-handed. In the end she managed to put together a satisfactory gift bag, and went to sleep that night more content than she'd felt in a long time.

*   *   *

Kitty and Uncle Chow were surprised and happy to see her, but were unable to completely hide their concern.

"Is everything okay, Granny?" they asked. "Did you get evicted again?"

"No, no. I'm fine," said Granny Ng. "I just wanted to pay you a visit. I'm sorry I didn't give you any notice."

"Are you sure you're okay? Do you have somewhere to stay?" asked Kitty.

"Yes, yes, a very good place," said Granny Ng. "If you don't believe me, look."

She opened up the plastic garbage bag full of gifts and laid out the contents on the ground: a barely used towel, two bars of soap, four tins of pork cubes, four packets of instant ramen, a packet of AA batteries, three airline cosmetics bags with facecloths, razors, toothbrushes, and cotton buds, and half a bottle of laundry detergent.

"That's all for you," said Granny Ng. "If I had nowhere to stay, I'd be standing here with a bag full of my own things, wouldn't I?"

"Well, I feel reassured," said Uncle Chow.

"Thank you for these things, Granny. You really shouldn't have," said Kitty. Granny Ng noticed that Kitty didn't seem that pleased, and she tried not to be upset by her friend's lack of enthusiasm. She sensed there must be something else.

Upon her arrival, it appeared to Granny Ng that not much had changed in the tent village. She'd found Uncle Chow cooking soup on the stove, and Kitty at her tent a few spots over, cutting someone's hair. She was in a bright blue tracksuit, chatting animatedly with her customer. The only noticeable difference was that there seemed to be slightly fewer tents in the village.

Uncle Chow handed her a bowl of soup. "Careful, it's hot."

"Beef?" asked Granny Ng.

"Vegetable," said Uncle Chow. "I'm trying to lose weight." He winked and patted his stomach, and it was then that Granny Ng noticed: his cheeks had a hollowness that she hadn't seen before, and the silver specks in his beard seemed to have dulled.

"Times are getting tougher." Kitty sighed. "The butcher used to give us his off-cuts for cheap, and the grocer would give us a good deal on rice and tinned food. We used to have friends around here. But last month, city officials did another sweep of the area. They not only evicted thirteen residents; they also went to the local businesses that were helping us and threatened them with fines."

Uncle Chow shot a scowl at Kitty for revealing so much of their situation. He cleared his throat and smiled at Granny Ng.

"And you, Granny?" he asked. "You seem to be in very good health."

"How are things at the other tent village?" asked Kitty.

Granny Ng shook her head. "I was evicted from there not long after I arrived."

"Oh dear!" said Kitty.

"I went to another village. But I had to leave there, too, after a while. And then another village. I suppose I didn't have much luck in those places."

"But you seem fine now," said Uncle Chow. "Did you go back to your son's? Is that where you got all these things?"

Granny Ng looked at Uncle Chow's thinned face and at Kitty, still so well-meaning and eager to help. They didn't really know one another that well, and actually had little in common. However, they were the first people in years that she'd considered her friends, and she wanted to be honest with them. She wondered how she could explain her situation. On the one hand, it would be a relief to share her secret, and perhaps they would be pleased for her. On the other hand, she might be burdening them with this information. Kitty in particular would doubtless overlook the benefits of her situation and focus instead on the risks, and try and persuade her to leave the young man's home before she got into trouble.

"Yes," said Granny Ng. "I'm living at my son's again. Don't worry, he knows that I took all these things, and he's very glad to help. Things are much better between us now."

Granny Ng made sure to visit Kitty and Uncle Chow every few weeks. Each time, she brought something for them, usually tins of food, or fruit. But she knew the really useful items—firewood, gasoline—she had no way to carry by herself. Eventually she started looking around the house for money that the young man had absentmindedly left out. There was a large glass jar on the kitchen counter full of coins. He automatically stopped there on his way in from work, pulled out loose change from his trouser and jacket pockets, and threw it into the jar. It was a little over half full, and every week Granny Ng noticed a small dip where the cleaner had scooped a few coins from it—little enough to escape the young man's notice, but enough, Granny Ng supposed, to make it worth her while. Granny Ng thought she could probably get away with taking a few coins as well. She felt guilty about it, and a little ashamed. But she told herself it was for a good cause, and that failing to share her good fortune with her less-fortunate friends was a greater crime.

After three weeks, she had collected a little over two hundred HKD. She took this money to Kitty and Uncle Chow, who refused to accept it, claiming they were already uncomfortable enough accepting her gifts. Although disappointed, Granny Ng felt it was important to relieve this awkwardness and did not insist. Instead, she began taking small electrical items from the house—a flashlight, a calculator, a handheld fan—and dropping them on the ground, shaking them, or throwing water on them. Then she took them to Uncle Chow to repair for a fee. Uncle Chow reluctantly accepted these jobs, but only after Granny Ng told him that if he didn't, her son and daughter-in-law would find out about her clumsiness and get angry with her. He also insisted that she take a flask of soup back with her after each visit. She began adding the soup to the meals she left in the fridge for the young man, whose thank-you notes the following day became increasingly appreciative.

As much as Granny Ng was dedicated to helping her friends, she knew the visits were as much for her as they were for them. She looked forward to seeing them every few weeks, bringing food or supplies or damaged electrical items. While Uncle Chow worked on a newly battered radio or electric kettle, Granny Ng made soup in the communal kitchen, or drank tea and chatted with Kitty while she cooked some lunch or cut a neighbor's hair. In the summer, she helped Kitty sew a new lining for her tent, and had her hair cut into a neat bob that let her feel a pleasant coolness on the back of her neck.

OCTOBER

In the second week of October, the local homeless coalition held a community fair in the park. There were more than twenty different stalls that the tent villagers could visit, which offered free haircuts, vaccines, basic medical checkups, and eye tests. Although Granny Ng could no longer claim to be a tent villager, with Kitty's help she managed to get a free pair of reading glasses and a medical checkup (the doctor gave her a clean bill of health, except for slightly low blood pressure). Uncle Chow had to be persuaded by Kitty to get a checkup, and was told he had high cholesterol and high blood pressure. "I don't see the use of being told these things if you can't do anything about them," he grumbled.

Kitty persuaded Granny Ng to stay for the barbecue party. Granny Ng acquiesced, but urged Kitty to go and chat with her neighbors; she wasn't feeling particularly sociable, and was happy to sit and listen to the music playing on the stereo. She settled herself on a plastic stool and nibbled on a single chicken kebab, balancing a paper bowl of soup on her lap that she intended to eat to keep her going for the rest of the night. She had felt fine about getting free tests and a pair of glasses from the fair, but now she suddenly felt like an interloper, taking from the needy. It was best, she thought, to stay on the sidelines and not draw attention to herself.

Her plan was not successful. Tent village residents and coalition volunteers kept coming up to her and asking if they could get her anything, why was she eating so little, did she need a blanket? Finally, the only way to reassure them and deflect their attention was to accept their food-laden plates, and to pretend she was chewing whenever they checked up on her.

Rocky, the construction worker, greeted Granny Ng and took a seat next to her. He was carrying a short-necked lute.

"Nice to see you again, Granny. Maybe I've had one too many beers, but I'm in such a good mood that I have to inflict my playing on our friends. You don't mind, do you?"

Granny Ng shook her head, and surprised herself with a giggle that was almost girlish. Rocky stood up and announced, "I hope no one objects to my amateurish playing," to which villagers responded with enthusiastic cheers. Rocky started playing and leading the others in renditions of popular folk songs and theme tunes from old television serials. At Rocky's invitation, Kitty got up and sang the solo from one of these songs, startling Granny Ng with the melodiousness of her voice. The crowd urged her to sing the next one, then the next. She was a confident and theatrical performer, inviting the villagers to clap along and pausing to tease several of them with the song's romantic lyrics. Kitty received her standing ovation with the effortless grace of a seasoned performer.

Rocky leaned over to Granny Ng and said, "It's a shame she doesn't sing more often. I hear she used to be a regular on the hotel circuit. Now it's all karaoke machines."

"I thought she was a hairdresser," said Granny Ng.

"She *was*." It was Rocky's wife. Granny Ng had not noticed until now that she'd taken a seat beside her. She looked a little more plump than before, though it might have been the billowy floral shirt she was wearing.

"She just sang for fun," asserted Rocky's wife. "She never made it as a real singer."

When Kitty came back to the group, she was a little breathless and excited, her face flushed. "I hope I didn't make a nuisance of myself out there." She smiled.

"We were saying what a shame it is that you don't sing for us more often," said Rocky.

"You have a very smooth voice," added Granny Ng.

"You're so kind," said Kitty. "It's nice to have an appreciative audience."

At the request of her neighbors, Kitty agreed to an encore. She chose a folk song, which Granny Ng recognized as a popular tune from the '70s. As Kitty sang, the melodious strains of her voice spun and floated above them all, toward the darkening sky, like an invocation to an unknown god.

DECEMBER

On the third day of December, Granny Ng was caught and arrested. The young man had installed a surveillance system, whose cameras had recorded the movements of a small, elderly woman wandering around the house. The police found her in the closet, curled up on her side. She looked up nervously at the officers, a middle-aged male and a younger female, who stared back in surprise. Finally, the female officer called the young man from the living room.

"Looks like we've found your burglar, sir."

The female police officer—she introduced herself as Officer Wong—helped Granny Ng up, and apologized when she handcuffed her. She asked her to sit down on the white futon sofa. The young man stood by the computer table, regarding her warily, as if she were a wild animal. Granny Ng avoided the young man's stare, although she would have liked nothing better than to get a proper look at him. While Officer Wong surveyed the inside of the closet, she said to her colleague, "Officer Tang, would you like to begin?"

Officer Tang was standing over Granny Ng, scratching his balding head and seemingly at a loss for words. Finally, he squatted down in front of her and said, "Granny, are you comfortable?"

Granny Ng nodded. "Quite comfortable, thank you. But these handcuffs…"

"Yes, I'm sorry about that," said Officer Tang. He pulled a slim notebook and pen from his jacket pocket. He tapped the pad a few times before asking, "Do you realize, Granny, that you've broken the law?"

Granny Ng bit her lip. She stared at the edge of a small half-moon indentation in the carpet, where one of the legs of the computer table had shifted.

"This is private property," he continued, "belonging to this gentleman here. If Mr. Mok decides to press charges—"

"Why did you say my name?!" said the young man, at a volume that seemed to surprise even himself.

"I think it's a bit late for that," said Officer Wong, peeling a Post-it note from the closet wall. "I imagine she knows quite a lot about you already."

Officer Tang continued, "If Mr. Mok decides to press charges, you could be up for counts of breaking and entering, trespassing—"

"And theft," added the young man.

"What items have been stolen, Mr. Mok?" asked Officer Wong.

"Well, food, mostly."

"*Mostly*? Anything else? Anything of value?"

The young man hesitated, then shook his head.

"I see." Officer Tang noted this in his book, then stood up and rubbed his knees, which were sore from squatting. "Granny, my colleague and I here need to fill out a report, and for that we need to ask you some simple questions. It would be much better if you could cooperate with us on this."

Granny Ng nodded.

"Good. Now, can you please tell me your full name?"

"Ng Shui Lin."

"Age?"

"Sixty-three. No, wait—sixty-four."

"How long have you been living here?"

Granny Ng finally stole a glance at the young man, who was staring at the wall over her shoulder with an expression of nervousness and quiet anger.

She answered softly. "One year."

"What!" The young man was almost shouting, his face reddened. "Why did you do this? Is this your idea of fun? Why aren't you at home with your children and grandchildren? Do they even know where you are?"

The officers asked the young man to calm down, and suggested that they continue the investigation at the station.

Granny Ng and the young man were each interviewed for half an hour. The young man told Officer Tang that for the past few months, he had begun to notice that food was going missing. He also noticed that household supplies like soap and toilet paper were getting used up a lot more quickly than usual. At first he'd thought little of it, putting it down to his own absentmindedness; perhaps Mrs. Lee, the cleaner, had left him a note about it and he'd forgotten. After all, he would also lose track of other things: he'd forget where he'd put a flashlight or an extension cable, for example, and then after a few weeks it would turn up on its own. But after some time, a vague, nagging doubt began to visit him just before falling asleep at night. The following morning, before leaving for work, he would quickly check around the house for signs of disturbance, but found none.

Again, he tried to put it down to his own paranoia, and reasoned that he'd probably been working too hard and spending too much time alone. But once in a while he would check the rooms, the cupboards, the closets, finding nothing. He never found anything, but the nagging doubt continued to visit him at night, and during the weekend, at certain times in the day, he would get the feeling that he was not alone. The surveillance system was expensive, but it gave him some peace of mind. He said he only wished he'd thought of it sooner.

By the time the officers had finished their interrogation, the young man had learned some more details about the old woman: that she was homeless and had broken into his home the previous winter, had set up a sleeping space for herself in the spare closet, where she had managed to live undetected for almost a year. He found this difficult to accept, as he was sure he'd checked that closet, but then admitted that, yes, perhaps in his haste he hadn't bothered to push the hanging clothes aside to check behind the plastic storage boxes. He also learned that she'd spent her days cooking, cleaning, doing chores around the house, and getting electrical items repaired for him. His cleaner had not, as he'd believed, had a surge of conscientiousness. After coming home from the police station, he opened up the closet and, overcoming his feelings of queasiness, gathered the old woman's things into a garbage bag. There wasn't much there—a sleeping bag, some clothes, two empty water bottles, a thin stack of letters addressed to her son, and some drawings and Post-it notes lining the walls.

Ken Mok spent the following week in a state of indignation and embarrassment. He wanted to share the burden of his victimhood with other people—his father, his coworkers, the woman who no longer wanted to speak to him—but he decided against it. His father would see this incident as further proof of his son's stupidity and incompetence. *How can a person not know that a stranger is living in their house? For a year!* His coworkers would no doubt see this as a ripe opportunity for ridicule. The day after the arrest, there was a small article in several newspapers, which identified the young man as "a 33-year-old IT professional. The old woman was identified as Ng Shui Lin, 64 years old. The woman appeared to be of normal mental health. When police asked her why she had lived in secrecy at the man's home for almost a year, she replied, 'I had nowhere to live.'"

A few days later, a colleague emailed him another article about the incident, which someone else had sent him from a news website. The subject line read, "How Dumb Is This Guy?" Mr. Mok assured himself that this wasn't directed at him personally. It would be impossible for anyone to know the true details of the incident; there must be hundreds of thirty-three-year-old IT professionals living in the area. He searched for the story online and found that brief articles had appeared in some sixty-seven news outlets, mostly Chinese websites. To his relief, he found that in all of them, he remained anonymous.

After some time and, he thought, an unusual amount of persuasion from the police officers handling the case, Mr. Mok decided to drop the charges against the old woman. The officers managed to convince him that she posed no real danger to him, and that they would make sure she was returned to the care of her son and daughter-in-law. Immediately after agreeing to drop the charges, Mr. Mok installed a more advanced security system in his home. Any instance of the alarm going off would send an alert straight to his cell phone, so that even at work he could feel reassured.

Mr. Mok tried to return to his old routines with the same normalcy and thoughtlessness as before, but found that a new nagging feeling had replaced the old one. This manifested as a dense weight in his lungs, like a cloud of stone, and seemed to appear at odd, inexplicable moments: when he set foot in the house after work; when he stepped out of the steam of the bathroom; when he dropped a cake of ramen noodles into a pan of boiling water. This gradually affected his posture, and he developed a slight stoop.

From time to time, he opened the closet door and peered inside. It still seemed unbelievable to him that a person could have stowed herself away there for all that time. The inhumanity of it both saddened and repulsed him. There was no trace at all of the stranger having lived there, and this unnerved him more than if he'd found some scrap of evidence—a hairpin, or a stray button.

He had trouble sleeping. He would wake in the middle of the night and feverishly check the closet, then the doors, the windows, even the cupboards. After a few weeks, the house had fallen into its former state of subtle disarray. His habit of looking for things and expecting to find them in their right places was gradually undermined by his tendency to distractedly throw things in any available cupboard or drawer space. One day, upon arriving home, he caught his brief moment of disappointment when he noticed there was no Post-it note on the fridge, and realized that he'd hoped this act of care and attention had somehow magically transferred to Mrs. Lee.

Eventually Mr. Mok acknowledged how much the old woman had been taking care of things, and how little Mrs. Lee had been doing all these years. He fired her, and placed an advertisement for her replacement in the local classifieds. He called the newspaper the next day to withdraw the ad, deciding he would rather not have another stranger in his house. The house fell into further disarray. That dense, weighted feeling grew stronger, and his stoop grew a little deeper, so he had the air of someone perpetually cold.

One Saturday morning, Mr. Mok phoned the police station and asked for the officers in charge of the case. Officer Wong took his call. She barely concealed her surprise, but was guarded when answering his questions about the old woman. Finally, after several minutes of assuring her of his benign intentions, she told him to come down to the station. There, she and Officer Tang told him that soon after the old woman's arrest, a search had gone out for her next of kin (she had refused to tell them the whereabouts of her son, claiming she had forgotten). It was outside of their normal scope of involvement, but the officers felt badly for the old woman, and posted an appeal for her relatives to contact the police.

After a week with no reply, during which time the old woman was placed in a shelter, Officer Wong managed to track down the old woman's son and daughter-in-law. They claimed to have been completely ignorant of the situation. When questioned about their lack of action at the time of her disappearance, they said she'd left a note about visiting a relative. They added that they'd received a letter from her some time later, informing them of her decision to live at a friend's house, and that she was quite happy there.

"The funny thing," said Officer Tang, "is that on the surface they looked like such a nice, respectable sort of couple. He's a teacher, and she works for one of those fashion places—"

"Louis Vuitton," said Officer Wong. "But nothing too exciting; she works in the accounting department."

"They just didn't look like the kind of people who'd let their own mother wander the streets," said Officer Tang.

"If you don't mind me asking," said Officer Wong, "why exactly are you trying to find her?"

"I just want to make sure she's all right," said Mr. Mok, surprised to hear the words come out of his mouth. "Believe it or not, I feel a little responsible." Before he could help himself, he blurted out, "I was thinking of giving her a job."

The police officers looked dubious.

"As a housekeeper," he continued. "She did a good job of keeping the place in order. I suppose I never fully appreciated it at the time." As soon as he heard himself saying it, it really didn't seem like such a bad idea.

The police officers told him the son and daughter-in-law had placed her in a nursing home, which, in the end, said Officer Wong, was probably no better for her than if they'd never tracked them down. "You know the kinds of things that happen in there."

The officers helped Mr. Mok find the name and number of the nursing home. He called that day, pretending to be the old woman's son. The receptionist sounded surprised to hear from him. He asked if he could visit her that day. The receptionist told him visiting hours were over, and when he asked if he could come by the next morning, she informed him that the home needed at least twenty-four hours' notice to prepare the residents for visitors.

"What do you mean, 'prepare'?" asked Mr. Mok.

The receptionist responded with an edge of impatience to her voice. "Some of our residents have very particular needs. We prefer to avoid making family members distressed, particularly young children. Some of our residents have difficulty controlling their behavior."

"Well, it's just me, and I don't mind," said Mr. Mok.

"It's company policy," snapped the receptionist. Then, in a gentler, rehearsed voice, "Please call at least twenty-four hours in advance to schedule a visit. Thank you."

She hung up before Mr. Mok could reply. When he called the number again, it went straight to a recorded message: a softer, kinder version of the receptionist's voice. Mr. Mok was left wondering uneasily about the kind of place the old woman was staying in. Well, I suppose I'll find out soon enough, he thought. He made a mental note to call the following morning and schedule a visit for the weekend. That night, however, he received a call from his mother telling him that his Aunt Flora had died, and the funeral rites would take place that Saturday and Sunday. Mr. Mok promptly gave his assurance that he would be there. He briefly considered visiting the old woman after his return, but remembered that it was generally considered bad luck to visit someone after a funeral. Or was that limited to visiting pregnant women and people with young children? Whatever the case, he decided he would have to postpone it. He spent the following weekend fishing with his father, who chastised him for his poor technique but otherwise didn't complain about his company.

When the next weekend was almost upon him, his colleagues reminded him of the company softball game against the accounting and sales divisions. His division won, and a colleague whom he believed had never thought much of him patted him on the back and said, "Good game." The following weekend, the woman who'd stood him up several months ago invited him to a weekend away at her favorite hot-springs resort. He learned that she had just split up with her boyfriend, and suspected that he would be no more than a distraction for her, but he agreed anyway. The touch of another person, even without emotion, was better than nothing. And so it happened: one thing after another prevented him from arranging a visit to the old woman, and as his life became filled with more and more vaguely pleasing distractions, the thought of her began to grow ever more distant, and the cloud of stone that resided in his lungs seemed to lighten a little every day.

BEARS AMONG THE LIVING

by KEVIN MOFFETT

(This story, from McSweeney's 63, *was a finalist for the
2022 National Magazine Award in Fiction.)*

THEY CALL OUR TOWN the City of Trees because
of the trees. Along Harrison Avenue, sycamores
with their tops sheared to accommodate power
lines overhead. On Foothill, massive peeling euca-
lyptuses. On Mills, prim maidenhairs dropping their rancid
berries. Our town is a page, its streets are the lines, houses are
words, and the people: punctuation. Trees are just trees. We
hear church bells on Sunday but never see anyone coming out or
going in. The Church of Christ has a new sign in front that says

HE'S STILL LISTENING, which makes me a little sad. It makes me want to say something worth listening to. Less and less, I'm in control of what I broadcast. At a park the other day I was reading on a bench while my wife pushed our son on the swings. A woman walked up to her and said, Just a heads-up: There's a man reading over there on the bench and he's not with anybody. We're all keeping an eye on him. His zipper's wide-open.

It was true. I mean, it's true. Lately, while walking, I'll sometimes feel a suspect breeze on my groin and look down to find my zipper open and I haven't used the bathroom in hours. Either the crafts-manship of zippers has declined or I've been neglecting to zip. A friend tells me not to worry, that it's an evolutionary adaptation, like pattern baldness or the gluey odor certain old men acquire. My friend (his name's Andrew—calling him my friend makes him sound imaginary) thinks it's a way of keeping undesirable DNA out of the gene pool. Besides, there's no law that says you have to keep your zipper up, he says.

I'd never thought there was, but he says it so defensively, as if he were dispelling a widely held opinion. Sunday mornings, we walk our dogs together, and whenever a car in a driveway is block-ing part of the sidewalk, he'll kick the bumper as we walk past.

Bad car, he tells his dog.

The limits of my language, Wittgenstein said, are the limits of my town. Something to that effect. We are bisected by freeways, circled by helicopters, tilted up toward the foothills, snug in our stalls. Will we die in our beds? Will we die in our cars? Will loved ones surround us waiting for frank instructions? Our town: a blend of street noise and birdsong, a flurry of signs, an algebra problem. People call it a bedroom community, a phrase I used to repeat because it sounded kind of lurid until I finally looked up what it meant. Asleep at night, I plot and replot my jogging circuit. Seventh to Mountain, Mountain to Baseline, Baseline to Mills, Mills to Bonita... I wake up exhausted.

Mornings, when my family's still asleep, I survey my modest claim, purposeful and sincere as a lighthouse keeper. I walk Otis into the park across from our house and we watch the overtrained border collie fetch Frisbees, catching them, stacking them one by one, and then carrying them home in his mouth. You're a good boy, too, I assure Otis, even though both of us know the only thing keeping him from sprinting toward the foothills, never to return, is the frayed orange leash clipped to his collar.

Yesterday a local man was arrested for lewd and lascivious conduct. The newspaper said that after getting a *personal body part* stuck in a park bench, he needed the help of some bystanders to free it. Such a strange euphemism: *personal body part*. Isn't every body part personal? No wonder schizophrenics think newspapers transmit coded messages: there's too much casual ambiguity. Before I learned to read, I remember seeing a grainy photograph of a teenage boy on the front page of the paper. I asked my mother what the story was about, and she skimmed it and said, He won a prize at school. For what? I asked. Her eyes were fixed on the boy's picture. For some vegetables he grew, she said finally, and folded the newspaper and tucked it under her arm, but I could still see the doomed boy peeking out, and for the first time I noticed how the seeds of future misfortune are hidden in photographs. Only in retrospect can they be detected.

I don't have all that many memories of my father. He died a few weeks before I turned eleven. I remember him sitting in a La-Z-Boy and laughing loudly at the nightly news, and feeling kind of resentful because I couldn't figure out what was so funny. I remember overhearing him say to a friend from the track: I don't like being drunk. But I do like getting drunk. I also remember trying to watch Halley's Comet with him. He woke me at three in the morning and we sat on cabana chairs in the driveway, him sipping from a tall glass of Regal Blend, trying to get drunk but not be drunk, and me shivering and anticipating the moment the comet would scream across the atmosphere, spraying shards of fire and dust and ice. The stars pulsed. An hour passed. The moon hung there, dumb as always.

He woke me again at dawn and pointed to a faint blue scribble in the sky. Barely scratched us, he said. He handed me a chunk of charcoal, freezing cold. I found this in the front yard, he told me. I held it to my nose. Charred rock, a molar plucked from the jaw of an old god. I carried it to school in the side pocket of my backpack but forgot about it until after lunch, and by then the chunk was lost, dust.

Probably just a briquette from the grill, my mother says when I call to ask her about it. She's been drinking Gallo wine again.

When she's been drinking Gallo wine, she tends not to indulge my sentimentality. Your father always had an antisocial sense of humor, she says. One summer the singer Freddy Fender performed at the horse racing track he managed, and she couldn't go, but she really wanted a signed picture. Though my father didn't want to ask for one, eventually, he gave in and got one for her: *You're the Tear in My Eye. With All My Love. Freddy Fender.* Later, years after he died, she looked at it more closely and realized it was my father's handwriting. Simply to amuse himself, he'd asked Freddy Fender for the picture but not the signature.

Laughter's supposed to be shared, she says. She tells me she accidentally watched a documentary about it. It's like a universal language, she says. Even before humans could talk, we laughed; I can't remember why. Something to do with showing we mean one another no harm, or surviving danger, the overwhelming relief of it.

She tells me how on their second date, he suddenly started laughing, and when she asked what was so funny he said, Nothing. She kept pressing him and he finally told her he'd been thinking about the sun. Whose son? she asked. No, *the* sun. What about it? she said. I just realized there's an object in the sky that will blind you if you stare straight at it. And? she asked him. You don't think that's a little amusing? he said.

And that, she says, was your father. It's how she concludes every story about him: And that was your father.

What else? she says to fill the silence (when she's been drinking Gallo wine, it's difficult to get her off the phone), and she waits and I wait to see which of us knows the answer.

* * *

The summer he died is a smear of wildfires and hostile fauna. Miles north of us, the pinewoods burned, clotting the central coast of Florida with a scorched haze. My mother, sister, and I moved to a cul-de-sac of gravy-brown condos, drew straws for the smallest bedroom (I lost), sat inside awaiting instructions from the proper authorities, and watched pine ash fall and fall. Then it rained. The fires smoldered and finally went out, and I spent the summer selling off my baseball cards and hunting snakes in the palmetto scrub behind our condo. When I came home one night covered in chigger bites, my mother brushed clear nail polish over the welts and I lay shirtless and miserable as the chiggers suffocated in their hidey-holes. My body was a decoy, a trap made of meat. I scratched off the scabs of dried polish one by one. Years later someone told me chiggers don't burrow inside skin, and that the welts, which were actually full of chigger saliva, would've healed quicker if we'd left them alone. The summer he died, I watched the retired bail bondsman next door bludgeon a cottonmouth with a shovel—the snake's severed head kept snapping while its headless body slithered away, and the retired bail bondsman grinned and gestured with the shovel as if he'd orchestrated this educational display just for me.

A sign in front of the Methodist church: GOD ISN'T ANGRY. Whenever I pass it, I say it aloud, God isn't angry, adding the unspoken verdict: He's just… disappointed.

Lately I've been thinking about the ice cream man. The ice cream man, he tunnels into our town, solves our streets, turns on his music, and waits like a spider. Nothing's more inscrutable than a darkened house. Nothing except a whole street of darkened houses. Some of us sleep, some lie in bed counting their resting heart rate. Every website agrees: its rhythm is unusual. This isn't good. We like our refrigerator magnets and our dental hygienists' hairstyles to be unusual, not our resting heart rates. I remember when sleep was so easy, a nice calm pool warmed by humming turbines… Now sleep is a panicked rabbit clutched tight to my chest. Just keep still and I won't hurt you, I tell my rabbit, but you can't calm the thing you're clutching. That's been true for years. If we let him, the ice cream man would notice even the faintest tremor of need and drive toward it at once. What a fireman is to a burning building, an ice cream man is to our desire for ice cream.

Coyotes eat the cats, cats eat the songbirds, songbirds eat the morning quiet. Nothing eats the coyotes. Last year some homeowner tried poisoning them but only succeeded in making them more ornery. Our coyotes are not noble mascots. They look like starved and hunted dogs.

My son plays a song that goes, *I am, I am, I am Superman, and I can do anything*, and he asks if the singer is saying *can* or *can't*. Can, I say. The chorus repeats and he asks me again and I reassure him again. He has no tolerance yet for brooding superheroes who can't do certain things. He likes Superman. He suspects he's only pretending to be scared of Kryptonite, the way he pretends to be Clark Kent. The characters in his cartoon shows never use words like *kill* or *die*. We must eliminate them! says the skeleton lord. Punish them, destroy them, vanquish them. Temporarily, of course. Even the worst villains survive into the next week, and the next. When the skeleton lord's air fleet is brought down, the sky blooms with the black parachutes of healthy skeletons. My son leans closer to the television, willing each of them safely back to their evil lair.

I was standing around with some other parents, waiting for the kids to be released from school. I miss maps, one of them said. You know, the kind you kept in the glove compartment and had to unfold, and when you were done with them you could never quite figure out how to refold them. We all remembered those. Then everyone started sharing nostalgic artifacts from childhood. I miss thinking Columbus discovered America, someone said. I miss using my mom's makeup mirror to pretend I was walking on the ceiling. I miss getting lost. I miss feeding my neighbor's dog chicken bones through the fence. I miss carrying money loose in my pocket, back when three or four dollars was so *powerful*. I miss invisible ink. I miss feeling loyal toward my breakfast cereal. I miss getting all dressed up to have my picture taken. I miss friendship bracelets, extra credit, merit badges, participation trophies. I miss being rewarded just for following along. I miss ant farms. I miss having my foot measured. I miss thinking every rabbit I saw was the Velveteen Rabbit.

I miss when my future was more interesting to me than my past, I thought. The other parents paused and looked at me, which meant I'd said it out loud as well. They waited for an explanation. The least I could do was tell them how I used to dream of being a landscape architect, as opposed to dreaming of when I used to dream of being an landscape architect. Dreaming ahead instead of dreaming behind. I kept my eyes on the sidewalk and finally said, I also miss scratch-and-sniff stickers. Sighs of relief from the other parents, robust communal nodding. It felt good to think about things you hadn't thought about in a while. Harmless, nearly forgotten things. Some of the stickers smelled like what they were supposed to smell like and some didn't, and every time you scratched them the smell grew fainter. Remember that? You had to make sure to ration it out because the stickers wouldn't last long. It was an object lesson. Remember? Scratching and knowing that every time you scratched you were erasing the very thing you were savoring.

Where were we? That's another phrase my mother repeats when we talk on the phone. Now, where were we? As if conversation is this punishing labyrinth we're navigating together. Careful not to lose our way, careful to measure where we're going against where we've been. Oh, now I remember, she tells me. I was telling you about those sounds coming from the roof. I thought something was trying to claw its way in—turns out something was trying to claw its way *out*...

A friend gave her a book called *When Bad Things Happen to Good People* after he died. She never read it. She put it on the only bookshelf in our house, which happened to be in my bedroom, next to the only other book we owned: *The Good Earth* by Pearl S. Buck. I must've scanned its title a thousand times before falling asleep. As a kid I imagined it as a jingle: *Bad things happen to good people in monsoons, hot-air balloons. Ancient tombs, hospital rooms.* Another friend came to the house during the funeral and took away all my father's clothes, donated them to the Salvation Army. She thought she was doing us a favor, scrubbing our closet of unwanted reminders. Years later we'd still see his golf shirts all around town. On a man pumping gas into a motorcycle. On a supermarket bag boy. Another friend leaned in close to her after the service and whispered, They say the grieving process lasts six months for every year you were together.

She was forty-two years old when he died and she never dated again. She begrudgingly went to one Parents Without Partners meeting and came home with some pamphlets and a coupon for three free karate lessons. She had eight hundred dollars in the bank, monthly social security checks, a job at a betting window at the racetrack. Everyone at the meeting seemed so plodding and glib, brimming with false light. Boys need positive male role models, a fellow partner-less parent told her at the meeting. She thought at first he was hitting on her, but it turned out he was recruiting boys for his martial arts dojo. Relieved, disappointed, she took the coupon he offered her. At River of Tradition we teach the four pillars of respect, he said, pointing to the patch on his coat, where the four pillars were listed. She wasn't wearing her glasses so she couldn't make them out, but it looked like one of them was CUSTARD. He's at an age where he should be working hard on his belief system, the man said, though she'd never told him how old I was.

My birthday parties, until I stopped having them, were always at Top Dogs. It had a special party room in the back and everyone got a footlong except the birthday boy, who got a birthday foot-long, which was just a footlong with special birthday toppings. I remember eating at Top Dogs a lot as a child, but I don't think we went there an unusual amount—I just remember every single trip there. The greasy, ass-buffed smoothness of the booth seats, the ritualized dressing of the footlong. Years after he died, when my mother was going through her born-again phase, she made us pray before we ate them. No one ever explained the mechanics of prayer to me, so I treated it like a wish list, closing my eyes and telling God everything I wanted. We quit one church for another and then quit church altogether, but the idea that I was born incomplete and that my natural inclinations are faulty, damnable even, has always rung true to me. Especially when I'm inside a Top Dogs. Our town council banned all fast-food chains within city limits, but the nearest Top Dogs isn't far. Just across the border in a grubby, makeshift red-light district: strip club, suspect massage parlor, marijuana factory outlet (ice cream man idling in the parking lot), Top Dogs. I eat quickly, hunched like a scavenger bird, and tell no one I've gone. I don't pray before eating my footlong but I tell myself that tomorrow I'll atone by running six miles instead of three. In my head I'm already running, absolving myself stride by stride for my casual trespasses into nostalgia.

In a booth nearby, a woman wearing a shredded golf visor says to another woman, Did you hear about the boy whose last wish was to die in Santa's lap? Turns out he was faking. It was just something he started saying and his parents went along with it. The other woman considers this and I sense everyone in our jetty of booths leaning in to hear her response. Top Dogs isn't the sort of place that abides deliberation—the woman's silence pulls at us like the branching limbo before a diagnosis. She reaches behind her ear and brings a tress of hair to her nose and sniffs at it. You know, she finally says, it's almost impossible to actually smell yourself.

Here's what I've been wondering, my mother said to me once over the phone. Here's what's been bugging me. Do you think he'd be dead by now if he didn't already die?

One year my sister and I dressed as boxes of laundry detergent for Halloween. She was Rinso, I was Biz. We made the costumes ourselves out of old cardboard boxes. Our mother thought it was so clever she sent a photo of us to the multinational conglomerate that manufactures Rinso and Biz and received, in return, a coupon for $1.50 off her next purchase. She was livid, she ranted about it for years afterward... but what had she expected? Free Rinso for life? She never could shed her unblinking faith in products she saw advertised on television. She knew Ivory was 99.44 percent pure and Calgon would take her away. When I was an infant she fed me Tang in a baby bottle because the commercials said it was healthy. The astronauts drank it, she'd say whenever she was pressed about feeding a newborn sugar water. That neon orange space powder rotted my baby teeth down to the root. Nowadays she watches the wholesale jewelry network, where the commercials are the show, and all the shows are about jewelry. She still wears her engagement ring, which she's had resized twice to fit her shrinking finger. The only other keepsake she has of my father, besides pictures, is his name on a yellowed slip of paper. After their first date she wrote it down and wedged it between her mattress and box spring because she heard that's what Janet Leigh did the night she met Tony Curtis.

Listening to my wife and son try to reach a compromise about how many toys he's allowed to bring to bed with him, I think: The sheer number of words it takes to raise a child—it's absurd. *Can*, I repeat when the song comes on. He *can* do anything. Escorting him through childhood on a flotilla of words. I remember the wannabe Amish guy who tended the video store cash register while his daughter lay next to him in a playpen. One night I came in and he was showing her trading cards with pictures of crying dwarves on them. Silently he'd hand her a card and silently she'd study it and hand it back to him. When he noticed me he said, I want to teach her that the world isn't as uncomplicated as she thinks it is.

A worthy enough goal, I guess. My son says he and a friend watched footage of ocean trenches, and there are these blind white eels that break apart if you bring them to the surface— they're held together by water pressure—and they terrified him. I tell him he shouldn't worry because he'll never have to go to the bottom of the ocean. You're better off worrying about the DMV, I say. He walks off without asking what *DMV* stands for, because he doesn't need to. His sense of danger is prehistoric, wiser than words.

And what to say about my half brother, my father's first son, who showed up at my college graduation and gave me a hundred-dollar bill in a bank envelope? He's ten years older than me, and I'd only met him a few times and haven't seen him since. He looked unnervingly like our father. He had a thin scar on his cheek and the skin on either side of it was misaligned, like patterned wallpaper not quite matched at the seam. The thing you should know about our dad (he told me when we were alone)—and you might not remember this because you were pretty young when he died—but that man was hung like a goddamn grandfather clock.

On my morning run, I often imagine myself at age eight watching me run past. There he goes again, I think of me thinking. When I was eight I found a switchblade in a crumpled paper bag. I also found, in the glove compartment of an abandoned mail truck in the woods, a porno magazine full of pregnant women. Something like that is bound to leave a permanent stain... and now that I'm thinking about it, what was a mail truck doing abandoned in the woods? I remember how on my school bus someone wrote *Black Sabbath Rules* on the back of the seat in front of mine, and every day I returned to check if they'd written anything else. I wanted a list. I wanted to know exactly what the Black Sabbath rules were.

I called a phone sex hotline I found in the magazine, made my voice good and deep. When the woman came on the line she said, *Well, well, well, well, Mr. Motherfucker.*

Our streets, they were here when we got here. They channel us, keep us from scribbling in the margins. Just before two city buses cross paths on Indian Hill, there's a moment when it's unclear whether or not the bus drivers will wave to each other. It lasts for about two seconds. When they do wave, the moment is neatly resolved, allowed to vaporize. When they don't, it lingers like a failed sneeze and expands into an omen, a placeholder for everything dreaded, all the things that could end badly and do. Next to my father in his Skylark, I used to signal to semitruck drivers on the highway, trying to get them to blow their air horns. I wanted influence, I wanted to be recognized by the biggest things on the road. I did this recently with my son in the car, and when the truck driver answered with a sustained honk, my son sank low in his seat, mortified. He made me promise to never do it again. I promised I would try. My son tells me I say *maybe* too much. He tells me that *we'll see* is not a satisfying answer. He's already eight years old, older than I was when I started to understand the subtle language of the road, the exonerating and implicating notes passed wordlessly from driver to driver to driver.

At IKEA he asks why there are so many pregnant women shopping and I tell him I'm not sure. He asks if women go to IKEA to get pregnant, and although I'm intrigued by the idea of women going to IKEA to get pregnant, I restrain myself from telling him that yes, they do. I say maybe they do. He asks if I knew that French women are naked 30 percent of the time, and I tell him I did not. Where did he hear this? He says it's just something he knows. He says he knows a lot of things his mother and I don't. It seems like lately he's been trying to keep himself a mystery. When I tell him he needs to go brush his teeth, he says, Does a tiger brush his teeth?

*   *   *

I know there are other things I should be showing him—truths, values, important concepts—but how can I if I'm still not clear on the particulars myself? The other day he asked what Captain Hook's name was before he lost his hand. I checked into Hook's details and read out his birth name to my son: James Aloysius Hook. His name was Hook before the hook—having his hand cut off and fed to a crocodile was a terrible irony. Or a coincidence. Or an ironic coincidence.

In college, I tell him, I had a friend named George Blaze. Guess how he died? My son covers his ears. He doesn't want to guess, or know, how George Blaze died. Later he asks me if there's such a thing as a monster planet. I ask him to clarify what he means and he says, A planet with only monsters on it. How am I supposed to answer a question like this? I answer yes. Which makes him happy (I knew it would) and a little apprehensive. How close is it? I pause for some quick calculations. At least ninety-seven light-years away, I tell him. Which is very far, I say. A light-year's like a normal year but much longer because it's a distance. You know how long a year feels, January to December? Okay, so imagine that but you're walking the entire time, through space. For ninety-seven years. That's how far.

He asks why it's called a light-year and I say, No one's really sure, and put my hand on his shoulder, consoling him about all the things we want to know and cannot.

When my wife and I first met I told her I used to be pen pals with former president Ronald Reagan. She asked where the letters were and I tried to remember, growing annoyed at myself for being careless enough to misplace personal letters from former president Ronald Reagan, before remembering there were no letters. Truth is, I'd written to him once, after he tested the microphone at a radio address by saying, I've signed legislation to outlaw Russia forever. We begin bombing in five minutes. For a newly fatherless kid living fifty miles north of Cape Canaveral, which was a primary Russian target, who kept himself awake at night worrying about flash burn, air bursts, blast waves—phrases even the most unimaginative child could conjure viscerally—Reagan was a terrifying clown. The least he could have done was to write back and reassure me, tell me my fears were unreasonable. About a week later, I received a form letter on White House letterhead. I don't remember what it said. I read it quickly, licked my thumb and rubbed at the signature to see if it was real, then threw it away.

We are bears among the living, agile and fearsome. We range and rut. We hunt. We return to our dens to sleep and let torpid winters seal our wounds. When we die our pelts are stripped from our bones, draped over plausible likenesses, nailed to pedestals in telltale poses. Children still flinch at the sight of us, though our eyes are flat and lifeless. For now death seems to have perfectly arrested our essence. One day we're moved to the garage, replaced by a Christmas tree, and we stay there, surviving, yes, but shrinking. Time declaws us, softens our contours and our blood-matted fur, and it gives us a bow tie, and one day, where a life-size bear once stood, there's a cute little plush toy stuffed with foam and air, a harmless abbreviation consigned to spend a third life in the land of make-believe.

*　　*　　*

Sometimes I think I can I still summon the sound of his voice. A thin, distant rasp. My childhood is a song I've heard so many times I've stopped listening to the words. Probably half the things my father said to me he never said to me.

You're the man of the house now. Your duties consist of inward foraging, incubating petty grudges, and eating food before it expires. Fear not, I'll be watching over you until you're old enough to watch over yourself. Don't let that stop you from doing what, to the best of your knowledge, boys do. Become what you are, become what you are pretending to be. Learn something about everything and everything about something. Don't linger before mirrors. Appreciate rain. Take what scraps you have of me and raise them as a scarecrow against aspiring father figures. Make up some good shit. Never trust anyone who owns a reptile or a riding lawnmower. Is it my voice you're hearing right now or someone else's? And how old are you now? Old enough to watch over yourself? Old enough to watch over someone else? Children, and I quote, are the living messages we send to a time we will not see. Something along those lines. So what are you trying to say and why are you still trying to say it? Do you think this is a game, Kevin? Do you think you are winning?

BECOMING THE BABY GIRL

by ADACHIOMA EZEANO

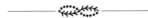

(This story, from McSweeney's 56,
was a 2021 O. Henry Prize winner.)

I. ME AND MUSCLED MAN

IT'S EXAM. TALL THIN girls don't show up. I wonder if they are all all right. I ask the course rep where they are. He's busy re-reading his worn-out, photocopied version of Iweka's *Introduction to Drama*. He doesn't even look at me. I sigh. Prof. Okafor comes in with muscled men. They come with guns and anger. They come with swearwords. They stand us up. They search us. The taller one searches me. He touches my breasts and my eyes bulge. My mouth forms a *whaat?* He says, "Why is it hard?" He asks, "Do you have expo there?" "No, I don't bring prohibited reading materials into the exam hall," I say. "You can," he says. "I don't see why you should not," he keeps on saying. "Everybody does it. Only, they have protectors. I will be your protector. Give me your phone number and yourself." I hiss. I call him idiot. I call him useless. I call him stupid. I call him a very, very useless man. My voice ascends with each word. He screams at me to shut up. He turns to Prof. Okafor, tells Prof. Okafor, "This girl carry expo oo."

"That's a lie! That's a lie!"

"Fill out the examination malpractice form, first of all," Prof. Okafor says to me.

"Why would I do that? This guy is just lyi—"

"No, no, you will not call this honorable man a liar. Fill this form out, young lady. Fill it!"

I take the malpractice form from where he piled them on the table, write my name, and wonder, Can they do this to tall thin girls? Tall thin girls wearing power as perfume and flipping long, dangling braids or costly wigs, brandishing beauty and snobbery like they are the only humans in this universe. This muscled man and this professor. Can they do this to tall thin girls?

2. ME ON MY FIRST DAYS HERE

I sway my hips past people with my lips slightly parted. I walk past people with grins on their faces, past people with inquisitive looks and no shame as they say, "Hey, fine girl." I say to them with determination that I'm not here to be fine girl and agree with myself: I am not here to be fine girl. I braid my hair in a Ghana weave with black Darling attachments, wear the long skirt Dad bought with the oversize shirt Mum bought. Both of them wiped tears with white handkerchiefs when I pulled out my traveling box. I left them behind with our thin yellow dog, Jack. Jack, with his pendant ears. I wear my mother's cat's-eyes and my pointed nose that everyone believes my father made possible. Dad fills me up with *don't forget* advice as he drives me to Lagos Park: "Don't forget where you come from." "Don't forget where you're going to." "Don't forget to choose the right company." When my bus pulls away from Enugu, I try everything I can think of to connect where I'm going with where I come from. When I dab my face with the white handkerchief Dad gave me before he swerved off in his car to go home, it is tears I wipe from my eyes. I hope never to forget.

3. I CAN'T BE TALL THIN GIRLS

Three tall thin girls who are colored like sun, who burn through the class, who let out loud clangs of laughter, who put on airs like they are Beyoncé, who say, "Yeah, you guys, what the fuck, yeah, yeah," who wear English like it is a song, who come to class in too few clothes, clothes that look like they'd fit a two-year-old, who wear long hair extensions worth as much as my father's bungalow, who wave their hands and their perfumes waft around and take over the class. These tall thin girls, who are liked by all the boys and all the men in this school, who bad-mouth Prof. Chris and boo Prof. Okafor, who make girls wish to be them. Those tall thin girls who call to me on the Monday of the first week I walk into this new school and say, "That forehead, oh my god, you look like you are Rihanna right now." Those tall thin girls who call to me on the Tuesday of the second week I walk into this new school and say, "Your shirt, girl, your shirt. Mehn, it looks damn so good, really, giirrl." I wear the loose-fitting white shirt Mum bought from her neighbor who sells imported secondhand wears. Those tall thin girls who call to me on the Thursday of the third week I walk into this school. They say, "Your hair, is that natural? The way it falls straight like a river, really, is it natural?" My hair has drunk uncountable cups of cheap relaxer. My hair doesn't fall straight like a river. My hair is not natural.

Now, those compliments have consequences: the urge to constantly google Rihanna. Place her picture side by side with mine. Compare and contrast. The urge to reshape my loose shirts, make them tighter. Starch them. Buy new ones. The urge to cut my hair. Patiently regrow it till it falls like a river. The urge to become tall thin girls, beautiful, effortlessly confident, eager to dole out compliments.

Who wouldn't want to be tall thin girls? Tall thin girls who drive around the school in Venzas and Lexuses; tall thin girls who are gold; tall thin girls who are bold. But I like to think I am not cut out to become tall thin girls. I am the girl who remembers where she is from and where she is going, who chooses who she goes there with. That is what my father has always said to me, and I am the girl who is her father's daughter, so I ignore tall thin girls on the Friday of the fourth week when they say, "We like you. Be us."

Well, I do not completely ignore them. The tallest of them, the one with the face shaped like an egg, skin the color of Angelina Jolie's, looks at me and says, "Heyy, my name is Ella. Can I have your phone number, please?" And my mouth goes to work telling it to her.

4. ME AND THE MIRACLES TALL THIN GIRLS MAKE

Now it is tears I wipe from my face again. It is holiday, though I am not going home. I am waiting for the school's disciplinary committee on exam misconduct to sit. No one knows when they will, or if they will, and only when they sit will I know if I will be rusticated from here. For now, I do not know. The letter I received many days ago orders me not to travel yet, orders me to stay till my fate is stated. I don't live off campus—only the rich students do that—and the school hostel is closed by management, to be reopened when school resumes in a month's time. So for now, I put up at my friend's house, and don't know where I will go from here. She says she is going to the village to help her mother with farming and trading so they can save for her school fees next session. They will harvest crops and sell vegetables and yams in the open market. She hasn't gone yet. I beg her not to, not to go yet, not until I find somewhere to stay. I like to think she will give me her key when she leaves. She hasn't said so yet. I only hope, keep saying, "Shebi, you'll leave your key for me when leaving, right?" But a daughter not yet free from her mother's loins will wear her mother's pants. So I wasn't surprised when, two days later, the earliest sun not yet blinding the moon, she sprang from her side of the bed and hit my bare shoulders over and over till I stretched and said, "Ah-ah!"

Her mother had called, had said, "It's either I see you here now or you see me there now." So, a girl goes home. She shrugs. I ask for her key. She says nothing. I ask for her key. She says nothing. I ask for her key. She breaks into a story of a young girl like us who made millions last month, just like that. So I pack my stuff as she packs her stuff. I stand by the back door, watch her apply her makeup, rub red lipstick, pencil her brows, wipe off the red lipstick, apply a pink stick, use contour on her face and look extra good. I want to tell her she looks extra good, but I'm not sure I want to talk to her yet. I stand there, watch her drag her Echolac out with lips tightly shut, beads of sweat forming on her forehead, wrinkled lines appearing on her face to form a plea, begging me to help with the heavy box. I press my phone instead because I am not here to help if you are not here to help. Still I stand there, hoping she will say, *Here, take my key. Always lock my door o.*

"Come out, I need to lock the door o." I grab my handbag and drag my box out by Papa Okey's shop, where she and I stood last night, talking about the things I don't care to remember now. She drags her Echolac to the street, flags a bike, tells the rider, a man in a black jean jacket, that she is going to wherever. They bid whatever whatever price, and the man in the black jean jacket climbs down, helps her pull the Echolac up onto the bike, and they zoom off, leaving me in what I want to assume is an intentionally collected swirl of dust. A mild way of telling me to fuck off.

I stand there for hours, watching everything: hurrying men and women, girls and boys, strangers zapping off in my dream cars—Venza, RX 350, Porsche, Range Rover, honking cars and buses and motorcycles, bus drivers cursing one another while struggling for passengers; everything, indications of people busy and life fleeting. I stand there, by the side, doing nothing. My mum calls. I ignore it. I ignore it because ignoring is what you do when you know why a particular call is coming in and you know you have no answers yet to those variegated *wh*- questions you are destined to listen to while pressing that phone to your ear. Mum wants to know when I will be home. Who knows?

I lean my box against the peeling wall and walk into Papa

Okey's shop, buy airtime, load the fifteen-digit pin into my phone, subscribe for a month's data, and open my WhatsApp. Maybe I can find someone I know who is still around, someone who could save me from sleeping on the street. Maybe. There are tons of new messages, from friends at home, course mates asking for this textbook or that, men who want, people who claim they care, then these messages from this I-don't-know-whose number. I check the profile picture. My eyes swell! It is Ella! Ella of the tall thin girls. Like, who in the class gets messaged by Ella?

MON., 2 MAR.

Hey Bby Gal 11:41 AM
Yeah..... Ella,, here 11:41 AM
Chat me up asaq. 11:50 AM
Asap** 11:51 AM

THU., 5 MAR.

Heyyy, 10:15 PM
Your ignoring my chats now or they are just not delivering? That's fucked up tbh 10:15 PM
This is Ella tho. Don't be a bitch, yeah? 10:15 PM

FRIDAY

Hey!!!!! 10:17 PM
You don't remember me or what? Gal. It's Ella. Ella! 10:27 PM
Audrey's friend. Queen's friend. Ella! Ella!!! 10:28 PM
Are you really ignoring my text 10:28 PM

YESTERDAY

Babes, 10:01 AM
I called you. You didn't pick. 10:01 AM

TODAY

Someone just told me the issue you had with Prof Okafor. 12:05 AM
Call me ASAP. We can help you deal. 12:05 AM

THIS SENDER IS NOT IN YOUR CONTACTS
BLOCK   REPORT
ADD TO CONTACTS

Ella! 10:20 AM
I just saw your profile picture now! 10:20 AM
Ella! Queen + Audrey's friend? 11:07 AM
Jesus Jesus! I am so oo sorry!
Like how can I ignore you? 11:07 AM
I am so so sorry, ppleaad 11:07 AM
Please*** Biko 11:07 AM
I didn't have data,, haven't been here for ages now. 11:08 AM
Hello Ella, are you there? 11:08 AM

Heyy 6:06 PM
Sup with you and Prof Okafor? 6:06 PM

Eh! You heard? 6:06 PM

Lol Ofcoz I heard. Been meaning to reach U. 6:06 PM

Please, I beg you, help me with that man's issue o.

Please. I don't know any anyhow in this school. I cannot
afford to be rusticated or anything. biko 6:06 PM

Anyone** 6:06 PM

Where are you ATM? 6:07 PM

Papa Oks 6:07 PM

Papa Okey's** shop 6:07 PM

Kk 6:14 PM

You travelled? My battery is low. It shut down soon sef. 6:14 PM

Go and charge biko. 6:46 PM

Charge? No light here oo 6:46 PM

I don't even have a place to sleep 6:46 PM

Wot do u mean u dont hv place to sleep? 7:10 PM

I'll explain when we see 7:10 PM

Stay at that Papa Okey's shop. I'm driving down. 7:17 PM
Will call as soon as I am there 7:17 PM

OMG! OMG! ELLA!!! 7:17 PM

May God bless you eh. Thank youuu 7:17 PM

Ella? Are you here yet? 8:00 PM

Ella?? 8:17 PM

Ella??? 8:25 PM

I am at Papa Okey's shop 8:30 PM
I am parked where he sells kero. Where you dey? 8:30 PM
Are you there??? your phone off already??? 8:31 PM

MISSED VOICE CALL AT 8:32 PM

TAKE YOUR CALLS!! 8:33 PM

I see you. I see you. In brown Venza 8:33 PM

Yea. get in here. I didn't park well. 8:33 PM

    I squint as I look into the night, partially blinded by the sparkly streetlights. I pull up my box and drag it to where she has parked. I am a little scared of these tall thin girls. She opens the passenger door for me to get in once I've pushed my box into the backseat. I resist asking for the name of her perfume that makes the inside of this Venza smell like it is a room in heaven. "Thank you very much, Ella. I don't know what I did right to deserve stressing you like this." She says nothing, nods and keeps bending toward her steering wheel, pressing her phone. It is an iPhone, those long, fine ones that are new and make you drool. We sit in silence. Well, more truthfully, I sit in silence. She is on her phone, pressing, exhaling now and then, smiling mild smiles. I stay quiet, don't know how to be next, yet.

    Ella coughs before she says, "So where... do... we go from here, yeah?" This is our very first real conversation and right now I feel her accent. It sounds like she learned from someone who learned from someone who learned from an Americanah, a

complete been-to who thinks staying in America is all we have
to do to become Jesus.

"I dunno. I had…"

"Fuck it! My house. Where are your stuffs?"

"Oh, in the back here."

"By the way, your name is Akunne, right?"

My name is not Akunne. I don't say this. I don't tell her my
name is Ofunne either. I only wait for her to buckle her seat belt
before I begin to tell the story nobody asked of me. I tell of my
temporary roommate, a.k.a. friend, who left me on the street.
I tell of Prof. I tell of standing a whole day and watching the
world pass.

"Wow," she says. I talk for close to thirty minutes. She says,
"Wow." I say how honored I am to be helped by her, how grateful,
how I deeply admire her and everything she stands for. She says,
"Wow." I tell more because I do not want to sit and say nothing.
I talk on: Whatever, whatever, yada, yada, Buhari Buhari. Prof.
Okafor is worse than a corrupt president. You know, you know.
EFCC should not only drag around politicians that misappropri-
ate funds. Blah, blah. They should also handle humans who are
mean to other humans. Or better still, there be a body for this.
Yada, yada.

Ella just drives. No more *wow*s. No nod. No *yeah*. No *fuck it*.
But her silence sways me as much as she sways her head, which
she does a lot, using her green-painted, long nails to brush her
long, straight extensions from her face. But before she starts
playing Davido's "Nwa Baby," she says, "Baby girl, you don't
mind staying in my house, yeah? And yeah, the number I chatted
you up with, yeah? Save it, yeah? And yeah, I hope you got sexy
pictures on your profile, yeah? Because I want to see all them

sexiness you got, yeah?" She swiftly sways her head, uses her green nails to push back her hair again before she winks at me. It looks like she's saying: *Welcome to being a god.* I am still wondering if I am ready for this.

5. ME AND TALL THIN GIRLS ARE *WE* NOW

We wear black dresses. We strut. We go to Prof. Okafor's office. Ella, Audrey, and Queen say I should stay in the hallway. It is nearly empty now, everyone still on break. A few weeks ago, students studded this place, strutting and carrying their files with pride because it is not easy to beat out a million candidates to secure a spot here. It doesn't matter whether that aunt or uncle of yours who knows a someone who knows a someone that collected something small, maybe money or kindness, worked it out for you, and now here you are, an undergraduate. No, it doesn't matter. We are here now, that's all. The future leaders of Nigeria.

Tall thin girls open the door to Prof.'s office. Audrey drags me into the room by my right hand, saying, "Come here, baby girl, come here." My eyes meet Prof.'s. He looks away immediately, says to Ella, "See to it that she writes fast, extraordinarily fast." He stands up from his chair, opens his cabinet, brings out the question papers, selects one, and gives it to me. He leaves his office. Ella takes out a textbook, throws it to me. "Use it. Don't waste my time, please."

"You know we will graduate top of our class, yeah?" Audrey says, smiles, pouts her mouth, winks at me.

"Leave her alone! She needs to concentrate," Queen says to Audrey.

"Is she writing with her ears?" Audrey says.

"You guys, don't be like that now!" Ella says and then turns to me. "Be fast."

I sigh, write and write and write. Or maybe, copy and copy and copy. Once I finish, we pile into Queen's ash-colored Lexus RX 330. I ask, "So do you know when the disciplinary committee will sit?"

They look at me, those three tall thin girls. They laugh. They say, "What the fuck, whaa? What the fuck…"

6. BECOMING THE TALLEST THINNEST

I wear new tongues now as well as say "yeah," "you guys," "what the fuck," "yeah, yeah," as well as sing English as well as slap the driver who brings me home as well as become Rihanna and Beyoncé and Cardi B as well as wear too few clothes and hair extensions costing the price of ten plots of land as well as empty bottles of skin-toning creams onto my skin till I shine shine like I am sun as well as drain expensive perfumes till people stop to ask how I got such a fine smell as well as become more beautiful than tall thin girls. Even their men say so. They choose me over them. It makes them happy, though, so long as I get picked and they get paid. They say, "This is why we selected you, because you blaze so bright and your brain burns like fire. We know. We always know the right ones."

7. BAD GIRL GONE GOOD GONE BAD

I lose it and stab my shadows when I hear my father's baritone blare over the phone. He calls more now, and when he is done asking how is school, how is class, how are you coping, my university daughter, he says, "Ofunne, be good. Be godly, okay? You will be home for the holiday this time around, right?" When he calls, I hear him; when he ends the call, I hear him. I remember the last time I saw him, his hands on the steering wheel, his mouth telling me not to forget where I am from. Right now, I am wondering how a girl from where I am from did forget. I am thinking of all the men I have come to know over the past three months. Chief with the stomach like he swallows the continent for breakfast. He was my first. He was my very first because Ella says it brings good luck; having a wealthy man rip your hymen means you will never meet a poor man. Ever! I didn't tell her of Joshua, the boy living behind my new two-bedroom apartment who sneaks in after these chiefs have gone. He begs for tea and t-fare. I give him tea and t-fare and kiss and me. We moan together and I know that even if he had money, I wouldn't want him for that. Then there is Prof. Okafor. And the man with white beards. And the man who pays for the two-bedroom apartment. And this other guy, Igwe Obiora, who Ella made sure I'd never see again. All he gave me were multiple orgasms and cowries. He said the cowries were original, the original cowries my ancestors harvested human heads for. There are other men, too, people I work hard to forget. The only person I am working hard not to forget is me. I fear that in trying to be me, I missed, became tall thin girls instead.

I stand from my bed, go to church. I kneel. I say, "Heavenly father, forgive me, forget the things I did, accept me back." I skip classes. And when I don't, I sit far, far from tall thin girls. But they come. They knock and knock and knock and knock till I know I can't really dodge tall thin girls.

"Don't call me baby girl. My name is Ofunne." But tall thin girls don't care. They say, "Ofunne is bush, something the governor would not like to call you."

"Which governor?"

They tell me how the minister of education celebrated his birthday when I was idling out. They didn't call me, because I was idling out. They tell me the governor looked through Queen's phone while they gisted, chewed gum, and sipped rum. They tell me that among many pictures, it was my picture he saw and liked. They tell me he said, "Get this one for me na. Ha! See big ikebe! What, what will she cost me?" They tell me they are here to break my idling. When Ella says, "You are going to South Africa with him," I nod, forget my father in heaven, forget the one in Enugu, and say, "Please, call me baby girl once again."

8. IT'S JOHANNESBURG, BABY

So the governor calls my phone, calls me baby girl. So he says it this way: "beibei girl," like he lacks something in his mouth, teeth or tongue. When he first calls, I wonder which governor this is. I listen as he tells me, "Keep our relationship to yourself, just you should know it." I put everything he tells me in my mouth and swallow it with water. I prepare for the South Africa trip. I ride to the newest boutique in Lekki with tall thin girls. Once we've burned the money he sends for my prepping, we return so I can pack, and for the first time, tall thin girls don't look so glamorous, not more than me. I know they are jealous, not just because they say it and laugh but because I see it in their eyes. I sleep in Lagos today and know that tomorrow I will be sleeping in Johannesburg.

The governor calls. He says to me, "Beibei, we will not go to Johannesburg right now, but we will go very soon." He sends enough money to buy ten Venza cars. Tall thin girls say maybe he saw a thicker girl with a bigger ikebe, oh yeah. They laugh with their mouths wide enough to swallow a river. I want to tell them to get out of my flat, but my voice is too tiny to start a war. I say I want to go see my mum this weekend since the Johannesburg trip is off. Tall thin girls say, "For what?" We sit in my living room, quiet, wearing too few clothes, pressing our phones till Audrey reads out from a popular blog that there is a strike now. We google it and learn that the Academic Staff Union of Universities is negotiating higher salaries for lecturers, and they're meeting with governors. I smile. I say this is really why he postponed Johannesburg. Tall thin girls press their iPhones. I stand to turn on my AC; there is too much going on right now.

9. JOHANNESBURG, FOR REAL

10. PUKING OUT THE PARTY

The governor buys me a white Crosstour and says, "Keep this car. But keep us to yourself." And so I'm keeping the month we spent in Johannesburg after the strike ended to myself. I mean, I did not even tell tall thin girls what went down there, or else they would be minding me like I was a baby: "Have you taken pills, eh? How much did he give you, eh? Will you see him again, eh?" Well, now I am bigger, from all the dinners, I think, and I am back and yay, I have my own car, and the strike is off, and I am here at a very depressing party at Nkem's house. Nkem is the friend of Aboy, the senior special adviser to the minister of foreign duties. Aboy understands the real meaning of foreign duties. Apart from linking us up with the minister himself, Aboy has connections and gets me and tall thin girls influential men who reek of power and hard currencies and hardness. His ride or die babe, Nkem, is drama, and her house is for showing off, with her plasma TV and her washing machine and her Indian hair and her fake smile and her Aboy. I drink vodka and rum and run to the toilet because I retch, and then puke. I don't know why I puke, but I puke again. Nkem comes in to her toilet. I am facing the bowl and puking, and the bitch looks at me and says, "What the hell? You've got AIDS now? You slutting tall thin girls! What the hell. What the hell."

11. A DRUG AND A DRINK TO DRINK

It is exam. I am the only tall thin girl in the exam hall because I tell tall thin girls I want to write all my exams in the hall and not in the office so no lecturer will have the chance to grab my ass. Ella shrugs, says, "Your choice." Now I think I shouldn't have had such guts. It is a difficult exam. My hands shake and seem to be afraid of holding things. My pen won't stay put, keeps slipping through my fingers. In my head, there sit a million humans with hammers and they hit the hammers, and each hitting leaves my head thinner. I want to die, and that is the only feeling that comes close to describing it. That and the hollowness that hugs you only when you lose someone who you once breathed like the air. I lost myself, but I am not sure this is why I feel like I am holding hands with the butchered parts of my body. One of the invigilators taps me from behind, asks me,

"Are you okay, dear?" Her voice is soft and patronizing. I am not a charity case and I do not know the best way to say *get lost* if not by handing in my blank papers to this thin woman. She collects them, walks to the end of the hall, and hands them over to the new professor, who doesn't know me and who doesn't know tall thin girls. I stand from my chair, hold the other students' gazes. I am used to holding the other students' gazes. I have become for many girls the star now. If they only knew what it's like. Like being a perfumed dead rat. I go to the table where an invigilator had earlier ordered we drop our bags and phones, grab mine, leave. It is an original Louis Vuitton Saintonge. The other tall thin girls would never keep a Louis Vuitton Saintonge, with its smooth calfskin and its soft tassels and its expensive price, on the same table where cheap secondhand bags cluster. Ella would have found handing over her bag a very valid reason to leave the exam. But not me, and this is one of the many things that worries Ella about me. I pull out my phone, an iPhone XS, dial my mother's number, walk to my car. When she says, "Hello, Ofunne m," I pause, exhale, say, "Hello, Mummy."

"Omalicha m, kedu? How was your exam? When are you coming home sef? Ha! It's going to a century since I saw you last o."

"Mummy, my exam, it was bad."

"How? What is the problem? Ogini?"

"I—I don't know. I don't know what I'm doing."

"What's the problem, nne'm?"

"Mummy, I don't know."

"Are you sick? Are you eating well?"

"I am tired, Mummy, very very."

I hear her exhale. She keeps quiet for some time. Then she

asks again when I am coming home. I don't know if I am going home. I don't have plans of going home, but I say, "In two weeks' time, Mummy." And nod repeatedly when she asks, "I hope you are still prayerful eh?"

"I will be praying for you here, too, I nula? I will pray. Just have faith. Your exam will be okay."

"Okay, Ma."

"You will pass. Ah! Our king of kings. He's all-knowing, a miracle worker! Have faith, I nula?"

And I have faith. I have faith that the all-knowing king of kings will not make known to my mother the reason I am so tired, the reason I wasn't able to finish the test. He won't make known to her that I haven't stopped puking since Nkem's party; that when we hang up, I will drive straight to Ella's house for some drink she promised will stop my stomach from growing. Because the only thing I need to grow as a baby girl is my bank account, and maybe my breasts and, yeah, my ass. I don't actually think I'm pregnant. I took all measures. But I go to Ella's house because nobody tells Ella no.

Tall thin girls are splayed out on Ella's couch when I open her door that afternoon: Ella reading my worn-out copy of *Purple Hibiscus*, Audrey lying on the floor pressing her phone, Queen holding up a miniature mirror to her face. They want to know how my exam went. I am too tired to recount. Ella repeats, do I know my constant tiredness and headaches and constipations and swollen breasts and vomits and every other whatever can only be attributed to pregnancy? I roll my eyes. Earlier, when Ella said this, I ignored her, as I want to now. But she has a pregnancy test and as soon as I urinate into the brown cup she hands me and return it to her, she immerses the colored end of the strip into the cup. She pulls out the strip and we wait, her singing Ada's "I Testify" and laughing, me sweating and telling her, "Stop, stop, stop that song right now." And then she cackles, holding up the strip and pointing at the two colored lines.

"Oh, yes! Now drink this," she says, handing me a mug. "I will not have a pregnant baby girl."

I have faith that the all-knowing God will not show my mother this, either: me grabbing the mug, drinking the damn thing, wanting to vomit, the taste like rotten fish; me ignoring Ella as she says, "Don't even think about it" when I run past her to the toilet.

When I come out a minute later, Ella doesn't believe me that I didn't puke it up.

"Take this drug." I eye her. Look at Queen and Audrey to say something. Audrey speedily turns to her phone. Queen speedily turns to her phone. I sigh. I throw the drug into my mouth and drink my water. And I say to Ella, "Anything else?"

"No, my madam. Meanwhile, you left your small phone here yesterday o. See it on top of that table."

"I did? Are you serious? I didn't even know to look for it. Ha!"

"Na so the exam do you? So, this is how bad this exam got to you eh?" Audrey says.

"Or is it the pregnancy?" Queen says, throws her head back and laughs.

Audrey says, "A number you saved as 'Gov' kept calling and calling, like he owns you for real. Is that the governor?"

"I thought you said you were no longer seeing the governor," Ella said.

"I am not seeing any governor. Give me my phone."

Audrey runs to the glassy center table, collects the phone, and puts it into her pocket. I sigh, walk to where she stands. She makes to walk farther, to make me chase her. But then suddenly she stops, pulls the phone out of her pocket, and begins pressing it.

"Give me my phone, Audrey. Ella, please talk to Audrey."

"Audrey, give the phone to her now now."

Audrey throws the phone at me. I dodge it and it hits the floor. The battery and the phone's back fall out. I pick them up, panting as I do so.

"I hope you're not hiding anything from us like this. Ella, see your babe o," Audrey says.

Ella looks at me and looks back at her book, which she is now pretending to read. I enter Ella's room, lock the door, sit there for a while. My mind runs around. I need to sleep, but I don't want to. I unlock the door, go to the living room, where tall thin girls are still lying around, grab my original Louis Vuitton Saintonge, pick up my car key, put on my slippers, open the door, and leave the house.

When I get into my car and lock my door, I dial the governor's number and listen to his campaign song till the governor says, "Hello." I do not let him start up with his usual boring "How thou art, my sugar, you know I love you, my sugar, blah blah, sugar, yada yada, sugar."

"I am pregnant," I say to him immediately, though I don't know why.

He keeps quiet for some time before he says, "You are supposed to be a secret. You are supposed to be secret, sugar."

I want to say I guess this sugar is too sweet to stay secret.

"Is he a boy?" he asks.

"I don't know yet na."

Nothing comes from him for a moment, and I wonder if the network is bad. But it's not. He sighs loudly.

"You are good, all right?" he says. I want to tell him about the drug and drink from Ella, but I worry that will worry him too much and he will worry Ella too much and Ella will worry me too much.

"Don't panic, sugar, tomorrow eh I will come. We will go and see the doctor together. I want a boy. You will remove the baby if the baby is not a boy, you hear?" I don't say anything. He repeats the question, asking, "You hear?" This time I say, "Till tomorrow, please."

He sighs, says he will talk to me later. I want to call my mother, tell her, but I know she will cry that her daughter has lost her faith, has brought dishonor to the family. I want to call my father, tell him, but I know he will sigh severely, say his daughter forgot where she comes from, brought dishonor to the family. I start my car, drive away from Ella's house. I want to go home, but I am not sure home is the two-bedroom apartment I can afford because my body houses an abundance of men. So I keep driving, and keep driving. And keep driving. And keep driving.

UNSOUND

by MARIA REVA

(This story, from McSweeney's *53, was a winner
of the 2019 National Magazine Award in Fiction.)*

SOMETIMES THEY ARRIVE IN vans from the maternity ward. Sometimes in strollers, or inside shawls wrapped around waists. Sometimes from the village, sometimes from the town. Few of the babies have names. If they arrive healthy, they were born unwanted; if wanted, then unhealthy.

The baby house sits tucked behind a hill, out of sight of the village and the town.

It's bad luck to talk about or show pictures of the babies living at the baby house, like it's bad luck to talk about or show pictures of a train wreck or a natural disaster.

The main hall of the building has bright windows and three rows of beds, and a *sanitarka* who makes rounds with a milk bottle. She strokes the babies, talks to each in turn.

She says, "My kitten."

She says, "I wish I could keep you for myself."

She says, "They told your mother to try again."

The director of the baby house is young, eager, and progressive. He's the darling of the Ministry of Health and Social Labor. The beam of light piercing the fog. The broom battling the cobwebs. During the first year of his tenure, he urges the Ministry to take a holistic approach to the issue of invalidism. Since adult invalids are classified as Group Ones, Twos, and Threes according to their labor capacity, the director believes their group number can be predicted—projected—at birth. That way the Ministry can project the resources necessary for lifelong collective care.

According to the director's classification of infants, the Threes have a minor defect. It may be cosmetic—webbed fingers, a misshapen ear—but when has that helped a person land a job? Even the outwardly normal babies pose a risk. Abandonment is trying; there's always the chance of a depressive mother, an alcoholic father lurking in the genes. So the director deems the healthy but abandoned babies Threes as well, just in case.

Twos are blind, deaf, and/or mute. Skin disorders and ambiguous genitalia fit the bill too.

Ones simply lie there.

An aerial view of the baby beds looks like this:

```
[ ][ ][ ][ ][ ][ ][ ]
[ ][ ][ ][ ][ ][ ][ ]
[ ][ ][ ][ ][ ][ ][ ]
```

This year, the Ones, Twos, and Threes sleeping in their beds look like this:

```
[3] [3] [2] [3] [2] [3] [3]
[2] [1] [1] [1] [1] [1] [2]
[3] [2] [3] [3] [3] [2] [3]
```

The director would deny any pattern to the distribution of the babies. If the healthier babies lie next to the great bright windows where they can chatter with the magpies, and next to the doors where the occasional Ministry inspector can see them best, it's surely a coincidence. Pick any other room where the older children sleep—except they rarely sleep, not all at once—and try to find a pattern in that jumble.

And anyway, it's the *sanitarki* who assign the babies to their beds, not he.

In this particular batch of babies, the loudest voice comes from row three, bed seven. The puzzle pieces of her face didn't seal together in her mother's womb. The cleft begins at the right nostril, plunges down the upper lip and into the hole of her mouth. A boisterous Three, just on the edge of invalidism, the girl is one of the favorites. She coos and babbles and peek-a-boos, flirts a little with the *sanitarki*, grips their fingers with iron strength when they pass by.

*   *   *

At six to ten months, the babies begin to crawl. Hands and knees patter on the vinyl floors. Today the distribution of the crawling babies looks like this:

```
      3   2   3   2 33
   3   2 3     3
      3   2 2    3 2                              3
```

On the far right is the lone baby: she's the lively Three. Faster than the others, the girl has slipped out of the baby house. She's cruising along the wooden picket fence, eyes set on a gap wide enough to squeeze through. Pine trees tower beyond it, beckon her with their syrupy smell. Four pickets to go, three, two... The same *sanitarka* who found the girl inside the medicine cabinet yesterday, the over-turned dustbin the day before yesterday, catches up to her now. The girl sticks her head through the gap—the air feels different on the other side, less dense—but as she pushes herself forward, the collar of her romper tightens around her neck and the pines slide away.

The *sanitarka* doubles over, panting. "You'll be the end of me." She lets go of the romper. The baby looks up at her and a flutter of giggles escapes her mouth, wins her captor over like it did yesterday and the day before.

A small, secret relief for the overworked attendants: not all the babies learn to crawl. If some of them aren't let down from their beds, it's because they'll never be able to walk anyway. Only natural, for those with clubfeet or spinal conditions. If everyone learned to crawl, where would they go? Beds take up most of the space, and there aren't enough *sanitarki* eyes to watch over everyone.

*   *   *

The older children name her Zaya. Little rabbit. Her mouth is a crooked assemblage of teeth and gums. As the teeth grow they poke through the slit in her lip. At breakfast, half her porridge oozes from her nose.

The name starts with a letter she can't pronounce, and the other children delight in hearing her try. There are many letters the girl can't pronounce, because they require both sets of lips and a complete upper jaw.

Whenever a *sanitarka* goes for a smoke in the courtyard, Zaya follows. Most of the time the woman sits in silence, staring at the wall opposite, taking grateful pulls on her cigarette. On good days she reads a magazine or a book; on the best days she reads aloud to Zaya, who learns to follow the words.

Every New Year's Eve, the baby house receives a donation from the Transport Workers Union. A six-wheeled truck sighs to a stop in front of the gates, envelops the waiting children in a great diesel plume. Grandfather Frost—whom a recently orphaned boy calls Saint Nicholas before receiving a prompt correction—descends from the passenger side. He has a long white beard and wears a tall boyar hat, a blue velvet coat, and felt boots.

Grandfather Frost beams down at the children. "Who's been good this year?"

The children shrink back, alarmed by the question.

Grandfather Frost recoils, too, unaccustomed to children unmoved by the prospect of gifts. He whistles up to the pock-faced man behind the wheel, who wears a plastic crown festooned with a shiny blond braid—the Snow Maiden. The bed of the truck lifts, dumps a pile of old tires over the fence. Grandfather Frost uses shears to cut the tires into swans.

"It's a miracle," says a *sanitarka*, and so it is. The children keep silent, watching the miracle unfold. This is how he does it:

Soon the courtyard is littered with dusty brown swans. The children paint the swans red or blue or yellow. Zaya mixes red and yellow in her tin to make a radiant orange, but an experimental dab of blue turns the mixture brown.

When the director of the baby house comes to Zaya's swan, he says, "That's a shame. Grandfather Frost gave you three bright colors to choose from."

Zaya invents an explanation. The director would find the explanation very clever, and would surely repeat it to his colleagues at the Ministry, who would find it very clever also, but the trouble is, of the sounds that slosh out of Zaya's mouth, the director understands none.

So he asks, "Why not just paint the swan yellow?"

Every spring, the *sanitarki* trim the hedges alongside the building, pull weeds around the tulips. They bleach and starch the curtains, pour ammonia over the floors, shine the doorknobs, wipe the babies down.

The Psychological-Medical-Pedagogical Commission arrives in a procession of three cars. Zaya and the other four-year-olds press themselves against the windows of the baby house, watching the procession in a quiet panic. They are about to be redistributed.

The Threes shouldn't worry. Unless they freeze up during the test, they'll move on to the children's house.

The Ones can't even get out of their beds, and no one can do anything about that now, so they'll be transferred to the psycho-neurological *internat*.

"What's at the *internat*?" asks one of the children.

"It's a delightful place where children run barefoot, pick berries," says the director, who has popped in for the day. "Commune with nature, and so on."

A *sanitarka* starts to weep.

"Happy tears," the director explains.

The Twos are the wild cards. Sometimes the Commission sends them to the children's house, sometimes to the *internat*.

Zaya, our solid Three just a few months back, has slid to a Two. She has abandoned speech in favor of writing, but few of the children know how to read yet, so most of the time she points and grunts.

When it's Zaya's turn with the Commission, the director escorts her to the back of the building to a small room that smells like moldy onions. The Commission sits at the head of a long table. They've arranged themselves in descending order of height, like nesting dolls. The largest man, who has a thick mustache cascading from his nostrils, asks Zaya to confirm her name.

Zaya hopes this isn't part of the test. She has to answer every question, without exception. She feels as though her bottom is about to give out like a trapdoor. Afraid of wetting herself, she clenches her knees together. To deflect the question, Zaya does what she saw a *sanitarka* do once, with the director, to get an extra day off. The girl twists her finger in her curls, peeks at the men through her thick lashes. She leans in, coy, as if she wanted to tell them a secret. The men lean in too. First she raises three fingers, then seven. When no one says anything, Zaya forces out a giggle: *Silly, can't you understand?*

The largest man looks down at the file in front of him and laughs. "Row three, bed seven. Her sleeping assignment." The answer satisfies the Commission.

The man in the middle, with oily, porous cheeks, pushes four puzzle pieces across the table. Zaya fits them together. It's a picture of a cat, a dog, and a parrot.

"Can you tell us what you see?"

Zaya stares at the cat, the dog, and the parrot. She feels the shape of the first word inside her mouth, whispers it into her hand. It doesn't come out right, so she moves on to the next word, then the next.

> Cat
> Dog
> Parrot
> Bird
> Thing
> With
> Feathers
> Pets

~~Zoo~~
~~Animals~~
~~Fluffy~~
~~Friends~~

The Commission watches the clock above the girl's head. The inside of Zaya's palm is warm and wet from her breath. The smallest of the men says, "One more question and you're free to go. What's the weather like outside?"

Zaya swivels around, looks out the window. All she wants is to run out of the building, where the weather is. Instead she turns back to the Commission, presses her hands to her ears to keep from hearing herself, starts pushing the first word out. Its mangled syllables resonate between her palms. She wishes the Commission wouldn't look. She shuts her eyes, bangs her fist against the table, louder, louder, to keep from hearing herself, until the pressure in her chest breaks and the words fire out. *How bright and beautiful the sun*, she cries. *Not one cloud can cover it up!*

The psychoneurological *internat* stands at the edge of a cliff, overlooking the Dnieper River. Patches of white plaster flake off the walls to reveal pink brick underneath, as if the building suffered from a skin condition. Long ago, before its gold-plated cupolas were dismantled and its eighteen copper bells were melted down to canteen pots, before its monks were shot, it was a monastery. An iron fence, a recent addition, surrounds the grounds. Its spiked rods rise high enough to keep in the tallest of the children, the space between them narrow enough to keep in the smallest.

The fresh batch of five-year-olds arrives in the back of a decommissioned camo truck, hair and faces dusty from the road. A tall woman in a dark green suit, their new director, orders the children to gather round in the courtyard. Her large, smooth forehead has a plastic sheen. One hand rises in greeting as the other does a head count. The children who can stand prop up those who can't against the fence.

Zaya watches a group of teenagers blow dandelion fluff at each other in the distance, two of them barefoot, just as the previous director promised. She scans the courtyard for tire animals, sees in their stead fresh mounds of earth.

The woman points to a sheet-metal sign nailed to the arched entrance of the decommissioned monastery. "Can anyone tell me what that says?"

When no volunteers come forward, she reads the sign herself: "There is no easy way from the earth to the stars."

A voice to Zaya's left asks what are stars.

"To reach the stars you need to build a rocket. And we did that," the new director says. "But let me tell you a secret." She lowers her voice, and the circle of children tightens around her. "To build a rocket you need parts, and sometimes you get a crooked bolt, a leaky valve. These have to be thrown away. If they aren't, the rocket is unsound, and won't launch. And if it does launch, it might explode into a million pieces."

The children nod along.

"That's just the way it is when you're reaching for the stars." She casts a magnanimous glance over the group. "Sometimes you get defective parts."

The children nod along.

"But we don't throw people away. We take care of them. You can bet on that for the rest of your life." She straightens up. "When you're feeling blue, it's something to think about."

The children follow her into the building. They file along a corridor, past the canteen; past the storage room, containing a blackboard; past the latrine, where a bald boy squats in the shadows, gargoyle-like, his shoulder blades jutting out; past a pair of twin girls balancing on one leg each; past a door with a tiny square window too high for Zaya to see through. They reach a cavernous hall crowded with beds and children. The painted walls are crowded too: flames rise from the floor; a red snake wraps its tongue around a thrashing figure; above them, curly clouds, men with wings, men without wings, disembodied wings twisting around each other, stretching to the domed ceiling, at the center of which is a woman cradling a baby. The baby stares down at Zaya day and night wherever she is in the hall, its hand up, on the verge of uttering something important.

In the following months, Zaya adds to the pictures to pass time. Using a sharp stone, she scratches the men's mouths open to let them speak. She wishes she could reach the never-sleeping baby but it sits very high.

When winter comes, the cold whistles through the cracks in the windows and into the lungs of the children. Zaya develops a cough, then double pneumonia. She drifts in and out of a fevered fog. Noises filter into her dreams—the rustle of sheets, snot bubbling up and down endless nasal passages, the distant cowbells from the village, the clack of trains heading to the town.

Outside the window, a couple of older, healthier children chatter as they dig another pit. When she hears them shoveling earth back into the hole, Zaya feels for the damp soil on her hot face, but it isn't there; it's for someone else.

Green buds erupt on the branches outside. Sun rays on bedsheets shine brighter.

When Zaya awakes between fevers, she sees a pair of withered arms and legs on her bed. She tries to move; the matchstick limbs answer. She covers them with her sheet.

The girl looks at the beds around her. Given the hush of the room, she's surprised to find most of her neighbors awake, blinking at the ceiling. She's in a different room, a white-tiled room, the room on the other side of the door with the tiny square window.

[1] [1] [1] [1] [1] [1] [1]
[1] [1] [1] [1] [1] [1] [1]
[1] [1] [1] [1] [1] [1] [1]

Zaya could try walking again, but where would she go? Everything aches, as if a fire had ravaged her insides. She lays her head down and goes back to sleep.

She awakes when a pair of fingers presses on her wrist, checking for a pulse.

She awakes when the corners of her sheet lift and she floats in the air for an instant. She screams and falls back down onto the mattress.

She wakes writhing in hot, wet sheets. Something hard slams into her side. When she disentangles herself, she is on the floor. Her sweaty palms slip on the pale pink vinyl as she crawls to the door with the square window. She tries the knob, beats her fists against the door. She slumps back down to the floor, a heap of bones. The coughs erupt through her mouth and nose in painful spasms. Two limp-faced girls gaze down at her from their beds, peaceful. All she needs to do is let it happen, their heavy-lidded eyes tell her. Give in, melt into the floor. Isn't that what this room is for—a long rest? She need only let her lungs clench, wring themselves out, and two pairs of hands will take her away. That's when the parents will come; she's seen them visit when their child is safe in a little box. Someone might even sew up her lip for the occasion.

Her head rolls to the right. In the corner of the room, a crack in the vinyl floor glows.

What she has to do is crawl toward that crack. The need is bodily, instinctual. She has seen it in every moth and mosquito bewitched by a flame.

Right hand, left knee, left hand, right knee. Her joints grind painfully, her elbows buckle, but she keeps moving.

Zaya lifts the corner of the vinyl off, then a pair of loose planks. A small hole in the floor opens up to a set of stone steps leading underground. The tunnel's cool breath gives the girl a burst of strength. She stands on shaky legs. Strings of cobweb cling to her arms and face as she follows the light down the cold steps, which level out into a chamber. Long, narrow shelves are carved into the stone walls. Broken candles and vases litter the floor—remnants of pillage. The air smells sweet, like an unwashed mouth.

The glow emanates from a corner of the chamber, from underneath a gray pile of robes. She wades through them—the cloth's folds retain a bluish luster—and the unsettled dust brings on another round of coughs. Inside is a mummy. Half of one. The legs appear to have been snapped off. The brown, leathery face squints up at Zaya. Its mouth, petrified mid-scream or mid-yawn, suggests that the creature met its end in wretched terror or sublime repose. Its hair and beard are the yellow of dead grass. The hands cross at the chest, skin stretched between knuckles like a bat's wings. Beside the creature lies a cylindrical hat that Zaya has seen before, atop the bishops painted on the monastery walls, but the jewels have been picked out.

Zaya stares back at the shriveled face and determines from its gaze that something awaits her, something important. She gathers the half saint in her arms, tugs the hat over its forehead. A century of desiccation has made its body very light. The saint pulls forward, as though tied to a string. The pair make their way through the tunnels, turning right here, left there, the bundle leading her through the dark, urging her toward the miracle. They totter up a set of steps to an opening. She smells the leaves before she sees them. She pulls branches and weeds apart with one hand, clutching the half saint with the other. They climb over a clutch of tree roots. The blue sky greets them. Zaya leaps forward, ready to run from the *internat*, run as far as her aching legs will take her, but she stops.

They're outside the building, but still inside the tall iron fence.

Before Zaya can feel the blow of defeat, the bundle pulls her back into the tunnel. Wrong, it was wrong, but it'll make it right again, if Zaya just follows.

Down the tunnel they go, then to the left, right, left again. They reach an opening in the cliff face. The only way down is a fall to the jagged rocks below. Back into the tunnel. The pull is stronger now, the pruney creature in her arms frantic to perform its marvel, and she is frantic to witness it. Right, left, another left. They're outside again, but still inside the fence, this time just a few steps shy of the forest beyond it.

Zaya waits for direction. The half saint, now inert, gives none. She shakes it. In the daylight its parched features look exhausted, accepting of their fate. Determined to have at least one of them escape, Zaya thrusts the bundle over the fence. The half saint lands faceup on the wild grass, its expression unchanged.

Someone calls the girl's name. Zaya turns to see a *sanitarka* running toward her. Just a few yards away now, the woman spreads her arms wide as though for an embrace.

When Zaya slides her leg between the rods of the fence, she doesn't expect the rest of her body to follow. But it does; it squeezes right through. With the *sanitarka* approaching, the girl can't think about what is and isn't possible. She thinks only of running.

THE NEXT DAY AND THE DAYS EVER AFTER

by ADRIENNE CELT

(This story appeared in McSweeney's 57.*)*

IN THE MORNING, A girl was running around the track. The sun was high enough to cast a shadow behind her as she moved, and the day was already getting warm. She wore track shorts—blue, with a white stripe along the hem—and a long-sleeved white T-shirt that looked iridescent, like the slime coming off a snail. Without articulating it, the workers assumed she was wearing a sports bra, but they were less sure about underwear, and they wondered. When the light hit her face, it was possible to see a trickle of sweat running down her cheek, which she would periodically wipe away with the sleeve of her T-shirt, never slowing down the pace of her jog.

School was out for the summer, so the workers had experienced very few distractions as they replaced the roof on the old auditorium. Apparently, the building was still functional enough to be repaired instead of torn down, but it looked out of place, looming over the slick new classroom structures like an ancient toad. The workers were bored. It would've been one thing if school were in session, with children screaming at one another in the halls and slamming their lockers for entertainment, but everything was empty and quiet, almost as if the space had never been inhabited at all. It unnerved the men, made them edgy. They kept their radio blaring from the moment they arrived until the moment they finished up each day, and took to leaving their tools around just to add a bit of clutter. Occasionally, they held contests of strength to see who could lob an empty Gatorade bottle the farthest off the roof, but the foreman always made them clean them up before they were allowed to go home. A couple of times, teachers had shown up to rummage through their classrooms, ducking through doorways and emerging a few minutes later with an armful of books or folders, but beyond that, the workers were alone.

Until today. When they arrived, at six forty-five, the girl was already there, stretching. Her heel was kicked up on a ribbed metal bench, and she wore tiny earphones. She didn't notice them, or didn't seem to, and soon enough she began moving around the track at a steady pace, her light-brown ponytail swinging behind her. She might've been eighteen or nineteen, maybe twenty; certainly not a student at the school, which offered only grades seven and eight. Her legs were tanned, even though the summer was just starting, and her fingernails were painted black. That morning, the men had intended to complete the flashing around the air conditioner on the southeast side of the building, but the track was located to the northwest, so the foreman agreed they could pull up old tiles from that side instead. The men were cheerful. The foreman was cheerful. The girl was muscular, and indifferent to them.

They started by securing a plywood jack near the edge of the roof, and then worked in teams, prying up shingles with a pitch-fork. One man would wedge the fork beneath the edge of a tile and lever it upward, then another would peel a whole strip away from the underlayment. They moved forward in this way until they reached the jack, at which point they had to reposition every-thing and start again. The jack kept the shingles from sliding to the ground, collecting them instead in an untidy pile, which the men then tossed into a dumpster. Since there was no one on the sidewalk below, it wouldn't really have mattered if a few shingles slipped, but the men were used to a particular protocol, from which they would never willingly vary. The girl was much too far away to be in danger from falling debris. A hundred feet from the roof there was a set of large concrete steps, which descended ten or twenty feet more, and below that was the red dirt track, with a grassy football field inside it. The girl moved around the track with an expression of focus and determination, her muscles flexing each time her feet hit the ground, and kicking up a small cloud of pink dust behind her. Hair switching back and forth. By now, she'd pushed her shirtsleeves up over her wrists, halfway to the elbow.

They speculated that she was in training for something. A marathon. A triathlon. One of the men, who went by Rodriguez, said he'd run in a marathon when he was younger, and the rest of the workers were surprised. Why would he waste the time? Or, more important, the money? But Rodriguez just laughed. "No, man," he said. "Not official. I was living in Chicago, right? And the race went by my building. I didn't even know it was happening, but then one day I'm home from my job—I was a night watchman, so I had to sleep during the day—and there was all this commotion. People lining the streets, kids holding signs, the whole thing. And at first I was mad because they were being really loud and I couldn't fall asleep. I even tried putting a pillow over my head, but then it was too hot, you know? Shit. So finally, after like an hour, I just gave up and went outside to see what it was about, and it was actually kind of exciting. There were these people jogging down the street looking totally miserable, like they were gonna pass out, but around them everyone was screaming their heads off and giving all the runners high fives and handing out little cups of water. And I just thought, I don't know. I thought I could do that. Like, it would be funny. So I walked a little ways away and found a part of the route where there weren't a lot of people watching, and I just snuck in and started running with them. I only made it a few blocks before someone kicked me out, but I got *so many high fives*."

The men laughed.

They considered other reasons why the girl might be running with such resolve, at an empty middle school, so early in the morning. Maybe she was getting married, or at the very least going on an important date, and she wanted to look good. Slim down in the hips or the waist, so she could fit into a dress she had on layaway at one of the department stores downtown. Maybe she had done some calculation about how many calories could be burned with each lap, provided she kept her speed fast and even. As the workers peeled another row of shingles off the roof, the movement of the girl's legs hitched her shorts up, and she had to tug the hem down to cover her upper thighs, after which they slowly migrated back up again. "I'll take you on a date, little girl," said a man named Maxwell. "I'll get your blood pumping." A few nervous giggles erupted around him. No one else had admitted out loud that they were watching her for any particular reason. But then again, she was out of earshot, so they could say whatever they wanted to, right? She was down there in the sunlight—tiny, like a toy—and they were up here.

"I don't think she needs to lose any weight," ventured a man named Simon Garcia. "I like a girl with a little oomph."

"Yeah," said another worker, name Bruzek. "Don't get rid of that butt! It's like an apple! All round."

"Don't you have a baby daughter, man?" someone asked him. But Bruzek just shrugged.

"That girl ain't my daughter. And I want to take a *bite* out of her."

They all laughed at this, too, before returning to the task at hand.

It was difficult work, jamming the tines of the fork beneath the tiles and tugging them loose in one big strip so they'd leave fewer pieces behind; corners and edges that stuck to the underlayment had to be picked off meticulously by the crew, sometimes with their fingernails, if the foreman was feeling especially OCD. A lot of bending, a lot of thrust was required to do the job right. It didn't take long before everyone's necks and backs began to ache, which they did almost simultaneously, as if the workers all shared one big body. Together, they complained about the heat, and the pitch of the roof, and passed around a bottle of ibuprofen, which they shook into their mouths like hard candy. Some of the men had messed-up knees, which made it difficult to crouch on the slanted surface, and one had the beginnings of arthritis in his hands, though he wouldn't admit this to anyone for several more years, when it got so bad that two of his fingers curled up on their own, the joints permanently swollen. They were all in pain. This was understood. Later, they'd drink whiskey and tequila and cheap beer—on this day, in fact, they would end up drinking more together than they ever had before—but for now the only distraction they had from the pain was talking.

"I wanna be the towel that wipes that girl's body clean."

"I'd like to stick my nose in those shorts and take a sniff."

"You know what I want to do? I want to pour honey on her legs and then take my time just licking it all off. Every single drop."

They hooted when someone came up with a particularly good idea, though they hooted quietly, so they wouldn't accidentally attract the girl's attention. She kept running, and her hands formed loose fists as she swung her arms in a steady rhythm. The men worked a little faster than usual, though also with a bit less precision. One worker poked another in the ass with his pitchfork, and a wave of hysteria swept through their ranks, making the men feel like they could do anything. They took turns spinning shingles through the air like Frisbees, trying to land them in the dumpster from greater and greater distances, or to thread them between various protuberances that jutted from the building's interior.

It wasn't until lunchtime that the workers began wondering how it was possible that the girl was still running.

"Don't white girls take breaks, man?" Maxwell asked Bruzek.

"Not while I'm around," Bruzek replied. "They beg me to keep going."

Eyes were rolled.

"Shut up, dude."

"Yeah, please, shut up."

"Whatever." He smirked. "You know it's true."

None of the men particularly liked Bruzek. When they passed around sandwiches, he always took the biggest one, and if they had a thermos of coffee, he poured himself an enormous cup without trying to figure out how much was left for everyone else. He wasn't all that nice to his wife, and they saw this, too, and judged him for it. But today they were inclined to forgive him his worst tendencies. They were in a beautiful mood with one another, and wanted to keep it alive, despite the aches and pains that radiated through their bodies, turning their skeletons electric. By this point it was high noon, and the girl's white shirt was blinding underneath the bright sun. If anything, they thought, she was going faster than before, speeding up with every lap she took. There was a water bottle on the bench where she'd done her stretching, and every so often—every five laps, or ten—she paused to sip from it, jogging in place, her cheeks never losing their rich flush of pink.

When she drank, her mouth puckered around the bottle's straw, and the men thought about all the women they'd loved, and whether any of them, ever, had worked as hard to keep herself beautiful as this girl was. None of them knew how Bruzek had met his wife, that she had been in love with his brother first, and that he had scooped her up in the fallout of her broken heart, and had then never quite forgiven her for failing to choose him first and only. He punished her with little comments and critiques, forgetting her birthday, their anniversary. Telling her that her pants looked too tight until she starved herself, and then getting her to believe the diets were her idea. "You know *I* think you're beautiful, baby," he'd say. "But there are guys out there who don't like it when their wives look pregnant all the time." She had a cute nose, he thought, cute eyes, cute hands and feet. He loved her fervently, and was terrified of losing her. Her name was Doreen, and when she really was pregnant he sang songs to her every morning, like: "Doreen, Doreen, the angel machine."

The men decided that probably, no, they'd never known a girl quite like this one, running on the track below them. Her body radiated care, in the curve of the muscles and the glow of her skin. So much so that it seemed to extend to them, too, as a kind of protection. They felt as if her body could drink up all their problems and sweat them back out without coming to any particular harm. She could undo every wrong that had happened to them, just by being what she was. So pristine.

The foreman let the men watch her for a while, while they all drank orange Gatorade—the worst but somehow the most abundant flavor—and tossed around a bag of chips and a sack full of bruised apples, which Maxwell's wife had gotten cheap from the Gleaners.

As the workers were pulling themselves up again, getting ready to push through the last few hours of work before they could climb down the ladders and go home, Simon Garcia broke the silence that had fallen over them. The other men were all stretching and moaning, but Simon stayed seated and finished his apple with great care, nibbling all the way down to the core.

"When I was in high school," he said, "there was this girl who did the long jump, who I was crazy about, Rafaela. Man, she was *strong*. Her thighs were almost as big as mine, but they were fine-ass thighs. She could've broken my neck with them." He sighed thoughtfully. "Sometimes I wish she did do that. Just squeeze and: *snap*. What a way to go."

"You know what I wish?" Rodriguez said. He was standing right on the edge of the roof, toes poking out over the gutter, weight propped against the pitchfork in his left hand. He could've been a farmer in some old painting, except he was wearing dirty jeans with holes in the knees, and a T-shirt advertising Jose Cuervo, which he'd acquired by accident, buying clothes by the pound at a Salvation Army store. It had been folded inside another shirt—a plain one, which was more acceptable by his mother's standards. But the Cuervo shirt was softer than anything else he owned, and he wore it almost every day, except when he went to visit his mother. "I want that girl to come pick me up in her arms and carry me away," he said.

For a long moment, no one replied. Some of the men were looking at Rodriguez, but most had turned back to look at the girl, who was now sprinting, her legs and arms pumping at a frightening speed. Her lips peeled back to reveal her teeth, which were clenched in such a way that they seemed to be holding some-thing in, something that was pounding and screaming inside her, which she would not release, not now, not ever. It looked painful, what she was doing. She looked tired. But she didn't slow down.

"Like, here?" Maxwell asked. "She'd come up here?"

"No," replied Rodriguez. "I'd be somewhere else. At a diner ordering a Coke, maybe. Or helping my mom with her groceries. Or maybe I'd be getting ready to come to work, like, about to get in the truck with all you guys. And then she'd suddenly be there, and she'd take me into her arms and she would start running, and she would hold me, and we would never come back."

"Oh," said Maxwell. He realized he wanted this, too, but didn't want to say so; he knew it would seem like he was only copying Rodriguez. The other man looked so certain of himself, as if by coming up with this idea he'd earned some kind of prize. It felt like he'd claimed the girl, and now she belonged to him more than she belonged to the rest of the men. As Maxwell considered what it might be like to just hang in someone else's arms, he turned away from Rodriguez, who was wearing an annoyingly happy expression. Maxwell stuck his own pitchfork beneath a shingle and slowly worked it up, focusing his energy on getting the angle exactly right.

Just then the foreman shouted, and the workers all spun around to face the track. The girl's feet had lifted off the ground. For a second they bicycled in space, just a few inches above the dirt, but then she gained some kind of traction and started going higher, fast. The men couldn't believe it. They let the tools they were holding clatter to the rooftop as they lifted their hands to shield their eyes from the sun. The girl shot up, straight into the light, which quickly obliterated all but her silhouette. Her blue shorts were lost to the workers. Her white shirt and teeth. Her long legs, made brown by the sun, and her feet, which had been pounding so sincerely against the earth all morning. The men screamed at one another and clutched their faces.

"Do you see this?" Bruzek asked. "This is insane! What is this?"

"What's happening?" asked Maxwell. "I don't— I can't—"

Rodriguez, though, was quiet. He watched her with great reverence, with the same beatific expression that had irritated

Maxwell just moments before. His chin tilted toward the cloud-less sky; his lips were slightly parted. The girl kept sailing upward, until she was just a tiny pinprick in the blue.

"No one's going to believe this," Bruzek said, thinking of his wife. For years afterward, he would consider telling her, just to see what she'd say: if she would take his word for it or think he was joking. "Jesus Christ."

The girl's water bottle was still on the bench, and her foot-prints littered the track. The workers surveyed the ground, surveyed the sky, their hearts beating frantically in their chests, but they could no longer see anything out of the ordinary—just a cheap plastic bottle that could've been left behind by anyone. The area of the roof they'd been concentrating on was almost com-plete: there were two more lines of shingles to strip off before the surface was clean and could be prepped for the next day's work. Tomorrow they would have to finish the flashing they'd neglected. They would have to come back here and do the same jobs they'd been doing for years, as if nothing had happened, because if they didn't, they wouldn't get paid.

Rodriguez stayed still.

"What do you think, man?" Simon Garcia asked him.

"About what?"

"Do you think she'll…"

Simon paused. He had been about to ask whether Rodriguez thought the girl would come back and take him with her, wher-ever she was going. Whether she would pick him up and hold him to her breast with those powerful arms, letting him rest his face against the sheen of her T-shirt. But he might as well have asked if she would toss them her shorts, present them with her underpants. Whether she'd choose to appear before them naked and invite them, gently, to take a turn with her, offering herself as a sweet relief from the endless grind of their existence. Whether she would strip the pain off their bodies, drink it into herself like wine, and then disappear, unharmed, unchanged. A vision that flickered into view just when they needed her, and asked nothing.

And that—he knew without finishing his question—would not happen. They'd been watching her all morning, and they hadn't seen the most important thing. The power inside her, which was not what they'd supposed. The next day they would come back to the school, hungover and exhausted from a mutually sleepless night, to pick pieces off an old building that was probably crumbling beneath their feet, fixing something that would eventually be destroyed and replaced with something better. They would work until they were tired, and then they'd go home, and start it all over again. They would do this for the rest of their lives.

And she wouldn't come back for any of them, because she didn't even know they were there.

PALAVER

by BRYAN WASHINGTON

(This story appeared in McSweeney's 62: The Queer
Fiction Issue, *edited by Patrick Cottrell. It was selected for*
The Best American Short Stories 2021.)

H E MADE HIS MOTHER a deal: for every story he
told, she'd give him one of her own.

That's hardly fair, she said.

Bullshit, he said.

It was the first time he'd used the word with her. And she let
it slide, the first of many firsts between them.

He'd been living in Shin-Ōkubo for the better part of three
years. She'd flown from Houston to Los Angeles to Taipei to

Tokyo to see him. Or at least that's what she'd said on the phone.
He knew that she and his father were going through it. This was
one of the reasons he'd left, although he hadn't thought about
that at the time.

Now his mom sat on the sofa, snacking on a bag of chips,
holding a magazine neither of them could read. Her son stood
beside a broom. His place was mostly plants and some shoes. He
had this balcony overlooking a bus stop, next to a convenience
store and a stairwell for the train station.

You go first, said the son.

Absolutely not, said his mother.

Fine. I'll start.

Jesus.

Once upon a time, said the son, I fell in love with a married man.

I don't need to hear this, said his mother.

We met in a bar one night, said the son. He bought me a
drink. Then he asked me to come home with him.

The mother looked at her son's face before she turned to the
wall, and then to the window beside them. The one thing his
apartment had going for it was the view. It'd drizzled her first
morning in the country, and she'd watched sheets of rain paint a
gaggle of grade schoolers by the stoplight.

You're serious, she asked.

No joke.

You aren't serious.

Why would I lie now?

Unbelievable. Were you safe?

I'll only tell if you play.

This isn't a fucking game.

Is that a yes?

God, said his mother.

Good, said her son, sweeping in what passed for his kitchen. We were safe. We're safe.

Is this a thing that's still happening, asked his mother. Are you still seeing him?

It's your turn, said the son. You give me one of yours first.

I'll make it easy for you, said the son a little later. Just tell me how you met Dad.

It was his day off. His mother sat beside him on a bench in the train station. They were waiting for the local line, just after rush hour, and he figured they must've made a funny picture, as his mom groaned with her arms crossed and he tapped away at his phone, leaping between a volley of apps.

Who the hell are you talking to? his mother said. How long were you living here before you lost your mind?

I only asked a question.

You're being fucking disrespectful.

Hardly.

Who are you texting?

My students.

Is that appropriate here? asked the mother.

It's fine, said the son. And it's your turn.

Gradually, the platform filled beside them. Every other occupant was a businessman of some sort. Every now and again, they'd chance a glance at the mother and her son, but at some point a lady rolled two twins in a stroller onto the platform.

The kids wouldn't stop crying. Everyone turned to glare at them. Eventually, gradually, the children settled down.

When the train arrived, tinkling a three-tone melody, the son and his mother waited a moment. Then they both stood, trailing the woman with the stroller, leaning into a pair of seats by the conductor's booth.

The woman with the twins turned their way, sighing. Both of her kids waved. So the mother and her son waved back.

Once upon a time, the mother didn't tell her son, I thought I'd take you back to Toronto. We'd live with my sister. The two of us would leave Texas, in the middle of the night. We wouldn't say a word to your father and we'd never come back.

Once upon a time, the mother didn't tell her son, I thought I'd become an opera singer.

Once upon a time, the mother didn't tell her son, I wrote poetry. I scribbled the words in a notebook and hid it in the guest room. But one day—you wouldn't remember this—I found you crying underneath the bed, and the pages were spread open, right at your feet. I think you were nine. I never wrote a poem again.

The son taught English at a juvenile detention center in Yanaka. His pay could've been better, but it was more than enough to live on. Most of his students would never have a reason to use the language, or at least that's what the son told his mom, but the teens still let him teach them, falling asleep only occasionally. They thought he was interesting. Every hour or so, he gave them breaks to use their phones.

That sounds depressing, said the mother.

Sometimes it is, said her son. But I like it.

You couldn't just have been depressed in Texas?

I was.

And whose fault is that?

The son opened his mouth, and then he closed it.

My students are funny, said the son. And they don't take any shit.

Impossible, said his mother.

How so?

They put up with *you*.

That isn't cute, said the son.

Anyway, said the mother. I thought you were an accountant or something.

Thanks for caring, said her son.

Don't act like you've ever kept me in the loop.

Whatever, said the son. I had another job the first few months.

And how'd that go?

It was fine. But one of the clients complained.

Because you're Black, said his mother.

No, said the son, but then he didn't say anything else.

Some nights, the son stayed out a bit later. His mother would walk to the convenience store for dinner, nodding at the cashier when he bowed. Sometimes her husband texted her, and she'd think about how to reply. But she never sent anything. It was enough, for now, for him to know she'd read it.

Then one evening, smoking on her son's balcony, the mother found, folded under her chair's leg, a crumpled Polaroid of two men. One of the men was her son. The other guy looked a little older. They both smiled, holding inflatable numbers on each other's shoulders, and the mother thought, briefly, that her son looked better unshaven, after all.

So she took a photo of the photo with her phone, and then she refolded it, slipping it under the seat. The mother started to light another cigarette, but then she thought better of it, and she stepped inside instead, kicking off her son's flip-flops, leaving a window open for the breeze.

The next evening, the son and his mother sat in a bar, one of the tiny enclaves lining the alleys of Ni-chōme. Posters and flyers showing men fucking in various positions were splayed across the walls, while a pulsing techno track thrummed from above. The son watched his mother eye each picture, and he winced at her, just a bit. But she didn't say anything about them.

The room was mostly empty. Two dudes fingered their drinks in the corner, whispering in each other's ears. The bartender, a bearish man, napped by the register. The son drank a frothy beer, calling out for a second, and his mother shocked him by raising her finger for one too.

The bartender said something in Japanese. It made the son laugh. He replied with something that made the bartender shake his head.

He thinks I'm charging you, said the son.

Don't lie, said the mother. I know where we are.

You didn't say anything.

It didn't need to be said.

Is this your first time in a gay bar?

Tell me about your married man, said the mother.

This made the son wince again. He fidgeted in his seat.

Once upon a time, he said, a boy met a man.

Here we go, said the mother.

The man promised this boy a kingdom, said the son. Or at least a house in the suburbs. And the boy thought this man was lying, but he wasn't. Which made the boy happy. Except the man maybe hadn't told the entire truth.

That he had a wife, said the mother.

And a child, said the son.

Jesus.

On the way.

That doesn't make a difference!

She hadn't meant to raise her voice. The son and his mother looked around the bar. But the two men in the corner only grinned, raising their beers.

I know you don't have any morals, said the mother, but do you think home-wrecking is a game?

You're asking the wrong question, said her son.

Does his wife know?

It's your turn, said the son, sipping his beer.

A little later, on the train home, the mother exhaled in her seat. Their car was packed with drunken businessmen patting one another's backs, and couples nosing each other's ears, and stragglers tapping at screens.

Fine, she said. Your father stole me from a tower.

We can't talk on here, said the son.

You asked me a question and this is your answer.

The game's no fun if you lie.

Your father plucked me from the top floor, said the mother.

Carried me all the way down. Slayed a dragon and all of the townspeople.

You're being sore, said the son. You didn't fly all this way to be sore.

I didn't fucking fly all this way to play games with you, said the mother. And how would you know, anyway?

Dad's not that kind of guy, said the son, and his mother started to say something else, but the train slowed to a stop, and his mom shifted in her seat, and he reached for the rail, steadying them both.

Most days, the son went to work. The mother followed him to the train station, where they diverged—and she rode from Shinjuku to Akihabara to Shibuya, funneling change into vending machines, walking in and out of shops, snapping photo after photo in Yoyogi Park. In front of the park's shrine, some women asked the mother to take their photo, so she did. When they asked the mother if she wanted one of herself, she smiled as they snapped about forty.

Some evenings, when the mother knew her son was finally asleep, she slipped on her sneakers, hopped down the stairs, and walked the strip lining the road by the station. Even on week-nights, the streetlights were always on. Traffic slowed to a trickle. The mother made bets with herself—she'd walk to the next inter-section, and then she'd turn right back around, but when she actually reached said intersection, it became the *next* intersection, and *that* one became the intersection that *followed*.

When the mother made it back to the apartment, she'd stand in the doorway, waiting to hear her son's snores. Once they returned, the mother settled back into bed, flipping her phone onto its side. There was a night when her husband texted her a single emoji, and she responded immediately, without even thinking about it, just as a reaction. She thought about how there are some things we simply can't shake.

Once upon a time, said the son, I spent the night on a bench in Montrose.

Once upon a time, said the son, I woke up in an entirely different part of Houston, in someone else's clothes.

Once upon a time, said the son, I brought a boy to the house. In high school, I think.

You didn't, said the mother.

This is a thing that happened.

Liar. When?

You were at work. Or something.

What? Where did he come from?

Who?

This boy.

Where they all come from. We met on an app.

Did you have sex? In the house?

Shit, said the son. Are you really asking me that?

You're the one who brought this up, said his mother. I'm asking because I'm worried about you.

You weren't worried then, detective.

I said I *am* worried, said the mother, you little shit.

Then don't be, said her son.

And anyway, said the son, Dad caught us. He told the guy to go home.

This made the mother open her mouth, but she didn't say anything. Her son waited for the words, but they just didn't come. So they both moved on.

Once upon a time, the mother didn't tell her son, my own mother tried to marry me off.

Once upon a time, the mother didn't tell her son, I couldn't have possibly made her life any more difficult: I broke every rule she ever put in front of me.

Once upon a time, the mother didn't tell her son, I introduced your grandmother to your father, and she told me she'd never approve. I laughed right in her face. And once I started, I simply never stopped. I laughed for weeks and weeks and weeks, until I ran out of breath, and then I started again.

Sometimes, in the evenings, they walked—usually in silence. They let the city do the talking between them. But this night was dimmer than most, and they'd chosen another club in Ni-chōme, and jazz drifted from the speakers, and the son looked entirely too distracted, flipping his phone on the bar counter.

Eventually, the soundtrack changed. When the mother said the singer's name aloud, her son made a face.

What, she asked.

Nothing, said the son. You're just full of surprises. Flying here. Listening to city pop.

Children are the least surprising parts of their parents' lives.

Also, said the mother, does your married man have a name?

This again, said the son.

You brought it up.

He does, said the son.

You don't have to tell me what it is, said the mother.

I wasn't going to.

What do you even do together?

Do I need to spell it out?

You know exactly what I'm asking you.

Well, said the son, once upon a time—

Enough with that.

He takes me to baseball games, said the son. He likes baseball. And we go for walks.

That's it?

Are you saying there should be more? Do you think we're aliens?

No, said the mother, but her son couldn't read her tone—it had a tenor he'd never heard her use before.

The son picked up his phone again. He tossed it back onto the counter.

Fine, said the mother. Then tell me a story about your students.

You don't want to hear about them, said the son.

Of course I do. And you clearly need something else to talk about.

They don't take me seriously, he said. It's like they know the whole thing's just an act. But they've taught me a lot.

The mother was about to ask what, specifically, the teens had taught him—but the son raised a finger, grabbing at his cell.

He spoke quickly and quietly. His tone reminded her of his father's. And then the son stepped across the room, down the stairs, and out of sight, whispering into his phone, leaving his mother alone.

He didn't come back for a while. Eventually, the mother realized that the bartender had been watching her. They made eye contact, and the bartender nodded, reaching for another glass.

That night, they walked back to the apartment in silence, and they'd nearly made it to the complex when the son sat on the bench out front, hiding his head in his hands. The mother eyed him, blinking. She thought about rubbing his back. She wasn't sure if she should.

Listen, said the mother. I won't claim to know what it's like. But I do know that disrupting a marriage could be the death of you. You have to trust me.

Is that why you flew here, asked the son. To lecture me?

I'm only telling you what I see. You have to take care of yourself.

You don't know anything about it.

I know that it's eating you up.

You don't know shit.

I know that it's got you crying at midnight halfway across the world.

What if I told you that everyone knows, said the son. Him and his wife? What if I told you that she doesn't mind? That she's got her own thing going on too? What if I told you that that's just the way it is, and I'm fine with that?

The son found himself breathing heavily, and the mother took a second to catch her own breath. A group of guys walked around them, smoking, and one of them looked their way, whistling. When the son stood up, the mother put her palm on his shoulder. He sat back down.

Maybe I should just go back, said his mother.

Maybe you should, said the son.

I left because you made me, he said.

No one made you do anything, said his mother.

No, said the son, you made me. I would've died. So you made me.

The mother wasn't sure if they were talking about the same thing, and before she could ask, the son shook his head. He stepped into the complex alone.

Once upon a time, the mother didn't tell her son, I caught you with a boy. You never knew that I knew.

Once upon a time, the mother didn't tell her son, I watched the way you looked out the window afterward, and I thought about cupping your cheeks in my palm, telling you to go where you wanted.

Once upon a time, the mother told her son, I flew halfway around the world to find you, and you were doing mostly fine. Or as fine as could be expected. I didn't know if I preferred that to finding you in a mess. I didn't know if one was better than the other. Wasn't sure if I should stay to find out.

His mother had planned to stay a week, but on her last morning she extended her ticket.

The airline didn't give her a hard time. Her son didn't say anything about it either. That evening, he didn't come back to the apartment, and she walked up the road to sit in a bar by herself. She ordered a glass of wine, watching the couples sitting across from each other. Another woman sitting alone made eye contact, and the mother nodded, and she nodded too.

The next morning, the son returned. He was brighter than when he'd left.

You weren't wearing those clothes yesterday, said the mother.

Another case closed, said the son.

I just don't think it's right.

Which part of it?

You know what I mean.

I don't think I do.

Then that's your problem, said the mother. It's your problem for not trusting me. It's your life. But you have to trust me to know that, at least.

And before her son could say anything else, the mother added, It wasn't my first time.

Your first time what, said the son, wiping at his face.

At one of those bars. At a bar like that.

Oh.

I'd been with my sister.

Oh.

She took me a few times, said the mother. Once, she took me and your father. We had a nice time.

The mother and her son stood across from each other. She glanced outside, through the window, at some kids hopscotching on the sidewalk.

Okay, said the son.

Okay, said the mother.

Well, said the son. That would've been nice to know. Before, I mean.

The son was still standing in the doorway, and when a man in the hallway passed behind him, he turned around, nodding and saying something his mother couldn't understand. Then the son turned to his mother. He stepped back outside and closed the door.

On the weekend, they went to the park. The mother watched her son pick up snack after snack in the convenience store, tossing them into his basket, bantering with the man behind the register. Neither of them said much as they took one train, and then another, filtering from her son's part of Tokyo, before walking through a handful of alleys that sprawled into an open field. A soccer game went on to their right, while a group of students danced to hip-hop in the foreground. What looked like the beginnings of a wedding photo session played out just beside the blanket they'd unfolded onto the grass.

The son spread the food across their blanket, opening boxes and shuffling silverware.

I forgot to bring a fork, he said.

I'll be fine, said the mother.

I meant for me.

Of course you did.

So, said the mother. What do you and your boyfriend eat together?

This was enough for the son to look up.

I've never heard you use that word, he said.

Well, said the mother.

The son grinned. His mother didn't.

He has a name, though, said the son. You can call him that.

Baby steps, said the mother.

The son watched the students as they made their way through their dance.

We go to bars, he said. We eat at stalls. Sometimes he cooks for me.

Do you ever cook for him?

Sure.

Often?

Often enough.

You should cook for the ones you love, said the mother.

Is there a story behind that?

The mother looked at her son, squinting. For the longest time, she'd thought he looked like his father, before deciding that she wasn't exactly sure *whom* he looked like. It would be a few years before she decided this was because of their own similarities.

Once upon a time, said the mother, I met your father in a library. He loved poetry. That was his thing. He saw that I loved it too. And that's when I knew—him seeing what I saw. That's what tipped me off.

Listen, said the mother. If you're ever in a relationship as long as the one I've been in with your father, you'll know what to look for. And you should trust yourself to know. Whatever that means to you. Whatever that looks like.

The son turned away from his mother. He wiped at his face. The married couple beside them stumbled around in front of the photographer.

That sounds sentimental, he said.

I didn't say it wasn't.

His mother looked over the top of his head at the newly-weds taking photos. When the woman looked up, they made eye contact. The mother smiled at her, and the woman smiled back.

Anyway, said the mother. I thought we were taking turns.

So now you want to play?

The son looked at his mother and then at the group of students, chanting and dancing. It felt like the temperature had fallen just a bit. The song sounded a little like one the mother knew, some tune she hadn't heard in a very long time, but as soon as the thought occurred to her, she cast it away, and she knew it couldn't have been possible.

Hey, he said. I'm sorry.

Yeah, she said. You should be.

No, he said. I meant for the other thing. For everything. You probably think I'm an idiot.

The teens in front of them slowed their dancing, falling all over one another. It was enough for the mother to grin despite herself. The world was bigger than anyone could ever know. Maybe that was hardly a bad thing.

You are an idiot, she said.

Thanks, said the son.

You're welcome.

Maybe you *should* leave, after all.

I don't think so, said his mother, grabbing another rice roll from the basket. Tell me something else.

FEAR OF LOOSE TONGUE

by LYDIA DAVIS

(This story appeared in McSweeney's 50.*)*

PLEASE BE KIND, RON, she says—
no mention of *anything*
that may or may not have occurred
at Hamburger Mary's.

OPPORTUNISTIC SEED

by LYDIA DAVIS

(This story appeared in McSweeney's 50.*)*

SHE HOLDS THE DOOR for him as he carries a case of wine into the house.

A seed floating on its bit of fluff takes the opportunity to enter the house behind him

(though this will not turn out to be, for the seed, a good move).

PHILOSOPHICAL QUESTION POSED BY STRANGER IN PAMPHLET

by LYDIA DAVIS

(This story appeared in McSweeney's 50.*)*

WILL SUFFERING EVER END?
Would you say:
    yes?
    no?
    maybe?

AN UNLUCKY MAN

by SAMANTA SCHWEBLIN
translated by MEGAN McDOWELL

(This story is from McSweeney's 65: Plundered,
edited by Valeria Luiselli. It was a 2022
O. Henry Prize winner, as well as a finalist for the
2022 National Magazine Award in Fiction.)

THE DAY I TURNED EIGHT, my sister—who absolutely always had to be the center of attention— swallowed an entire cup of bleach. Abi was three. First she smiled, maybe a little disgusted at the nasty taste; then her face crumpled in a frightened grimace of pain. When Mom saw the empty cup hanging from Abi's hand, she turned as white as my sister.

"Abi-my-god" was all Mom said. "Abi-my-god," and it took her a few seconds longer to spring into action.

She shook Abi by the shoulders, but my sister didn't respond. She yelled, but Abi still didn't react. She ran to the phone and called Dad, and when she came running back Abi was still standing there, the cup just dangling from her hand. Mom grabbed the cup and threw it into the sink. She opened the fridge, took out the milk, and poured a glass. She stood looking at the glass, then looked at Abi, then back at the glass, and finally dropped the glass into the sink as well. Dad worked very close by and got home quickly, but Mom still had time to do the whole show with the glass of milk again before he pulled up in the car and started honking the horn and yelling.

Mom lit out of the house like lightning with Abi clutched to her chest. The front door, the gate, and the car doors were all flung open. There was more horn honking and Mom, who was already sitting in the car, started to cry. Dad had to shout at me twice before I understood that I was the one who was supposed to close up.

We drove the first ten blocks in less time than it had taken me to close the car door and fasten my seat belt. But when we got to the main avenue, the traffic was practically stopped. Dad honked the horn and shouted out the window, "We have to get to the hospital! We have to get to the hospital!" The cars around us maneuvered and miraculously let us pass, but a couple cars ahead, we had to start the whole operation over again. Dad braked in the traffic, stopped honking, and pounded his head against the steering wheel. I had never seen him do such a thing. There was a moment of silence, and then he sat up and looked at me in the rearview mirror. He turned around and said to me:

"Take off your underpants."

I was wearing my school uniform. All my underwear was white, but I wasn't exactly thinking about that just then, and I couldn't understand Dad's request. I pressed my hands into the seat to support myself better. I looked at Mom and she shouted:

"Take off your damned underpants!"

I took them off. Dad grabbed them out of my hands. He rolled down the window, went back to honking, and started waving my underpants out the window. He raised them high while he yelled and kept honking, and it seemed like everyone on the avenue turned around to look at them. My underpants were small, but they were also very white. An ambulance a block behind us turned on its siren, caught up with us quickly, and started clearing a path. Dad kept on waving the underpants until we reached the hospital.

They parked the car by the ambulances and jumped out. Without waiting, Mom took Abi and ran straight into the hospital. I wasn't sure whether I should get out or not: I didn't have any underpants on and I looked around to see where Dad had left them, but they weren't on the seat or in his hand, which was already slamming his car door behind him.

"Come on, come on," said Dad.

He opened my door and helped me out. He gave my shoulder a few pats as we walked into the emergency room. Mom came through a doorway at the back and signaled to us. I was relieved to see she was talking again, giving explanations to the nurses.

"Stay here," said Dad, and he pointed to some orange chairs on the other side of the main waiting area.

I sat. Dad went into the consulting room with Mom and I waited for a while. I don't know how long, but it felt long. I pressed my knees together tightly and thought about everything that had happened so quickly, and about the possibility that any of the kids from school had seen the spectacle with my underpants. When I sat up straight, my jumper rode up and my bare bottom touched part of the plastic seat. Sometimes the nurse came in or out of the consulting room and I could hear my parents arguing. At one point I craned my neck and caught a glimpse of Abi moving restlessly on one of the cots, and I knew that, at least today, she wasn't going to die. And I still had to wait.

Then a man came and sat down next to me. I don't know where he came from; I hadn't noticed him before.

"How's it going?" he asked.

I thought about saying *very well*, which is what Mom always said if someone asked her that, even if she'd just told me and my sister that we were driving her insane.

"Okay," I said.

"Are you waiting for someone?"

I thought about it. I wasn't really waiting for anyone; at least, it wasn't what I wanted to be doing right then. So I shook my head, and he said:

"Why are you sitting in the waiting room, then?"

I understood it was a great contradiction. He opened a small bag he had on his lap and rummaged in it a bit, unhurried. Then he took a pink slip of paper from his wallet.

"Here it is. I knew I had it somewhere."

The paper was printed with the number 92.

"It's good for an ice cream cone. My treat," he said.

I told him no. You shouldn't accept things from strangers.

"But it's free. I won it."

"No." I looked straight ahead and we sat in silence.

"Suit yourself," he said, without getting angry.

He took a magazine from his bag and started to fill in a cross-word puzzle. The door to the consulting room opened again and I heard Dad say, "I will not condone such nonsense." That's Dad's clincher for ending almost any argument. The man sitting next to me didn't seem to hear it.

"It's my birthday," I said.

It's my birthday, I repeated to myself. What should I do?

The man held the pen to mark his place in a box on the puzzle and looked at me in surprise. I nodded without looking at him, aware I had his attention again.

"But...," he said, and he closed the magazine. "Sometimes I just don't understand women. If it's your birthday, what are you doing in a hospital waiting room?"

He was an observant man. I straightened up again in my seat and I saw that, even then, I barely came up to his shoulders. He smiled and I smoothed my hair. And then I said:

"I'm not wearing any underpants."

I don't know why I said it. It's just that it was my birthday and I wasn't wearing underpants, and I couldn't stop thinking about those circumstances. He was still looking at me. Maybe he was startled or offended, and I understood that, although it hadn't been my intention, there was something vulgar about what I had just said.

"But it's your birthday," he said.

I nodded.

"It's not fair. A person can't just go around without underpants when it's their birthday."

"I know," I said emphatically, because now I understood just how Abi's whole display was a personal affront to me.

He sat for a moment without saying anything. Then he glanced toward the big windows that looked out onto the parking lot.

"I know where to get you some underpants," he said.

"Where?"

"Problem solved." He stowed his things and stood up.

I hesitated. Precisely because I wasn't wearing underpants, but also because I didn't know if he was telling the truth. He looked toward the front desk and waved one hand at the attendants.

"We'll be right back," he said, and he pointed to me. "It's her birthday." And then I thought, Oh, please, Jesus, don't let him say anything about my underpants, but he didn't: he opened the door and winked at me, and then I knew I could trust him.

We went out to the parking lot. Standing, I came up to a little above his waist. Dad's car was still next to the ambulances, and a policeman was circling it, annoyed. I kept looking over at the policeman, and he watched us walk away. The breeze wrapped around my legs and rose, making a tent out of my uniform. I had to hold it down while I walked, keeping my legs awkwardly close together.

He turned around to see if I was following him, and he saw me fighting with my skirt.

"We'd better stick close to the wall."

"I want to know where we're going."

"Don't get persnickety with me now, darling."

We crossed the avenue and went into a shopping center. It was an uninviting place, and I was pretty sure Mom didn't go there. We walked to the back toward a big clothing store, a truly huge one that I don't think Mom had ever been to, either. Before we went in he said to me, "Don't get lost," and gave me his hand, which was cold and very soft. He waved to the cashiers the same way he waved to the desk attendants when we'd left the hospital, but no one responded. We walked down the aisles. In addition to dresses, pants, and shirts, there were work clothes: hard hats, yellow overalls like the ones trash collectors wear, smocks for cleaning ladies, plastic boots, and even some tools. I wondered if he bought his clothes there and if he would use any of those things in his job, and then I also wondered what his name was.

"Here we are," he said.

We were surrounded by tables of underwear for men and women. If I reached out, I could touch a large bin full of giant underpants, bigger than any I'd seen before, and they were only three pesos each. With one of those pairs of underpants, they could have made three for someone my size.

"Not those," he said. "Here." And he led me a little farther, to a section with smaller sizes. "Look at all the underpants they have. Which will you choose, my lady?"

I looked around a little. Almost all of them were white or pink. I pointed to a white pair, one of the few that didn't have a bow on them.

"These," I said. "But I can't pay for them."

He came a little closer and said into my ear:

"That doesn't matter."

"Are you the owner?"

"No. It's your birthday."

I smiled.

"But we have to find better ones. We need to be sure."

"Okay, darling," I ventured.

"Don't say 'darling,'" he said. "I'll get persnickety." And he imitated me holding down my skirt in the parking lot.

He made me laugh. When he finished clowning around, he held out two closed fists, and he stayed just like that until I understood; I touched the right one. He opened it: it was empty.

"You can still choose the other one."

I touched the other one. It took me a moment to realize it was a pair of underpants, because I had never seen black ones before. And they were for girls because they had white hearts on them, so small they looked like dots, and Hello Kitty's face was on the front, right where there was usually that bow that Mom and I don't like at all.

"You'll have to try them on," he said.

I held the underpants to my chest. He gave me his hand again and we went toward the changing rooms, which looked empty. We peered in. He said he didn't know if he could go in with me, because they were for women only. He said I would have to go alone. It was logical because, unless it's someone you know very well, it's not good for people to see you in your underpants. But I was afraid of going into the dressing room alone. Or something worse: coming out and not seeing him there.

"What's your name?" I asked.

"I can't tell you that."

"Why not?"

He knelt down. Then he was almost my height, or maybe I was a couple inches taller.

"Because I'm cursed."

"Cursed? What's cursed?"

"A woman who hates me said that the next time I say my name, I'm going to die."

I thought it might be another joke, but he said it very seriously.

"You could write it down for me."

"Write it down?"

"If you wrote it, you wouldn't say it: you'd be writing it. And if I know your name, I can call for you and I won't be so scared to go into the dressing room alone."

"But we can't be sure. What if this woman thinks writing my name is the same as saying it? What if by saying it, she meant letting someone else know, letting my name out into the world in any way?"

"But how would she know?"

"People don't trust me, and I'm the unluckiest man in the world."

"I don't believe you. There's no way she'd find out."

"I know what I'm talking about."

Together, we looked at the underpants in my hands. I thought my parents might be finished by now.

"But it's my birthday," I said.

And maybe I did it on purpose. At the time I felt like I did: my eyes filled with tears. Then he hugged me. It was a very fast movement; he crossed his arms behind my back and squeezed me so tight my face pressed into his chest. Then he let me go, took out his magazine and pen, and wrote something on the right edge of the cover. Then he tore it off and folded it three times before handing it to me.

"Don't read it," he said, and he stood up and pushed me gently toward the dressing room.

I passed four empty cubicles. Before gathering my courage and entering the fifth, I put the paper into the pocket of my jumper and turned to look at him, and we smiled at each other.

I tried on the underpants. They were perfect. I lifted up my jumper so I could see just how good they looked. They were so, so very perfect. They fit incredibly well, and because they were black,

Dad would never ask me for them so he could wave them out the window behind the ambulance. And even if he did, I wouldn't be so embarrassed if my classmates saw. *Just look at the underpants that girl has*, they'd all think. *Now, those are some perfect underpants.*

I realized I couldn't take them off now. And I realized something else: They didn't have a security tag. They had a little mark where the tag would usually go, but there was no alarm. I stood a moment longer looking at myself in the mirror, and then I couldn't stand it anymore and I took out the little paper, opened it, and read it.

I came out of the dressing room and he wasn't where I had left him, but then I saw him a little farther away, next to the bathing suits. He looked at me, and when he saw I wasn't carrying the underpants, he winked, and I was the one who took his hand. This time he held on to me tighter; we walked together toward the exit.

I trusted that he knew what he was doing, that a cursed man who had the world's worst luck knew how to do these things. We passed the line of registers at the main entrance. One of the security guards glanced at us and adjusted his belt. He would surely think the nameless man was my dad, and I felt proud.

We passed the sensors at the exit and went into the mall, and we kept walking in silence all the way back to the avenue. That was when I saw Abi, alone, in the middle of the hospital parking lot. And I saw Mom, on our side of the street, looking around frantically. Dad was also coming toward us from the parking lot. He was following fast behind the policeman who'd been looking at our car before, and who was now pointing at us. Everything happened very quickly. Dad saw us, yelled my name, and a few seconds later that policeman and two others who came out of nowhere were on top of us. The unlucky man let go of me, but I held my hand suspended toward him for a few seconds. They surrounded him and shoved him roughly. They asked what he was doing, they asked his name, but he didn't answer. Mom hugged me and checked me over from head to toe. She had my white underpants dangling from her right hand. Then, patting me all over, she noticed I was wearing a different pair. She lifted my jumper in a single movement: it was such a rude and vulgar thing to do, right there in front of everyone, that I jerked away and had to take a few steps backward to keep from falling down. The unlucky man looked at me and I looked at him. When Mom saw the black underpants, she screamed, "Son of a bitch, son of a bitch," and Dad lunged at him and tried to punch him. The cops moved to separate them.

I fished for the paper in my jumper pocket, put it in my mouth, and as I swallowed it I repeated his name in silence, several times, so I would never forget it.

DAD.ME

by C PAM ZHANG

(This story appeared in McSweeney's 53.*)*

MASHA IS WATCHING SUNSET bleed down the FOR LEASE sign and listening to the house's empty rooms echo. She's breathing the new-paint smell that always makes her chest ache. But most of all she's waiting for the Dad.

The sun dips. Outside the window, streetlights flicker into existence; inside the immaculate living room, he does the same.

The Dad who appears is a rare sight: Latino. Medium height, heavy shoulders. Black eyes in a brown face. No blood or mess. Just a faint pallor to his lips—she'd guess pills or a car left running. He chose a civilized exit. Masha reaches to silence her phone. Cynical as she likes to think she is, she feels the weight of this moment. He's more corporeal than most Dads. She can barely see the window through his shoulder. He's more—real. This thought she shuts off as easily as she does her phone.

From the room behind her, the realtor chuckles. "Oh, *that?* I take it this is your first house viewing."

Masha ignores the patronizing tone and nods, waiting for this Dad's quirk to surface. She hopes he's not a talker, though those with chatty Dads assure her she'll quit noticing. "Mine's like the fridge humming," one friend said, and another, "My fucking pipes are louder than he is. Do you know a plumber?" As the Dad paces the room, Masha's heart does a funny lurch: black shoes. The practical rubber kind worn by garbagemen, day laborers, waiters at cheap restaurants. She recognizes them.

The anticipation Masha feels in this moment is not unpleasant, not unlike waiting as a child beside a cluttered van while two brown hands cleared a space for her. But all that happens is that the Dad clutches his throat and *ahem*s, gurgling like a clogged drain.

"I'll think it over," Masha says. She gropes for her original excitement but shadows have claimed the house now, sliding up the corners and under the stairs.

If her realtor's pissed, he hides it behind a professional smile. He's in his late twenties or early thirties and impeccably groomed. His hair is a shiny carapace, beetled smooth by gel. Not a strand shifts. An eerie effect in the blank white house that listens in, hushed and solemn. *Shh, shh,* say the blinds.

"You know," her realtor says, unnecessarily, "the city's full of dead Dads."

Masha makes a small, noncommittal sound as she buttons her coat. Leaving, she glances back to see her realtor, who is still smiling. His teeth are big, white, square as tombstones.

That place is a steal, Oz texts when Masha recounts the full story. Or almost full. She hasn't gotten to the Dad's height, or the familiar brown of his skin. *Way nicer than your shithole. Be practical, Mash.*

His tone recalls the realtor's, and Masha bristles, formulates an acid response. Instead of sending it, she makes herself survey her apartment with Oz's practical eye. As usual the sink is stacked high with her roommate Ashley's plates, the coffee table littered with Ashley's yellow Believer pamphlets. Mold makes Rorschachs of the ceiling. The basement unit is murky, thanks to the oak tree that blocks the window. When Masha signed the lease it was a spring morning and green light filtered through the leaves, and the stack of Ashley's tasteful literary magazines seemed as bright as Ashley's smile, her blond hair. Masha could swear there was fucking *birdsong*. Too late she realized that light entered the apartment only in the spring, only when the leaves were budding, only during one morning hour. Even later she uncovered the evangelist's zeal behind her roommate's smile.

Now she's left with darkness and Ashley. Three years Masha has lived here, growing sick of mold and growing too old for roommates and growing, hopefully, wiser—even as the city refuses to grow. New arrivals pack its streets into a deadlock, yet still the buildings don't rise or expand. Plenty of friends from her small arts college have moved away. Those remaining cram into shared houses with shared hens and composts and arguments about toilet paper. That's not the future Masha sees for herself.

You should take it, Oz texts. *Or*

. . .

Three blinking dots watch Masha as Oz types, much as Oz watches her when he broaches this idea in person of moving in together. It began as a joke. Then Oz stopped laughing. Started blinking intently in a way that makes Masha want to either hug or slap him.

You're right, she texts quickly, before he can finish. *I could really use the space.*

The dots disappear.

And finally Masha takes a seat on the lumpy couch to look at—or rather, through—her apartment's resident Dad. He's on the translucent end of the spectrum, slumped on the rug so that its pattern bleeds through his arms. His quirk is the bottle-shaped bulge under his shirt that he massages in slow circles. An alcoholic, Masha guesses, who drank his way to his death. At first he made her sad. Now she just sighs and heads out before Ashley can commandeer the space for her nightly Believer ritual—that lengthy, one-sided conversation with the Dad who never responds. None of them ever do.

The Dads turned up two years ago and there's still no satisfactory *why*. Only the *what* is certain, and the *where*: in this city, and nowhere else. In approximately fifty thousand residences, and never businesses, parks, train stations, grocery stores, public squares. Collected from the last few decades and appearing in random homes, Dads manifest standing or sitting or draped over the couch, the translucent but otherwise spitting images of the dads they once were—complete with bald spots and spattered shirts and the marks of their self-inflicted deaths. But whatever managed to squeeze through the chink between this world and the next is flat. Each Dad has exactly one quirk: a story to tell, an action to retrace. They play on a loop, shadows projected on an apartment wall. In the first thrilling weeks, sites sprang up like mushrooms after a rain: DadFinder.org, WhosYourDaddy.com, Dad.Me. Family members traveled across neighborhoods, states, continents to visit a dad, but found only a Dad. Accusations, apologies, tears, hurled vases, brandished grandchildren, old fridge drawings failed to make any impression. The Dads are harmless.

So when Masha weighs a new Dad against big bay windows and a proximity to good restaurants and affordable housing prices and her age and Ashley and her sense of what adulthood should be, her initial reservations fade fast. She calls her realtor.

Like his smile, the realtor's voice is far too bright. "Splendid! I trust you got over your, ah, reservations?" He drops to a stage whisper. "Very few people look at them, and I mean *really* look. But I understand why you—"

"I'm good." Masha doesn't want to hear whatever story he's manufactured to gain her sympathies.

The lease, when it arrives, stipulates the Dad and his quirk in a section right below "Utilities" and right above "Pets."

Two weeks later, Oz raises a last toast in Masha's old kitchen. "To adulting!" Masha rolls her eyes, leans in for a kiss, scrambles for balance on his thigh. He's already hard. Why not? she thinks, emboldened by the champagne, by the taste of imminent freedom.

Parts of Oz melt under her roving hand, other parts swell. She's just beginning to float pleasantly on the slosh of wine and summer humidity when he pushes her back.

"Let's go to your room," Oz mumbles, glancing toward the Dad in the corner. From her kneeling position Masha can see the window through the Dad's torso, the oak tree twined in his plaid shirt. Oz is suddenly, adorably, serious, and Masha tries not to grin as she reminds him about the current scientific consensus that Dads aren't what we used to call ghosts, aren't human or interactive as the Believers claim, just some kind of waveform or light pattern that coincidentally pulls from a point in the past.

"What, are you converting to Ashley's cult *now?*" Masha turns to the Dad and clasps her hands together in parody. *"Thank you for sharing your presence with me."* The intonation is perfect; God knows, she's heard Ashley say the words often enough. But Oz just blinks until she snaps, "Fine, I'll get rid of him."

Their four-year relationship is one of equals. Masha's proud of the way they split checks, swap unisex sweaters, switch positions in bed, accept social invitations independently. When she was promoted to senior consultant and started to outearn Oz, nothing appeared to change. No lumps in the Jell-O of their relationship, which continued to be smooth, sweet, maybe slightly bland. But tonight Oz has adopted a look of patient maturity that shrinks her into feeling sullen, childish. All of a sudden she resents how his lanky form looms over her, despite the fact that she was the one who had gotten onto her knees. Acknowledging the irrationality doesn't help. The glow is ebbing; she's twenty-nine, her relationship with alcohol no longer so simple. She hasn't drunk any water and she can feel the ominous pressure of tomorrow's hangover behind her eyes. Fucking Ashley, she thinks bitterly at the bleat of another Believer lecture coming from a laptop in Ashley's bedroom. She realizes her resentment is misplaced, but the vindictiveness feels good, and anyway her roommate has ruined plenty of evenings with her presence, if not exactly this evening. Fucking *Ashley*. This rekindles some impulse, not quite the same one Masha started out with but close enough. "Fine."

She doesn't use this trick often. No one does and no one likes to speak of it, though it's common knowledge, seemingly easy. A harmless incantation. Certainly Ashley's never used it. Masha takes a deep breath and speaks clearly into the corner.

"Love you, Dad."

And then the Dad evaporates until tomorrow at sunset, and they're left alone with their bodies, the gloomy oak tree.

Who's afraid of death these days, anyhow? Masha asks herself when the movers come the next morning. She's feeling giddy and as queerly light as her bank account. Death is just a passé fear amongst the uneducated—you might as well fear the dark, or gays, or women presidents. Any thinking person got used to death standing in front of the TV, death by the sink when you got a drink of water, death hovering at the edge of the dinner party. Most adjusted without a hitch, while extremists like the Believers outright embraced it. A college friend likened the cultural shift to that of eating fish whole instead of filleted. Waxing lyrical about mindfulness, looking truth in the eye, honoring origins, et cetera. This friend was a Connecticut WASP who never once in his childhood stared as she did into the milky eye of a fish steamed whole with ginger and scallions. This friend's dad lived corporeally in

Greenwich, had steely hair and a bottling business, and called his son three times a year: birthday, Christmas, Super Bowl.

Of course, some people froze in the presence of Dads. Tight smiles, tinned laughs. The first city report showed these people represented 10.3 percent of the population. Half a year later, 0 percent. The fearful moved on to smaller towns, duller lives. One of them was a junior VP at Masha's office, caught sobbing in the boardroom; his resignation left a fizz of speculation and an empty corner office. Survival, Masha and her coworkers agreed, of the fittest.

"Out with the old," Masha declares as she enters her new house—hers! In the mail slot: the former tenant's phone bill, an ad, and a yellow flyer from the Believers. As if Ashley, who had waved to Masha's moving van with a look of near-parental disappointment, had followed her. *Do You Believe?* Masha should return the bill to the sender, but instead she rips the lot up. Out with the old. She uncorks a bottle of celebratory wine. And why not: when he appears at dark, she toasts the new Dad too.

Masha leaves for work just before sunrise the next morning. She smiles into her new neighborhood's fresh, urine-free breeze and sees the Dad in the front yard, seated in midair. Four feet of empty space separate the grass from the seat of his nearly solid jeans. His legs form a ninety-degree angle, as if he were sitting on an invisible chair.

She drops her bag. He doesn't turn at the thud; Dads are deaf, blind. The long javelin of her shadow stabs straight through him. He casts none. She exhales; he doesn't.

Masha takes a deep, stern breath. Of course the Dad isn't *levitating* or *flying*—that spooky-story language is from another era. He must be interacting with an unseen prop, like the bottle-shaped absence that the Dad at Masha's old apartment liked to massage. Masha's manager, who lives in a penthouse with a downtown view, likes to tell new recruits about his own Dad, who each night climbs two invisible steps over and over to reach the height required to produce the broken angle of his rope-burned neck. In response, the manager installed a small home gym complete with a StairMaster. "He's a great workout buddy" is the manager's punch line. He delivers it with a wink.

This Dad doesn't step. He advances smoothly in midair without the use of his feet, legs locked in position and hands held stiff in front of him. Laughing a jittery laugh, Masha forces herself to stay in place. He's not *coming for her*; of course not. His eyes won't meet hers—their eyes never do. His brown hands are set at ten and two, his posture unchanging.

He's holding a steering wheel, Masha realizes. He's driving. The unseen vehicle is some kind of truck or van, to gauge from the height.

A truck, she decides.

Her phone buzzes: she's running late for a meeting. She bites her lip, then swipes the notification away. She finishes watching the quirk.

Masha comes to know it well. In the predawn light the Dad drives around the yard, stopping once to leap to the ground. He bends to lift an invisible burden. His knuckles strain, gnarled and brown. When it's over he walks inside, clearing his throat. If Masha doesn't move from her perch at the front door, his shoulder petals over hers. Always she steels herself, expecting a jolt of cold, an electric tingle. Always, nothing.

Masha considers calling her realtor and accusing him of— what? Deception? Malice? The man probably never saw the lawn at six in the morning. Probably has a list of eager buyers ready to take her place. For a moment she considers, bizarrely, calling Ashley. She doesn't even entertain Oz's maddeningly logical voice. She can already hear him telling her to calm down.

No, Masha can handle this, just like she handled the black mold at her old place. She tries to focus on the mystery of the quirk: how do the throat-clearing and the truck fit together? Did he kill himself in the truck? Did he choke? She tries to focus on this Dad's differences: two inches too short, hair too curly, nose too broad. But. That exercise was easier with the Dad in her old apartment, and easier with every other Dad she's seen. Their pale or ruddy skin. This Dad circles the yard in work jeans, a T-shirt. Heavy black shoes. Though he drives a truck and not a van, she knows those familiar motions as he stoops and lifts, stoops and lifts. She recognizes them.

Masha spent twelve days feigning pneumonia when the Dads first appeared two years ago. She holed up in her and Ashley's apartment, pajama-clad and browsing DadFinder.org, WhosYourDaddy.com, Dad.Me. Some sites employed clever taglines and well-lit photos; most didn't. The users came anyway. Masha filtered for *Ethnicity: Chinese*; *Age: 40–60*; *Eyes: Brown*; *Hair: Black*; *Skin Tone: Medium*; *Height: 5'11"*. She kept the door to her bedroom locked until, in the middle of the second day, she heard a thump from the living room. And there, wearing pajamas, too, was Ashley. She had her fingers extended toward the resident Dad, as if she were a moment away from grasping his incorporeal hand. That moment would never come, Masha knew, having tried it herself on the first night.

"Hey," Ashley said. She snatched up her fallen laptop, but not before Masha saw the familiar Comic Sans font of the Dad.Me site.

"Hey," Masha said back, suddenly shy.

For ten blissful days the roommates operated like the friends Masha had seen only on cheesy sitcoms. They finished each other's sentences. Passed the same bong. Subsisted late into the night on delivery and cereal. Side by side they clicked through the sites, and each evening they looked up at sunset for their resident Dad to appear. They made a game of guessing the contents of his invisible bottle: Ashley settled on cheap Jameson, while Masha suspected some home-brewed liquor, biting and white.

But then Masha opened her door for the pizza guy and Oz strode through. He shook her, hard. Like you would shake a child. Ashley studied Masha's face over Oz's shoulder, then turned back to her computer.

Oz waited for Masha to pack an overnight bag as Ashley calmly continued clicking. Her spine was unbent, her screen undimmed. Oz's throat-clearing, his stares, had no effect. Eventually he turned his back on Ashley. Masha followed his lead, followed him out of the house, returned to work on Monday.

Ashley and Masha spoke less and less often. And after Ashley quit her job to take a position with the Believers, Ashley and the Dad spoke more and more—at least, so Ashley claimed. Masha, silently watching the two of them from the doorway, never saying, *Hey*, saw no evidence that the Dad spoke back.

Ashley and Masha never did speak of the obvious. But if they had, Masha might have told her this:

Years earlier, when Masha got the call and drove to the shipping warehouse where her dad had worked and where his corpse had lain decomposing over the long holiday weekend, the building superintendent stopped her as she carried her dad's jacket out. The superintendent was an owlish man with pale, stunned eyes. In his creaky voice he confessed that he had worried about her dad. He'd noticed her dad sleeping in his office, noticed the empty takeout boxes piling up. Noticed Masha visiting, first every week, then less often. Noticed her dad crippled by the foot surgery, by a heaviness of spirit. Noticed the medication her dad took in yellow pill bottles, and wondered how many of those pills were left... Masha said nothing, but tears dripped down her chin and the jacket in her arms grew wetter and heavier as the horrible little man unloaded his conscience on her rickety heart. She got away, but not before suspicion had wormed its way to her core. Even after her eyes quit looking raw, even after the mortician scanned her dad's history of diabetes and high cholesterol and wrote "Heart failure likely," even after Masha seemed smooth and whole again, she felt certain she was rotting from the inside. Swelling soundtracks, men limping off the bus, corny cards with small hands in big ones: the gentlest of prods triggered collapse. She was structurally unsound. She shook at night.

But after the Dads appeared, after twelve days spent scanning every listing without finding a familiar face, with an answer, at last, to the superintendent's question, Masha slept through the night for the first time in years. And since then no one has knocked on the door of her dreams, no one has called in an accented voice, no one has stepped forward in plain black shoes. Until now.

Beginning with the shoes, similarities pile on. Workman's hands, cut and scarred. Slight hunch. Weathered neck. Unfashionable hair. Grim economy of movement. Soon Masha begins to feel her way through the realm of unseen similarities. As bad at emotional chores as he was

good at manual ones. Cooked for his children, but left them starved
for talk, tuition. Probably drove a white van as generic as his shoes.

Oz asks when he'll be invited over. Masha mentions unopened
boxes, unbought furniture. The time-consuming chores of home-
ownership. And it's true that Masha leaves work promptly at five
these days, ignoring her manager's passive-aggressive "Another busy
night?" She pushes past the yellow BELIEVE! shirts at the subway
and arrives home before sunset to pour a glass of wine. She talks to
the Dad. Not like Ashley did; those ritual phrases about "respect"
and "safe space" feel soggy, wrong. Masha gives detailed accounts
of internecine office politics and company events, how it feels to
be the youngest person in her position, not quite dwelling on how
this is the opposite of the way she spoke with her working-class
dad. The thought is always on the horizon but she looks away from
it, as she looks away from a too-bright sun. Once her career's been
covered, she moves on to Oz, their comfortable but maybe stagnant
relationship, her friends, her set-aside screenplay. The Dad's throat
gurgles, *Hrm, ahem*, and she accepts the encouragement, plunges
on. She falls asleep with her glass in her hand. When her alarm
screeches, she sprints to the lawn to watch the Dad's slow circuit.

When asked about her new house, she mentions the balcony
(which she doesn't sit on) and the backyard (which she doesn't
water) and the huge, sunny bedroom (which she doesn't sleep in
because she sleeps in the living room, on the couch, where the
last thing she sees before she drifts off is the black shoes pacing
back and forth and back and forth).

And then she's late to work again, mad dash through the subway,
crashing into a smiling girl in yellow. Somehow, in ducking the

hug the girl tries to give her, a pamphlet ends up in Masha's hand.

Trash! But all day it winks at her. A flash of yellow crammed under her reports, stuffed into her gym bag. *Do You Believe?* Trash. She wedges it into her garbage can. Scrapes her plate over it vengefully. Turns. Turns back. Starts to read the pamphlet's centerfold. "Tips for Talking to Dad."

This was all Ashley wanted to discuss, after: the Believers' theory that Dads could hear and, in their own way, speak. Language as subtle finger movements, the changing opacity of an eye. Learning to interpret these responses took no small amount of time or Believer membership fees. Ashley's salon-blond hair faded back to brown, unattended to, and the glossy magazines disappeared. But Ashley's smile only grew.

Meanwhile, Masha and her friends discussed the city's newest religious group with amused derision. The Believers are closer to a fashion and lifestyle movement than a Kool-Aid-drinking cult. They've never threatened to blow up a building or kidnap children. They enjoy enormous barbecues, plaid shirts, games of catch. Last year they rented an entire baseball stadium. "At least my bullshit's free," Masha said then, sneering. Her Ashley impressions sent her friends into conniptions.

But now Masha senses the alluring darkness in the Believers' cheerful laughter, in the hunger that takes the shape of smoke rising off their endless grills, week after week after week.

"Welcome home, Masha!"

Her trained smile works. The Believers let her into their park after a bear hug. No Ashley, thankfully—Masha chose an out-of-the-way meeting for that reason. Masha moves awkwardly to the buffet line. There's too much food. It's all grilled. It's all bland. She doesn't know what she wants.

"Hey," says a voice from behind a curtain of gingery hair. A pimpled teenage girl.

"Hi."

"Your first barbecue, right? I can tell, you know. I'm Trisha."

"Masha."

"Mine offed himself with *fire*," Trisha says lazily. Her mascaraed eyes blink like a bush baby's. "It was pretty horrible, I guess. The funeral was closed-casket. You know? So that no one would barf or freak out. My mom tried to throw his things out. She can be such a *bitch*."

"I'm sure she had her reasons," Masha offers. The words sound robotic and Trisha looks deeply offended. She rushes through the rest of her speech.

"So I'm really grateful for the male presence in my life, you know; even my stupid mom agrees." Trisha takes a swig of soda. This talk of *presence* comes straight from Ashley's pamphlets. It makes Masha uncomfortable, as Ashley's crystals and sage made Masha uncomfortable even before the Dads appeared. She doesn't know what to say—or rather, the ritual words feel wooden in her mouth. The silence stretches and stretches.

"How'd yours die?" Trisha asks.

Masha's mouth drops slightly open.

"Yours is gone, amirite?" Trisha says, leaning closer over the hot dogs. "I can just *sense* it. Plenty of them, they come for other reasons." Her gaze roams coolly around the field. Something regal and slightly aloof takes up residence in her despite the teenage slouch, the awkward fall of her hair. When her attention returns to Masha, it's more uncomfortable than the afternoon heat. "I mean, that's cool too. But people like us have a kind of… aura, you know."

"Um. Well." Masha leans back from Trisha's intensity, the too-close cheek with its thick spackle of concealer over acne. Did she do that when she was sixteen? "I don't know that I want to discuss that. Um. No offense."

"You're here, aren't you?" Trisha's arms swing to indicate the green field, the grills, the attendees with their pale necks baking pink in the heat. "So, like, *be* here."

"I'm not quite… I'm not—" *Ready* is on Masha's lips, but that seems like a jinx. Will she ever be ready? She and Ashley spent the same two weeks with the same Dad, and look at them now. Maybe there's something missing in people like Masha. Oz accuses her of being stubborn. Never satisfied. "I'm not really like you people."

Trisha's eyes widen. Masha has plenty of experience with what comes after this realization, but she's never witnessed its inception until now. Trisha seeing past her own concerns to *see* Masha's hair (straight, black), Masha's skin (yellow undertones). Masha's Chineseness.

Like the Dads themselves, almost every Believer Masha has met is white.

Masha babbles, "That's not what I mean. I mean, I'm not sure that I Believe all the way. Like you do. I'm just here to check it out." Pauses. Pathetically: "You know."

"Well… good luck," Trisha says uncomfortably, speeding toward the desserts.

"Leaving so soon?" a cheery volunteer asks Masha at the gate. Like many attendees, he wears a T-shirt bearing a terrible pun. DON'T TRUST ATOMS. THEY MAKE UP EVERYTHING! "Would you like a game of catch before you go?"

Something's been upsetting Masha's stomach since she got

here. Maybe too much cheese. When she opens her mouth, she's surprised to see that what spills free is anger, thick and frothy.

"No. I wouldn't. I've never played catch in my fucking life. That's what you think fatherhood is? Barbecue and—and—and—*Frisbee?*"

This isn't the man she wants to scream at. She knows it even as she jabs at the words on his chest—Dad jokes, they're called. She hates the humor, the blissed-out way these Believers talk and eat and throw softballs with gentle motions of their shoulders—almost shrugs. They shrug things off and Masha is sticky, prickly. *Xiao haozhu*, little porcupine, someone once called her. The volunteer smiles peaceably in the sunshine.

"All members have an equal voice here. We rotate one new activity each quarter, based on popular vote. Would you like to add to the suggestion box?"

One activity, they say. One quirk, they say. One? Masha could laugh if laughing weren't so close to crying. One? The anger's broken through a dam years in the making and now other things flood through. She could suggest that they replace catch with fetch-the-poker-chip, a game of scrabbling under a fold-up table in the cigarette-wreathed air of a warehouse. She could suggest they replace ketchup with acid-yellow mustard pickles, see if their smiles pucker. Replace plaid with nondescript T-shirts, nondescript white trucks loaded with boxes, rugs, eager child assistants. Replace grills with spitting woks, puns with accented English, baseball mitts with rough brown hands smacking your hand away, teaching not catch but the stinging difference between wrong and right. One? The volunteer's sentiment is well meant, but then again the sentiments always are, aren't they? "You must miss him," they all said, Oz included. How to explain that she didn't quite miss him, that missing was too neat, too easy. How could she miss someone with whom she couldn't sustain a conversation (his English poor, her Chinese poorer); someone she rarely hugged, rarely visited; someone to whom she didn't say, *Love you, Dad*. Didn't. No. Nope. Nada, zilch, *bu xin*. They just—didn't. The volunteer opens his mitt in invitation. Like Ashley's, his ease gleams. And this is the danger of the Believers, who lull you into lowering your spikes, only to realize, too late, that the scent of pine or cologne is wrong, all wrong. That what you need is sesame oil. She walks past him, his symbol that has no power for her.

For the first time in years Masha visits the Dad.Me site. Four failed passwords later, she makes a new listing. *Ethnicity: Latino*; *Height: 5' 9"*; *Hair: Black*; *Eyes: Black*; *Quirk: Drives a garbage truck (?)*. Her fingers shake on the keyboard. She waits.

Meanwhile she goes to work, goes to the gym, goes to Oz's clean and Dad-free place and listens to him drone on about his law office. What once bored her now soothes. If she listens long enough she can burrow into the ordinariness of it, like a worn blanket. Her stomach churns constantly. She loses weight. Oz pretends to cut his palm on her hip. She laughs at his clowning but acid bubbles at the back of her throat. He doesn't notice. She wonders what he notices. Nothing, she thinks, until he texts:

Hey how's the dad btw?

You mean Dad.

Oops my bad. Tired.

You can be so fucking insensitive. I've told you how I feel. If you can't understand where I come from then maybe we should—she stops, deletes it all, begins again. *If you're so tired then don't text me.*

Oz starts to type. The three dots blink for a long, long time. Masha can picture the curls falling over Oz's face as he pecks out an articulate response. A digital version of how he argues: so rationally, biting through each word like a crisp piece of fruit. Oz got this coolness from his own dad, who lives in Chicago. A professor with a booming laugh, an eye for human flaws, and a barbed wit that keeps listeners howling until he turns the lash on them. Masha likes the man; Oz worships him. Thinks just a little too much of him. Rage flowers in Masha, withers, flowers again. She shuts off her phone. Far across the unfurnished room she senses the Dad's gaze, those tired black eyes. Their eyes are always tired.

She sits awake that night thinking of suicide. "The rate of suicide is highest in middle age—white men in particular," read that first city report. For this fact, as for the other strange facts, there was no *why*. Did that make her own dad braver? Masha wondered. Was she to applaud him for clinging on, never mind that he ended as he'd lived, alone in a warehouse with grubby boxes his only company? Did that elevate him above his job of stooping for other people's belongings?

In a triumphant report a year after the Dads appeared, the city revealed that suicide rates had plummeted among older men. Maybe the permanence of death got to them, sobered them. The realization that taking your own life condemned you to an eternity of drool-stained collars, strangers gawking at the embarrassing mess of your blown-off jaw. Living dads quietly went on living at higher rates. Waiting to go by natural means, which guaranteed a return only in respectable, unrecognizable forms: proteins in the soil, nitrates in the air. And Masha wondered, then, if other factors increased as suicides dropped: alcoholism or domestic abuse or skipped soccer games or fewer home-cooked meals, more fast food, a bloat, bad temper, diabetes, dragged footsteps, silences at tables where brown hands unpacked greasy takeout, the frequency of wounding words in the night.

The city was silent on these. *Be practical*, Oz might say. *Compromise.*

There are no updates from Dad.Me, she's ignored a string of lecturing texts from Oz, she's on her fifth glass, she's talking to Dad, and somehow it slips, she slips, glass shatters, she says, "Love you," and Dad disappears. She starts to shake, crouched in the corner of her new adult couch that's firm and shapely and refuses to sink in or cradle her the way Ashley's ugly old one did. Masha didn't mean the words as an incantation this time. Sorrow chews her up, hollows her out, shakes her in its wet jaws and still its appetite is undiminished, its murky depths unplumbed. She imagines Dad disintegrating into a billion fragments, dispersed like crematorium smoke. Where do they go? What do they do when they get there? Do they feel there, do they speak or see, are they happier than they were in chairs and kitchens, at graduation ceremonies and pink-slip meetings and DMV appointments, during the jumbled victories and disappointments of children's lives? She calls him back, apologizes, mixing up the words, her pidgin Chinese as broken as another's pidgin English, but he's gone. Speaking the emotion only makes the object of that emotion go silent, something she's known since she was twelve years old, watching brown hands dump shirts and jackets into boxes marked BEDROOM, marked KITCHEN, marked FRAGILE. THIS SIDE UP.

*   *   *

"I need a new place," Masha says once her realtor picks up the phone.

She expects protests, stunned silence. Instead he says, just like on the first day, "Ah, *that?*"

Though Masha sets her teeth against his unctuous, professional ooze, she can hardly be angry at him for being understanding. He says he'll be over at the end of the day.

It's right after sunset when the realtor knocks. Masha turns the knob and the door pushes hard from the other side, shoving her against the wall. The realtor doesn't notice. Doesn't notice the wine stain on the couch, the bandages on her hands, the broken glass in the corner. The day is suffocating, hot. The gel in his hair is melting. He stares at the Dad.

"He reminds you of someone," the realtor says.

"Yeah. Look, I can pay a fee to break the contract; that's fine. But you have to help me find another place. You must have at least one house in this neighborhood without a Dad."

"I don't."

"Please."

"I don't."

She reaches down her dark well of anger but it's run dry. She asks, "Why?"

The realtor finally tears his eyes from the Dad. His smile is dazzling. An actor's smile.

"I was once as lost as you are," the realtor says. "I was angry. I didn't find my way until the Dads appeared. Real estate was the perfect way to search."

And though Masha doesn't want to know, shouldn't want to know, she finds the Believers' question in her mouth:

"How did yours...?"

"Shotgun. When I was two. He was twenty-eight. Ma destroyed

all the photos, but she always said I'm his spitting image. I'll know. I'll know him when I see him."

The realtor rakes a hand through his collapsing hair, exposing its white roots. Sweat has melted the powder from around his eyes and mouth. Up close, the exposed skin is stamped with fine lines. As the mask comes off, Masha understands the source of his eeriness. Behind the makeup he uses to freeze himself in youth, at the magical age of twenty-eight, the realtor could be forty. Fifty. He could almost be her dad.

"Think of everything I can ask him," the realtor says.

The realtor folds his hands neatly. Gnarled old-man knuckles—hadn't she ever noticed? Maybe she had. He seems to be waiting for something from Masha, scanning her as Trisha did, as the volunteer did, as Ashley did those first weeks after the Dads appeared. Ashley's eyes had risen to welcome Masha home, a hope and a question. "We're so alike," Ashley had said one night, her face slackened by a few beers, her yellow pamphlets splayed between them. Masha's mouth had gone sour. "I don't know what you're talking about."

"Be practical," Oz said the night she told him about her dad, meaning the words as comfort. "There's no way you could have known."

Now Masha licks her lips. "You're insane," she says to the realtor.

The realtor neither confirms nor denies this. He smiles serenely, as if to soothe a mistrustful child. Why is it Masha who feels crazed, with her tremors, her lunatic bandages? A blinding light emanates from the realtor's smile, tugging Masha closer. How many times had she watched her own dad turn on the bug zapper, heard the tempted creatures fry? It almost doesn't matter. She wants to embrace the realtor like a brother or friend. She wants that blissful assurance. That madness that looks a lot like joy, or love.

She forces herself to take one step back, then another, until enough walls stand between them to shut out the realtor's smile, and she can call a cab to pick her up.

The lawyer Masha hires to break the lease assures her the case is solid, given what he calls the "unsafe conditions." He asks her to repeat the part about the realtor knocking her aside with the front door. Whistles.

"Crazy, huh, what these people will do?"

She looks at him. He's a clean-cut man in his late thirties, and in the slight wear around his eyes, the softness at his jowls, she can see the shape of his dad, who probably also sat behind a desk, who probably wore suits and had assistants and made these kinds of booming, jovial statements that his son learned to copy.

"Crazy," he repeats, more uneasily.

Masha doesn't say anything.

Her lease is terminated without her paying a cent. She doesn't tell the story in civil court, to her lawyer's disappointment. She does tell it (almost all of it) to Oz, and when he looks at her with sympathy, with patience, she doesn't dwell. "I shouldn't have pushed you to take it," he says. She trembles in his arms, and though by the unspoken rules of their relationship she should absolve him of responsibility, draw back, and assert the independence of her decision, she says nothing. She holds still. Later she moves her things into Oz's Dad-free apartment. Burrows into Oz at night and lets the rhythm of his voice—as slow and regular as pacing feet—lull her to sleep. "Temporarily," she says of the arrangement, until that understanding decays and what they're left with may be the foundation of something permanent.

Sometimes she lies awake worrying about it, the way she arrived at this decision after four years together, whether there is a difference between something brand-new and shiny and something flowered after the death of something else. Sometimes this leaves her angry. Sad. But most of the time things are pretty good with Oz, even really good, occasionally so good that when they make love Masha feels briefly seized by white light. She makes of this what she will. There are no eyes, tired or otherwise, to judge them here. She takes down the Dad.Me listing, which never got a response. She looks for a Chinese cooking class, and when the only one she finds is taught by an old Jewish widow, she signs up anyway.

One day a few years down the road, a middle-aged man kills himself in an empty apartment. Does it with a shotgun: *blam*. Maybe not quite empty, depending on whom you ask: there's a Dad in the room. One whose jaw and throat were also blasted away by a shotgun: *blam*. A few blogs pick up on this oddity and write about it. Masha—now pregnant, now committed to the idea of growing something new even if the only place to do so is the grave of something old—recognizes her realtor's blinding-white smile in the photos. She moves on, the world moves on. The story fades. Six months later it reflowers. The dead realtor's wife gave birth to a son and the dad has now materialized as a Dad. Two Dads stalk the one empty room, a first. They don't interact, as reporters are disappointed to discover. They only stare through and past each other, their two sets of tired eyes above their two destroyed faces, which lack the implements for speech.

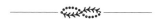

MY MOUNTAIN IS TALLER THAN ALL THE LIVING TREES

by ESKOR DAVID JOHNSON

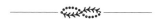

(This story appeared in McSweeney's 52:
In Their Faces a Landmark: Stories of Movement
and Displacement, *edited by Nyuol Lueth Tong.)*

MY MOUNTAIN THAT I LIVE on is not much to speak of and if you go by what some of the foreigners who come around this way say then it is really more of a hill, or even a mound. But I've never been anywhere foreign myself, nor do I want to at this point, and Barbados is about as flat as the bottom of a pan. Even on the ground you can see for miles around just by standing on the tips of your toes. So you can just imagine the view from my mountain, which is very near the town of Karata, whose people keep goats to race on weekends or to kill and cook if they are too slow. I know this because when I squint I can see all their business over that way, though it is not to say I recognize any faces from so high up. There was once a day when one of the goats escaped from its rope fence enclosure and wandered off into the confused roads, across the devilgreen land, up and down through ditch and hole until climbing my mountain and there licking my face where my cheek became my jaw. I did not have any sapodillas or oranges or cherries to give so it stayed with me only a few minutes before going back from where it came.

The people of Karata are aware that I live here and are on good terms with me. This began with them taking the detour during their walks to pass by my mountain and wave hello. Now they tend to shout from farther away. Sometimes they invite me down for a wedding or First Communion but I do not much like the taste of goat anymore and so I haven't been to Karata either. When I do need food, it is from the rainwater in my gourd or the trees around my mountain, which are sapodilla and orange and cherry—though some now have termites for veins and do not bear. I only take fruit from one of them a day, which I can look down and choose before making the walk. So you see? There are the birds and the sun and moon and the charcoaled corpse of a pine that was on its way to reach the clouds before it died, and that is it. My mountain is taller than all the living trees.

In general I do not face Karata because there is not much to look at apart from their lives and the beginnings of the sea on the horizon and also because most of the people who come to see me do so from the opposite way. I do not much like being snuck up upon and even though by the time someone is making their

way up my mountain it is quite impossible for me not to have
noticed, I would still rather see them coming from all the way.
The land in that direction is bush and farming plots cut from the
bush. For me to not spot a visitor approaching they would have
to not only avoid all the flattened clearings, but also hope it is a
windy day so I confuse their rustling of the bushes with nothing
special. I no longer sleep much and, in the hours I do, it is simply
ridiculous that anyone would think to visit, though life has not
been without its surprises. A woman was from Peru and a sleepwalker, moving like a drunk shadow in the field. I cannot say what
it is that woke her but she right away took to screaming so loud
the fireflies around her outed their lights. It was some time for
her to notice my mountain. She headed over and climbed up and
screamed again when she saw I was at the top. Who would have
thought I was there without first knowing it, a mole-faced man
whose hands have started to shake? She said she was camping and
was from Peru and was a sleepwalker and did I know where she
was. Over there is the town of Karata, I answered, but she'd come
from that way where the stars are bunched tightest. It had already
rained for the night, the cold dampness of a fever hung low.

She pondered the blackness. The grass here hides a tricky
beetle whose song is a long hiss, so at night it can sound as if my
mountain is in a nest of snakes. There are also snakes, real ones,
but not nearly as many as the hissing would have you think and
they do not have poison in them. But the woman from Peru did
not know any of this and I could see in the anxious way her eyes
darted to the insects' calls that she could not decide which terror
to brave between serpents and a man. She asked if I knew the time
and I told her I did not. "I never walk longer more than an hour,"
she said aloud, "so it is not more after than two. I would always

know the time when I am little." This talking as if she were alone calmed her and she went from a stand to a crouch, speaking at me about other childhood oddities: always knowing north even when spun around many times, walking in her sleep if she lay on her back. "But I am more comfortable if I sleep this way so this is the matter," she said. Then I told her that most people walk through their lives in a sleep, too, except they never get the chance to wake up. What bad manners of the mind to pass through life in a dream. She liked that.

When she slept it was with a rock as her pillow.

In the morning the sun faces my mountain from across the long yawn of land the woman from Peru had crossed. She grew sweaty with it and woke up itching and was making her way down before turning back to say thank you while once touching my foot. When I was sure she was gone I went down to pick my fruit. I do not know if her body still raises itself up to walk an hour north at night, but I do not see why it would.

Anyway, that meeting was a coincidence and you should not think I spend my time waiting for sleepwalkers to come my way. Most of my visitors believe I am where they find me. A few have believed it for so long they no longer expect to be proved right, as is true of those who go high enough in the air to see that the whole earth is round. On finding my mountain they do silly things like wet their pants or sing—not all lunacy comes from delusions. I can tell apart the foreigners from their walk, which not only lacks the waisty roll and tumble of the country people around here, but also wanders, searching for whichever direction is left. Even when they are still specks no bigger than a cherry seed I notice the vague maybeness of their steps, a tender shuffle that comes from trusting the current of a journey more than its sense.

When they reach my mountain there is always a pause while their senses catch up to where they stand.

Unless the opposite is true and it is instead a peppered heat that has driven them all this way. There were once two men approaching equally distant from each other and my mountain and running like maniacs. This was in the dry season, when footsteps crack like knuckles. I did not like their animal rush, even less so after the barrel-built one running through the canefields to my right galloped on all fours when he tripped, rather than right himself. I decided it was him I would hit with the rock I had picked up from my foot since he looked more solid of figure, better able to handle a misplaced throw to the head should I miss—my aim is not very good—and the other was already belabored by his own high-knee running.

Soon they were close enough. But when the space between them had narrowed as at the bottom of a valley, they set upon each other with the futility of wave and shore, one too persistent and the other too stubborn, and I could not throw my stone in the tangle of limbs. Neither wanted to hurt the other man but instead keep him back from my mountain. I would not say the burly one won, though it was he who first touched the bottom of my mountain, for as he climbed closer I saw how deeply his face had been shred open by the ground and how pebbles poked from his cheek. Through spittle and blood he spoke of their race across three continents and an ocean, then of the fellowship between them that had turned sour. They were both without names—he on my mountain had never had one and he below had had so many as to not remember which was first—and had come in search of new ones. "True ones," said my bald, bloody fellow. "How can a man speak with certainty when there is not a word to know that man by?"

My name is Itawadilela, which means he who greets with fire. I know it is mine as a child comes to know its own reflection: it moves as I do. And as there is no place for another to tell you which figure you are in a mirror, so is there no allowance for them to pin your fate to a word.

I said this loud enough that they could both hear. The lower one, lanky as a vine, crept up my mountain to be nearer. I asked why they did such terrible battle against the other when their hopes were the same and they said, "The news is that you speak to but one visitor a year," which was a little true, because after the man with two limbs I saw no one else for thirteen full moons. "I have nothing to call you," I said, but in their pleading and crying and reaching for my hands my heart was moved. "Your names are Wax and Wane," I said, and when each asked which was for whom I took a sapodilla from my lap and bit into it. A quick cloud made the sun blink.

I believe I am the center of a game played by the children of Karata, though the rules are still not clear to me. In it, they send an emissary to ask me questions, but only to get a particular answer, or maybe as a distraction. Even now, schoolchildren from Karata are coming with giggles in their uniforms. I can see them: khaki shorts and skirts just above the knees, button-down shirts the yellow of fallen bananas. They sing for most of the way, a birdsong babbling that is still music. The smaller ones are in danger of becoming stragglers, and must often catch up to the rest with quick little steps that leave them panting. The taller bunch wear their bags with just one strap on the shoulder. All their collective courage stalls closer to my mountain until, a few feet from the bottom, they are silent.

A girl shouts up, "Afternoon, sir."

I nod.

"Sir, you know it have a big storm coming this way? The storm big so." She stretches her arms wide and spins around. Some of the others laugh and steal glances up at me. Their bravery spreads like a rumor.

Now that she has found her voice (and her voice is the voice of them all), she dares some steps uphill. She has a shallow chin that causes her mouth to hang open when not speaking. Black blemishes spot the skin on her arms.

"Well if is look you need to look for a place to stay from the rain it always have by my Granddad house. You must be know him, he pass this way before. He does wear a hat like in them cowboy films and have a dog big so. You know who I talking about, right? A curly hair man, but he have a baldhead in the front."

By now she is well close to my feet and talking all the louder. Her head mirrors mine to occupy my vision. I have not said anything.

"You don't want to listen to what I saying, sir? You come to stay forever, eh? How you going to stay forever? Just like that?"

I do not much believe in the wisdom of children, as others seem to, nor do I believe in their innocence. Down there, some of them have made their way to the other side of my mountain and are picking up pebbles to fit in their pockets. As I turn to see, I hear the loud girl taking more steps up.

"What you go do with all the time if you stay forever, sir? You don't want to go?"

More of them scurry around. A girl climbs the sapodilla tree. Boys throw pebbles. Everywhere I hear them bleating.

"You want to watch everybody go and you don't have to?"

I stand very quickly to push her down, and as she flails for a grip all she grasps are loose rocks that dislodge with her. She tumbles all the way, hitting the grass with a bounce on her shoulder. The rest of them scream and run away, trying to throw things up at me, but it is difficult to fight and flee. The talking girl is the last to leave, hanging the battered arm loose at her side, wincing when she tries to move it.

Sometimes the children come with good cheer and smaller numbers; these days are good. Sometimes it is with the malice of a wild herd and then I wish that they, too, could be kept behind rope, or done away with on weekends.

A big storm is coming this way. Two afternoons later the air smells of a cent pressed beneath the tongue. By the evening the beetles do not hiss the dark welcome. I spend the last hours of sunlight lashing together my shelter. Though it cannot grow anymore, the dead pine still has branches that are as strong as they are supple. Its body stands just beyond a rock's throw. The twine to knot the branches together I find in the farming plots, untying them from the waists of sapling plants and the sticks meant to keep them straight.

Going so far away from my mountain is a difficult thing to manage. Being on the ground means that I cannot tell as well who may be coming, and being on the side facing the field means that I cannot see Karata. In such moments the hours go faster if I stay facing my mountain and keep in mind how difficult it is for someone to climb it without practice.

What I make is a flap of branches tethered down by more twine, the gaps in its lattice padded by mud mixed from orange juice. It is fastened to the side of one of the giant stones that had been too heavy to move, so that once tucked under, my back to the stone, one arm holding my ceiling down tight, I am a bird beneath a wing. Along the branches are rows of termites, reminding me at once of a traveler from Africa who said how delicious a meal termites can be just before the rainy season, sautéed with no oil other than that from their flesh and promising a light, nutty flavor. Unlike ants, termites have been known to build nests taller than a man, piled together from chewed wood, dirt, and feces. The clouds pry low. When it starts to rain the hairs of the soil stand on edge.

Because the rains always come from the direction of the sea, I know that my mountain will protect me. For safety, I am not even at its foot, but still close enough to huddle in its wind-safe shadow. Pressing my ear to the dirt I listen for the sound of the thunder-before-thunder, as I know is done in some parts of Bangladesh. Nothing ever happens when you want it to.

What comfort could I have given the man with two limbs? One arm and one leg on opposite ends as if leaning diagonally. His skin was warped and dangled loose around the face and neck yet cinched tight everywhere else. He could have been a Blackman or an Indian but there was no hair on his head to tell. I mean to say that he was a fearful sight bobbing through the fields on his way to Karata. "No one," he would say to me afterward, "even help me get here." Unless you count the young boy along the way that had lent him a plank of wood to press on. "Man like me, you have to learn your way through the scruff." This story that I am telling you happened long before, in the year of the wildfires.

He had first been walking to the old pine, which still lived at the time, green as a frog's back. Then on getting close he paused, took in the tree, and changed course to come to my mountain. The sun at that hour was in his eyes: even squinting tightly he could not tell if I was there.

"Hello?" he said. "Hello!" he shouted.

"Hello, I am up here," I said. "You cannot see me because the sun is in your eyes."

He picked up his plank and shielded his brow with it. He balanced well without it.

"Well kill me dead!" he said. "Who gone and put you up there? They wasn't lying, no. Who gone and put you there?"

"Would you ask the same of that old pine you were just watching? My answer is the same as its own."

He laughed. "Oh yes it's some pretty lyrics you have. Pretty, pretty lyrics."

This man could not climb my mountain nor did he try. In fact even then he still seemed in a hurry. Between his laughs he glanced at the horizon from whence he'd come.

Seeing me seeing him, he began, "They send me to the jail for beating a man to blindness. They did. But you put a man in a room as long as he can reach lying flat on the ground, lock the door, and tell him he can't leave until you say so…"

His missing arm pointed to his missing leg. "They had do plenty to me before then. But you put a man in a room with no windows and tell him he can't leave? You don't need much more than that."

So he had escaped, and I could tell by his pause that he wanted me to ask him how, so I did not. Instead I asked of the arm and leg. He clenched up like a secret, the two rows of his teeth sliding together into one grimacing line.

"Gangrene," was all he said.

What a life to live, where even to see from a regular height is a day's worth of effort.

We could hear the cracking of bushfires coming to life now that the sun had found its angle. Most of the fires started with kudzu, which is like ivy, and fast-growing. Koreans had flown it in some months before to save the land from erosion. The kudzu spread and then died, drying up into waiting tinder as the days got hotter. At night the sky was kept awake by long legs of fire kicking its underbelly. I would remember the scent of those orange evenings. Nothing is malicious in the smell of a natural fire. Still, had the man with two limbs made his journey to me an hour later, he might well have found himself wrapped up by those burning vines.

He did not stay long that first day, hobbling on to Karata, where a cousin waited with ironed clothes. The next afternoon he was back in a one-armed blue shirt that crackled with starch when he moved.

"So it's how many questions I get to ask you?"

"People pick their own habits."

"Well my habits is I is a talker. You good with that? You like you could—aye—aye—aye—" A wind had come to push him down, and would have, had he not hop-hop-hopped and righted himself. "Ha!" he coughed a laugh. "I tell you it's plenty they do to me!"

He wanted to know if there was anything a man could do to forget everything but *now*, as an animal does. I told him even an agouti remembers where the traps from last year were set, so every new season hunters have to trick them in new ways. Still, he went on telling me about what he would forget if he could:

"It had a day I walked around with a gun in my pocket. You ever do that? Man, you can't watch people the same after." And the footrace he'd lost on the first day of school and seeing his brother get married and gangrene. He checked my face only whenever he said a joke, to see if I found it funny, and, though I did not, it was his constant checking that eventually made me smile.

"Ha!" he laughed.

Before leaving that day he whistled. The tune was blue as his shirt, cutting through sheets of night dark like a scythe. I did not know what song it was. When he shut his lips, I heard the whistle still ringing in my skull as if the bones in me were quivering.

"Boss," he took to calling me some days after, "I had come to ask you 'bout this dream I had last night. But you know what I figure on the way here?" He sometimes propped his plank behind him so that leaning back against it he could better look up when talking to me. After asking a question he would raise both his eyebrows until the wrinkles rippled past his forehead up to his exposed scalp.

I began: "A man came to me once who believed—"

"On the way here I figure your dreams don't mean nothin'. It just come like a reflex. Like if you smell pepper then you sneeze, that's all a dream is, your head sneezing at night. Somebody ever ask you to explain a sneeze? Right, right. I thought so." After that, if ever one of us sneezed, he shouted, "Wake up! Ha! Wake up!"

He could be serious, too. On a cool afternoon he came late and held a plastic flute in his hand. The mad chorus of birds were running their mouths.

"My cousin have a little daughter she raising over there. A bright girl, if you see she read... you does really wish they could stay just so. Watch what she give me today." He held up the flute and then played from it, a light tune that should have been happy—a song the sound of sweetbread left outside until the gnats found it. He did not laugh *Ha!* or look my way.

That night a jeep drove through the bush toward Karata, its lights howling terrible against the black. It parked and men got out. I watched them walk to one house and then another, knocking on doors and sometimes stepping in. Some hours later they left. The man with two limbs did not come the next day.

I asked him once if it would not have been easier for him to have stayed his time in the jail.

"Nah it could never really be easy so," he said soft, as if others were listening. "How that go look for them to do that?"

"But you do not think—"

"Chuh! I mean watch you and all. If I was to say you couldn't go past this little space so, how you go take that?"

"Yes, I would not like that," I lied.

"Yes man. You ever see what it does be like over so anyway?" He pointed beyond the horizon.

"Once," I said. I thought a little. "They tried to do plenty to me too."

"Ha!"

Always he made music. Sometimes from instruments he'd put together—pebbles in a bottle, rubber bands stretched over a can—but mostly from whistling. My bones would hear him when he walked from Karata and then shiver again later as he left, his high tones wavering away like a woman in a dress running. He did not always realize when it was he whistled. Now and again, looking silently at the dusk's flames, each of us deep in the solitude of his own longing, sound would come leaking from his mouth without tune or direction. If I pointed that out to him, he would not remember having done it.

I offered him this: suppose this power to forget, he had already learned it, and on so learning chose to turn it on itself, remembering it no more. He liked that. "That come like a bulb getting so bright it blows," he said. Yes, I said, but thought to myself, more like a snake swallowing itself from the tail up.

Then he brought me food. It was a grilled snapper on a plate he balanced on his head through his slow, slow progress. The fish was cherry-skin red and from where I sat looked tiny enough to fit whole into my mouth. He had two forks in his pocket, dropping his plank to offer me one. "She not too bad, you know, my cousin," he shouted. "You would have to be plenty terrible not to cook up a snapper right." Because of the plate on his head he could not look up as he normally did, staring straight into my mountain instead. How would he get it to me? The fish would fall flat into the dirt if he tried climbing. I wondered if his cousin had left it to soak in garlic and salt the night before or had tossed it fresh onto the fire as it was. When you eat fish, the smell stays on your lips for hours after and flies smell it on you. Right there on my lap I had a pile of peeled oranges, enough to last me until the new morning, when I would take from the cherry trees.

"Boss," said the man with two limbs. "It not gonna swim again if I throw it back in the water, you know."

So I went down from my mountain, and we ate.

※   ※   ※

By dark, I am soaked. The land is smothered by a wet night. The sky is bigger than it has ever been, big as a face leaning in so close its skin is all you see. Its thunder sounds personal—I want to shout back at it. My arms ache from keeping the roof above my head, one moment pulling it down from where the wind would snatch it away, then pushing it off my chest to keep from suffocating. So you see? Even the air can drown you. So much of the mud between the branches comes loose once dampened again that it is not at all difficult to keep an eye on my mountain. It shakes and leans along with the trees. When there is lightning I make the mistake of seeing somebody on top and start toward it, but the storm sits me down again. Who would be out on my mountain at a time like this? Still, when I sleep, I have the dream of going up my mountain and the top getting higher the more I climb.

This is better than the other dream I sometimes have, which is the dream of walking on the ground. In it, my mountain can be far away or it can be close. If it is far, I spend my time walking to it and do not make it. If it is close, when I make it, it is not my mountain. It is a different one.

It came to bother me, the lie I had given the man with two limbs. What was wrong with my space of land that I would want to find others?

We were eating from a bag of peewa and spitting the black seeds as far as we could. "Them men them still using stone to sharpen they blade," he said, spitting. "The best thing to do is use a piece of hard leather."

The farmers from Karata had spent a lot of the mornings cutting and clearing as much dried-up foliage as they could, leaving fewer targets for the heat to incite into fire. When he was with me, the man with two limbs commented on all the farmers' doings.

"It have plenty, plenty uses for them ashes too," he told me. "Mix that up in your soil so and your produce growing plenty, plenty."

As he talked more about his other life as a farmer, I began to choke on a peewa seed. Seeing my troubles, he used his plank to strike me on the back while I pressed at my stomach until, just as spots began to dot my sight, the seed popped out, dropping barely past my toes. His final tap with the plank threw him off balance and he fell to the ground. When I turned to thank him, as sprightly as he'd seemed, something in me could not stand the sight of his apparent decrepitude. I grew sad for seeing him on the ground. The hand I used to help him up I did not use for anything else the rest of the day.

That month he had come with food and music and I had grown fat on the ground. I learned the kind of woman his cousin was through her food. Her macaroni pie was light as a conversation and the bread soft as washed skin. But in the week that her daughter came down with a fever, the okra tasted of nights up late.

The habit I had picked was to eat with him, but what was down there that I had to go see? My appetite changed after the peewa seed. I noticed flavors in the food that had not been there before. Her worries became my own—I would finish only half the portions the man with two limbs brought me. Once, I took the meal into my hands (breadfruit oil down, broth leaking to my elbows) and climbed back uphill to eat it there alone. He looked at me only a little and coughed a lot when he spoke. We talked about more things to forget while the wildfires bloomed.

For five days he did not come. All the noises startled me, a loud bird screeching overheard, the high whine of a goat. My bones were waiting for his music and I chastised them for it. Once, the moon was low and close, filled to the brim with so much light it might have split at the sides. Carefully, after checking that no one was coming my way, I lifted my head to it and tried to whistle.

On the sixth day he came in silence and my hands started to shake on seeing him. "Boss," he said, "it's some real craziness in that house I in." I did not say anything. He lowered the plastic container from his head and put it on the ground to open its lid. In some seconds its scent had reached me, meat still warm and calling. My hands were shaking. Then I was on the ground with my back to him, eating.

"That same shortman I mentioned that does be coming to check my cousin"—the flesh was burnt-sugar brown and slipped right off the bones as my teeth touched it—"well he come the other night talking about how he could build her a house, he does do some building work"—the peppers made me warm up to the ears, I tasted cardamom and excitement—"and just so she have all this marriage talk up in she head. You would swear no man ever talk to her before"—my face low down into the bowl, slurping gravy from the edges between bites—"and you already know it's plenty quarrel between me and her over there… like that goat hitting your belly right. Ha! Yes, she start to outdo sheself cooking now that this shortman coming around talking about two-story house with gas oven"—to get to the marrow I had to close my lips tight around the end of a bone and suck it out, as a mongoose does to an egg—"but if I end up not able to talk some sense into her the wedding could be in two weeks and all. I come to check if you could make it? You hearing me? You go come?" I stopped.

What was wrong with my space of land that I would want to find others? What was down here that I had to go see? Suddenly I felt ashamed of my hunger, its weakness. Staring into the bowl made me dizzy. "Come, it's not like it's a far walk," said the man with two limbs. "And if you get lost on the way back, just watch for that pine tree over so. Ha! I swear you could see it from the next side of the island and all, never see something so tall."

I turned to face him. "Why did you come here?" It was strange to hear my voice this loud. I had forgotten it could echo.

He wobbled as he rattled away. "Easy easy it still have the two weeks to think it over one of them young boys say he looking to make the altar but the varnish they find old and dry up so they looking to get more plus it does take its time settling too—"

"Why did you come here?" I said again. He understood.

"Well, you know how they are so... man ask for a trial... thought we was free men here... spend my life in a room with no windows? Ha!... tell a man he can't leave?... Ha!... Ha." But he also saw that I would be of no help, the trickle of his words drying up as I stared. Then he turned around and began to hop away, and, as if waking up, I realized that he was about to climb my mountain and I realized that if he had had another leg and arm, he would have used them to climb my mountain while I was eating.

I picked up a rock near my foot and threw it against the back of his head. He fell and bled into the earth. All his sound spilled out of him. That night, for the first time, I had the dream of walking on the ground. In fact, this is why I do not sleep much anymore.

*　　*　　*

The main difficulty in building my mountain the first time was just finding the privacy to do so. No one will say much to a man they see carrying a stone in his hands, except if he carries it to a pile already higher than their waists. So whereas I had moved the first stone in peace, by the end of that day not a passerby could avoid involving themselves.

At the time, my strength could be seen through the skin. Most observers knew better than to offer their help. Those who brought me rocks anyway had them refused: to this day some of those rocks have remained just where they dropped them. To move the boulders, I had to flip them face over face from farther out in the bush, where they'd been nestled together in a wide cup of dirt. I could manage such an effort only twice, abandoning the third one but a few steps from the greater pile. "But look at this," someone had said, holding her son's hand to point it for him. "But look at thiiis."

I worked at night, sweating hot in the sky's shadow. The sun made too many people brave. Without it I could ignore whether or not it was blood running down my legs. In the light, I wiped away the red-crusted residue.

Each day they resurged:

"Don't stand so close before something fall on you."

"Excuse sir, what you doing this for? All this work and you could have built a house with a backyard already."

"Ask to see if he need water."

"The base he making not wide enough. That thing go fall."

"Look at this. Look. At. This."

"Go find the schoolmaster and tell her come."

Word was spreading that I was here.

They stopped when my mountain grew taller than them and

they grew silent in its shadow. One day I spoke for the first time in months: "All right, I am tired now. And over there are your homes." That is all it ever takes. They retreated like ripples from a stone. By the time the moon had shed five new faces, all the trees but one had received my words as they would rain.

But the morning after the storm my mountain is shorter than it should be, and on climbing it as soon as the winds tire, I see how much work I have to do, how much of its body has been scattered. There is no choice of food but cherries: most of the oranges and sapodillas have been stripped off their stems. I slip on the wet backs of rock on the way down and hit my head. I see the flash of stars behind the sky's veil.

All that day the people of Karata trek the mud road beyond my mountain to check their lands for damage. The cane stalks are strewn. Where there were farming plots there are now big brown puddles. What they can salvage, or what they need for rebuilding, they ferry back in long trains of men and goats.

Without the strength I had the first time, rebuilding is difficult. My joints are broken levers bending the wrong way. On each trip I leave soggy plops of footsteps in my wake. Twice more I fall, my face so low down to the earth I cannot see farther than a child can jump.

Seeing my mountain smaller than they have remembered it in a long time, some of the townspeople find their old courage and offer help from a shout away, perhaps thinking that I am not up to so solo an effort again. Always I turn away their friendliness with a wave, then, when they get closer, with soft words of independence.

I have heard it said that nothing that lives lives alone, but how can that be when I have seen snakes slide away from their broken shells at birth without a look back? Unlike ants, termites do a poor job of making their way home if separated, but, unlike ants, any termite can become king or queen and start building anew. If I did not finish, how would my visitors know where I am?

Usually from the top of my mountain I would have been able to tell much earlier that something was amiss with the people of Karata, but now that my vantage is on the ground it is easier for them to sneak on the edge of my vision. This begins in the evening, when still a man offers help, despite a day of my saying no. He does not move along. "That's too much to handle on your own," he shouts. "It's whole day you looking like you going to break your back."

To show him my back is fine I pick up the biggest stone near me and hold it with one hand straight above my head. He cannot hear my shoulder creak under the weight. He does not move along.

Another man with a big dog stops to whisper with the first. They have their hands on their hips and gesture with small movements. I realize I need to get on top of my mountain.

Once there I see two more men and a woman are on their way. I see, too, that there is no one left clearing out the farming plots, though the land is still ragged.

"Mr. Man." The second one tunnels his voice through his hands for it to reach me. "It's not no crime to need help. We going and start to walk over to you." I shout no. Those others have spread themselves out. Together, the five of them step toward my mountain.

A rock slips out beneath me and *clackclackclacks* down. The half-moon stares like a lazy eye. The hissing of snakes wells up in my ears; wings the weight of an eyelash flutter in the breeze. I feel the thunder-before-thunder in my soles.

"Look, you need help. Is just talk we looking to talk." It is the second man again, with the dog. His hands are up and open to show he holds nothing, grazing the edge of the dark curls past his hat. On his arms, I recognize blemished spots. I feel the thunder-before-thunder beneath me. They are all close. "You need help. Come down so we could talk. Let us help."

Why should I go anywhere when the world comes to me? Why should I be on the ground to talk? For people who do not have a mountain, the world is without knowing, like a book held too close to the eyes. How could their words make sense if I were down there pressed next to them? The thunder-before-thunder is beneath me.

What do they know of what I have done? "Were you there when I touched a cripple on the head with lavender oil?" I say, turning in tight circles to see them all. "She moved her toes for the first time. Did you know that?" Their steps are slower, but they do not stop.

"My mountain was in a magazine!" I say. This man and his dog do not know that. A Ghanaian with a heavy mustache had brought me a copy as a gift and showed me the double pages where from a distance someone had taken its picture (and though I have never been as far away from my mountain as the picture-taker must have been, still I could recognize it, because no other mountain looks like mine).

"How will anyone even find me, if I come down to talk?"

"You can always come back," says the spotted man. "No one taking nothing from you. It's just talk." The dog has run ahead. It has a black, sad face. They have sent it to bite me and dig up my mountain. I remember the stone from before is still in my hand and I take aim.

The man is stern now: "No more of that. Nothing else have to dead."

"Everything that lives long enough learns that life is elastic, like chewed-up sap," I say. "Its weakness is in trying too much to stretch longer."

To burn him: I had to cover the body with a bed of kudzu thick enough for anyone passing by not to notice. But no one did pass by on that day, a silent one with a sun ripe for arson. He was heavier than you might expect. It was not until I had let more of the blood seep of out his skull that I could even move him about to fold into those roots.

"What that have to do with it? You are idle and advantageous," says the spotted man. He points and he is clear: "That pine never bother nobody and look what you do."

There are many uses for dead trees, as any man of labor will tell you. Ash can give new life to fields when mixed into the mud with goat shit. It was with a terrible mercy that I had found embers from a just-dead blaze and breathed them back to life among the roots, his limbs. "That pine had reached for too much," I tell him.

They have spaced around my mountain on all sides. Their hands are behind their backs and that dog is pawing the ground before it. From beneath me there is the rumble of a laugh digging its way to the surface. I will throw the stone.

Some mountains are hot and tempestuous on the inside. Some volcanoes are best left sleeping. Where were these men to see how many before were willing to lose their way in finding my mountain? Had they faced the Turk with his loud questions and his pistol? The woman so light she gripped the soil during strong winds? Did they know what becomes of a life eaten from the inside until it is unable to climb, or the sound it makes in its final panic? Young elopers had arrived on a clogged night with the heat of lust all in their eyes. On the verge of my giving them my blessing, they screamed at the idea of joining lives, as if waking up, and parted in separate directions. Ha. So you see? Not everything you are looking for is what you want to find.

VINEGAR ON THE LIPS OF GIRLS

by JULIA DIXON EVANS

(This story, from McSweeney's 53, *was a winner of the 2019 National Magazine Award in Fiction.)*

THE FIRST BOY WHO'LL ever touch me between my legs asks me to go to the horror movie with him when we're standing in the church parking lot after the evening service, boxes of brand-new prayer books nestled in the crooks of our arms, stiffening our joints. I look at the boxed scripture, so close to my heart, convinced that God knows. Nearby, the municipal streetlights pour suburban stargazer–friendly orange into the parking lot but otherwise our world is dark. We aren't meant to use electricity during Lent. No luxury taken unsuffered.

"We can't," I whisper, without making eye contact.

"You said you wanted to," the first boy who will ever touch me says.

"I know," I say. I look up. His eyes are bright, green or brown or something in between. "But that's because we weren't here."

"I'm going to ask you again," he says. "Later. And then you'll agree to sneak out of your house tonight. It's at midnight."

"Okay," I say. I try not to smile. "I'll probably agree to that later."

"Claudia," the priest calls from the steps of the sanctuary. "Come now."

The priest doesn't say anything to the boy. The priest doesn't look at the boy.

"Unless I wash thee, thou hast no part in me," the priest says, the sanctuary dark everywhere except the altar, and even then it's just the underside of his face, angular shadows of jaw, nose, brow. His voice is soft and formidable. I fear him; I love him. Like Christ. I fear everyone here, all the girls, and I love them, too, already. I want to be taken in by them. Like Christ. I belong here.

The other girls stand, so I stand. The other girls walk to the space between the front pews and the step up to the altar, so I follow. The other girls space themselves out, so I space myself out against them.

The priest leans forward, a puff of air from his lips; the last thing we see is a fine strand of smoke from the candle, a bend toward us, the light finally gone. Then black.

The other girls move but I can't see what they're doing in the dark. I can only hear the rustle of their dresses against legs, against the floor. I blink repeatedly, quickly, willing my eyes to adjust, and then my dress pulls at the shoulder, tugged from the hem.

"Lie down." A whisper, unrecognizable.

Blindly, I lower myself to sit, then to lie, bumping my head on the wooden edge of the front pew. I shimmy forward, one leg at a time, one butt cheek at a time, until I can lie flat on my back. I try to relax, clutching my arms across my chest.

"Spread your arms to the sides." The same voice, quieter now, but closer. "Like Christ."

"No talking," the priest booms. He sounds distant. Deadly. "Blessed are the dead who die in the Lord," he says.

"Blessed are the dead who die in the Lord," all the girls repeat.

In silence, five minutes pass, at least. Maybe more. The only thing keeping me from moving or falling asleep is an intense fear of making noise.

"Blessed are the dead who die in the Lord," the priest says again, so much closer, right above me. My eyes are closed but I know if I opened them, I'd be able to see; they'd have adjusted to the dark by now, and I know that I'd be able to see the priest, right above me.

"Blessed are the dead who die in the Lord," all the girls repeat.

"Blessed are the *dead* who die in the *Lord*," the priest says, animated, theatrical, exuberant.

"Blessed are the dead who die in the Lord," all the girls repeat, the collective whisper a wall of soft noise, *s*'s and *wh*'s and *d*'s.

Finally, "Blessed are the dead who die in the Lord," the priest says.

"Bless—" I start to repeat, but nobody else does. I cough, a cover-up.

It seems final, we seem done, but nobody moves. This time I might have fallen asleep, because I awaken to a finger poking at my wrist and a quiet "Get up."

Outside, the sudden chill of night on our bare forearms, she says, "I'm Iris."

"I don't know what I'm doing," I say.

"I know," she says. "I barely do."

"Thank you," I say.

"Sit by me every time," she says.

I don't answer. I just look at her. Her skin, clear and dark; her hair, braided close to her temples and looped around into a knot at the crown. Her dress, as white as mine. Her eyes, somewhere between desperate and eager.

I wonder if I look desperate. Or eager. Or just lost.

"Okay," I say. "I'd love to."

"I don't really know anyone here yet," Iris says.

"Are you new too?" I ask. "You've just... always been here."

"Yeah," she says. "I started coming about a month before you."

When my parents hug me, I cringe, keep body contact minimal, and pull away as quickly as possible. I never hug friends. Maybe it's the sting of holy wine still on my lips or maybe it's Iris, but I want her to just hang on to me somehow.

"I need to go," I say.

Iris lifts her right hand, holds her left one at waist height, outstretched, and steps forward. Someone, a girl, a friend, a human being, is giving me a hug.

"Have a good night," she says, and for a moment, I panic, like, *How did she know.*

"You too," I say, barely a whisper, because that's all I can fake.

*   *   *

Outside the boy waits, leaning against a parking lot palm tree lit up from below, Malibu-lights style. Ankles crossed, arms crossed. Lanky ankles, lanky arms, a boy, but everything else about him seems ancient in that light.

"You're still here?" I ask.

"Just to ask you again," he says, pushing off from the tree and merging to my side as I walk. "Come with me tonight."

"We're still at church," I say.

"That makes it better."

"I'll sneak out. Wait on my street," I say. "Eleven."

We both look straight ahead, walking slowly toward the sidewalk. Out of the corner of my eye, I see him nod. I see him duck his chin. I wonder if he's smiling.

"I'm not gonna walk you home," he says.

"I don't want you to, anyway," I say.

"Yeah, well, I wasn't gonna."

"I would've run away if you did," I say.

We stop and face each other. Both of us out of control, both of us not even sure, both of us not even liking the other, both of us not even knowing what liking someone means, both of us bathed in stupid palm tree light from below, both of us just wanting to feel like the winner without knowing what or why or how.

"Okay, Claudia. Eleven p.m."

"I hope it's really scary," I say, and walk away.

*   *   *

I want to look away as soon as it's the dog in the frame, walking slowly toward the camera, toward us, the plasticky tap of claws on indoor flooring, the slight crescendo of scary-movie music. Look forward. Eyes on the screen. See it through.

The first boy ever to touch me between my legs chooses that moment. His hand, dry, hot, on my knee, his head bent toward my shoulder.

I don't turn my head, because I am determined. Watch this part. He wants to kiss me but I am determined. Watch. I can hardly see, can hardly think, I watch the screen, God watches me, God watches my parents at home asleep in their queen-size bed, facing opposite walls, God watches this boy with his hand on my leg, God watches this dog on the screen about to die. I don't turn my head. The boy's mouth on my neck instead of my mouth, wet and almost ticklish. His hand creeping up my leg, the inside of my thigh. I keep my eyes on the screen. But I uncross my legs.

The dog presumably dies, but all we see is blood flung everywhere, spouting, preternatural squeals and shrieks, cellos trembling, flashes of light, right when the boy's fingertips slip beneath my underwear.

"Oh god," I say, to the dog, to the gushes of blood, to our Savior, to the boy.

"Oh god," he says. "It's, like, runny."

He pulls my underwear down my legs, the stiff white cotton prescribed to us by the church for this season. We are not to discuss this underwear with anyone, the priest told the girls the day he handed out a small paper-wrapped parcel to each of us. Not even each other. The underwear pools on the sticky theater floor.

The boy leans toward me, his chin on my shoulder, and his breath smells like pizza but sweet.

"We're not even supposed to be using electricity," I say. "It's Lent."

He pushes a finger inside.

"Wait," I say. "My underwear."

We're almost to my street now, not talking, because I don't know what to talk about. When he steps closer to me and brushes against me, I can smell myself, the inside of me, all dried and crusted on his fingertips.

"What?"

"I left them. Where are they? Did you leave them on the floor?"

"Oh," he says. He shrugs. "I guess."

"I can't just leave them!" I say. I try to whisper. I try not to sound like a freak.

"It's not like we can go back. The theater is closed."

"Oh god," I say.

"We'd be like, *Excuse me, my friend left her sexy panties on the floor, can we come in*," he says, his voice somewhere between mocking and annoying. "Then you'd actually be in trouble, unlike now, when nobody needs to know."

"I need them."

"They sell underwear at, like, Target. The theater people will sweep yours up with all the popcorn trash, probably laugh and say, *Gross*, or maybe, *That's the third pair today*, but they'll still just put them in the trash."

"Are you sure?"

"Yeah."

"But I need them."

"So," he says. "You're not wearing panties right now?"

I don't answer.

"Hot," he whispers.

"I can walk the rest of the way by myself," I say.

I'm awake before the sun. I must've pulled off only four hours of sleep last night, if that, but the tiredness feels fleeting. The tiredness feels important. I climb out of bed and pull my pajamas off, standing naked in front of the mirror, orangey-gray light seeping in through the half-open blinds. Nothing feels different, nothing looks different. I try to look at my body like the boy would look at my body if he could ever see me naked, but I feel nothing.

I think about Iris seeing me naked. Would she compliment me? Would she look away? I think about the other girls, all lined up, seeing me naked. I think about them staring, some with arms outstretched, pointing. They lean close to one another and whisper.

I think about the priest seeing me naked, standing across the empty church and staring at me. It's the first time I feel anything. I feel anxious and afraid, but also like I'd want to see him naked, too, even though he is mostly ugly. I bet if he were naked, too, he would have an erection, jutting out like an arrow from his crotch. The other people at school look at porn on the internet but the only thing I have access to right now in my room is the biology textbook from last year, the sex-ed year, so I sit cross-legged on my bedroom rug in front of the bookshelf and flip to the page with the erection drawings. The pages make a high *brrrrr* noise as I flip until there it is, a sketch of a boy with a loose nest of pubic hair and a stiff penis pointing up and off to the side. Tiny lines run to all the anatomical vocab words and I feel ashamed.

I close the book, put it back in its spot on the shelf. I open my dresser and count the pairs of underwear, running my fingers across the perfect folds. We are taught to cherish what the church gives us, to treat these things with the respect a sacred object deserves. They're soft and crisp at the same time, like an old dress shirt. Four pairs here. Last time I did laundry was three days ago so there're two in the dirty-clothes hamper. Each week I will just have to wear one pair twice. Easy. Nobody will know. Nobody will ever find out. I pull a pair on (three left) and get dressed.

Each day's lessons, studies, and prayers are performed in the dark during Lent. We're supposed to come to church twice each day: first thing in the morning, and then in the evening, after dinner, but my parents think it's fucked-up to have to go to church in the morning when we can barely get ourselves ready to leave the house for work and school in time. I tell them I am always ready in time but then they say that I need to be reasonable, and then they say, "Everything in moderation," and then they say, "Look, it's one thing not to turn on your light at night and to eat only food that doesn't need to be in the fridge, but we're not driving you to church twice a day."

"Fine," I say.

This morning, I say, "Fine, I'll walk."

They don't know anything about church. I found this community on my own, eavesdropped on whispers in the bathroom at school, and I will walk to this place on my own. They don't really care and they don't understand. They don't know where I got the underwear.

*   *   *

"Hey," Iris says.

"Hey."

"You look like shit," she says. And then she covers her mouth with both hands, a little gasp. "Sorry. I'm used to my sisters. I... I don't know. You remind me of my sisters."

"It's fine, I know I look like shit," I say. Sisters. I have never had a sister and I think that's why I like this church so much, all the girls. All I've wanted is for someone to look at me and say, *You're like a sister to me,* and it might've just happened or maybe I'm so tired that I'm actually asleep and I dreamed it, I dreamed Iris up entirely. I consider telling her that I'm tired. I consider telling her that I'm tired because I went to the movies with a boy who put his finger in my vagina and I left my special church underwear there on the sticky floor. I consider telling her that I'm tired and down one pair of panties. "I think I'm getting a cold or something."

"Father is calling for a meeting after morning prayers," she says.

"After?"

"Yeah, right after. We're all to stick around."

"But I have to get to school. Don't you have to get to school?"

"We all do. Well, except for the ones who are residents."

"Residents," I say, not a question, more just remembering.

"Oh! I put my name on the list," she says, sort of like an aside. "For the next opening. You should too."

I start to laugh, but only because of my parents. Only because of the way they'd react and the ridiculousness of imagining asking them. Telling them. I'm not sure which of those two I'd do. Specifically, I'm not sure which of those two I'd be expected to do.

"Do your parents mind?" I speak slowly because I don't want to give anything away. "That you'd live here? With the church?"

Iris purses her lips and maybe she's sizing me up a little too.

"I'm waiting until I find out to talk to them," she says. "But anyway."

"What's the meeting about?"

"A breach."

"Of what...?" I ask.

"Nobody knows yet."

I want to ask her how long she's been here this morning, how long all the other girls have been here this morning. I want to ask if there's something I don't know, some sort of pre-morning prayer fun time. Or, more likely, some sort of pre-morning prayer prayer. I shift my weight along the line of my hips until the sun, due east, is directly behind Iris's head. She's silhouetted now, her hair just a glowing, scraggly outline. She's holy and pretty and I'm like a sister to her.

"Girls," the priest calls from the narthex, leaning against the arched entryway to the sanctuary. "It's time."

Prayer is terse.

The priest says, "Let us humbly confess our sins unto Almighty God."

And we recite, from heart, "Almighty and most merciful Father, we have erred and strayed from thy ways like lost sheep," but I don't make a sound. My mouth moves in the shape of each sound but no noise comes out, not even a whisper. He doesn't look at any one person. It's more like he's looking over our heads, but it still feels like he's staring right through me.

"We have followed too much the devices and desires of our own hearts," all the other girls say and I think of the boy's fingers poking at the wet parts like he's checking if his food's cool enough to eat yet.

"We have done those things which we ought not to have done," all the other girls say and I think of my underwear left on the movie theater floor, telltale, damning, and I like it and I don't think I'm okay with liking it, or maybe I am.

"And grant, O most merciful Father, for his sake, that we may hereafter live a godly, righteous, and sober life," all the other girls say.

After the communal confession the silence is long. We sit there, solemn, eyes fluttered shut, for the usual amount of time, until it drags on longer than usual, and then our eyes are pinched shut, and then we have one eye open, or maybe it's just me looking around, done with confessing, done with silence, done with closed eyes, wondering if anyone else is done with it too. With my one open eye I scan the room and land on the priest, staring right at me, his chapped lips a straight line, his liver-spotted hands folded across his lap, on top of the penis I am sure is in there, the penis I imagined jutting from his crotch just this morning. I close my eye again and my mouth moves in the shape of the words "I am a sinner, I am a sinner, I am a sinner."

"Girls," the priest says at the end of the morning prayer. "We will remain in the sanctuary for an important meeting."

He stands, walks forth from the altar.

"There has been wrongdoing amongst you," he says.

Whispers rise from the pews. The shapes of teenage girls lean toward each other, shimmer pink–tipped fingers cupped around berry-scented lips, breath like toothpaste and bagels against Q-tip-scrubbed ears of matching teenage girls, the air thick with fake-flower shampoo and benzoyl peroxide. Whispers of "How awful" and "Oh my goodness" and "Who is it?" and "Do you know?" and "I am praying for whoever has done this." And it goes on for a second too long before I lean toward Iris next to me and cup my pink-tipped fingers against toothpaste-bagel words: "Oh my goodness," I say. "Oh my goodness, oh my goodness, oh my goodness."

Iris nods and she has shimmer-blue fingernails, pale like Wite-Out against her brown skin when she whispers into my ear, "Was it you?"

"Girls," the priest says. "There has been a report from a parishioner that an indecent item of our sacred clothing has been found sullied and cast aside at—" he pauses against the silence. "At the *movie theater*."

And that's when the girls gasp. Electricity during Lent. I wish I had it in me to whisper back to Iris, *Yes, it was me. Do you understand? Yes or no or maybe?*

Finally, maybe because we aren't collectively understanding the scandal, the gravity of this perversion, he says: "Underwear. Panties. One of you removed her distinct underwear and left them on the floor while presumably doing something only God has seen and only God can forgive, yet you will never be pure again."

That boy would laugh right now, but I think mostly I'm scared of being seen by God, so instead I bring my hand to my mouth like all the other girls, a sea of pink (one set of blue) fingernails across a sea of berry lips across a sea of sharp inhales. I float, a dead fish on their seas.

"We stay here, God's sheep in a flock, together, as penance."

"For two days," he adds. "No sleep."

294 / VINEGAR ON THE LIPS OF GIRLS

I turn to Iris. "My parents will flip out."

"Parents aren't *allowed* to flip out," she whispers back, her shoulders lifting and lowering briskly. "He'll even call the schools for us. So we can, you know, relax."

I try not to smile. "Nice."

"No talking," the priest says. "From now on. You must remain in silence. I will return in three hours."

When he leaves I turn to Iris and mouth, "*Holy shit,*" but she's not looking at me; she's looking at her hands. I'm glad. It was a mistake and I'm glad nobody saw me cuss. Nobody but God.

At noon, his robes swiff against the wooden doorframe as he marches in holding a tray of small silver vessels and cloths.

"All rise," he says, his voice a flat line.

We rise. My knees almost give out from stiffness. I have to pee, desperately. There's pain in my lower back and just beneath my belly button and I think my period is starting.

He leaves the sanctuary again, reemerging barely thirty seconds later with a small cardboard box of nails from Ace Hardware, probably the one just down the street. We've all been sent (in pairs) on errands to Ace for the church, especially during official work days, dress pockets stuffed with church petty cash to buy tape and wood glue, tools and screws.

"Today we seek forgiveness from our Father as Christ did."

He opens the box and empties it into a silver chalice, metal chinking against metal.

"Today we suffer like Christ; today we are one in Christ."

I close my eyes.

*   *   *

He holds my left hand in his left hand and I stare, noticing how childish mine looks against his. He raises his right hand high above his head. The sunlight streams only in narrow channels in here, pinkish and orange from the small '80s artsy stained-glass inserts, but it glistens against the shiny tip of the long nail.

He drives his hand swiftly down toward mine, slowing only at the last second.

I flinch and he makes eye contact with me as he slowly presses the sharp nail into the center of my palm. My dry skin pinches and the metal is cool. He presses it firmly for one, two, three, four counts, and I trust the societal strictures that mean the priest will probably not draw blood, that mean the priest will probably not pierce this nail straight through the metacarpal bones in my hand.

"May you be pure in God's sight. Then, now, and always," he says, and briefly presses it harder into my palm, but then releases it, setting the nail lengthwise and wrapping my fingers closed around it.

"May you be pure always," he says.

"May I be pure always," I repeat, guessing, not knowing the liturgy, not knowing this part.

"Amen," he says, and "Amen," I repeat.

I fix my eyes on my curled-up fist and watch, in the periphery, as he takes a wide sidestep to my right, toward Iris, the next in line. She's crying, her shoulders lightly shaking.

"You have nothing to cry about, child, unless you are the wrongdoer."

It wasn't Iris, I want to say.

*   *   *

The second time the priest leaves us alone, we all form a circle after one of the older girls, a resident, Violet, herds us silently. We sit with our legs crisscrossed, knees touching our neighbors', fingertips entwined with one another's and resting in the crook where our knees join.

Some girls weep. Some girls keep their eyes closed and their mouths incessantly in prayer. Some are staid, staring straight ahead. Some turn to their neighbors, whispering kind words of God's peace and love. Some whisper damning words of God's reckoning. I roll my head to my right to look to Iris and squeeze her blue-tipped fingers.

"Will they let us out?" I whisper, knowing I should be in prayer. "To pee?"

"I don't know," she says. "I am so hungry."

"Me too," I say. I'm not hungry. She squeezes my fingertips and smiles, and I know I said the right thing. Lies are almost always a safe bet. "I'm worried that I'm in trouble."

"With God?" she asks and I realize I want to giggle, and I realize that if this were different, if Iris and I were just regular friends, acquired the regular way, we'd giggle about this. We'd watch it on a TV screen in one of our teenage bedrooms and giggle at the absurdity, and flip through magazines and complain about homework in the next breath and maybe that's when I realize I'm scared of everything about this.

"No," I say quickly. "I mean, with my parents and with school. My parents aren't very supportive of… of my faith."

"Really?" she whispers. She brings our entwined hands up between our faces and leans closer, her eyes closed reverently but she's not praying. I feel sisterhood. "Mine neither. I thought I was the only one."

I'm like a sister to her, I remind myself, and I feel warmer than during any moment with the boy, any moment with anything else.

"How about," Violet says, her voice low and serene, her eyes hard, on Iris and me, "we pray together."

When the priest returns he steps into the middle of the circle, over Violet and her neighbor's knee-junction, with a tray of cloths and small silver pitchers. He lifts a cork from one and it smells sharp with vinegar, and with the sourness and with the beginnings of hunger and thirst. It's somewhere between puckering and mouthwatering. Some girls cough.

"All rise."

"Oh God, make speed to save us," he says.

"Oh Lord, make haste to help us," we say. I barely whisper, some of us don't seem to talk, some of us are so loud, the words shouted, desperate.

"We—" and the priest stumbles and I wonder if he's off-script right now. I don't think there's liturgy for this or maybe there is. Maybe when they decided to give us all the same underwear they discussed it, generations ago, a meeting of the church elders, saying, *What if we find them cast aside after a boy fingered one of them in secret? What should we say, what should we write, what should we do?*

I clutch Iris's hand entirely.

"Today we suffer like Christ."

"Amen," the girls utter and maybe there is liturgy for this and maybe they've all done it before because they all seem to know what to say and do.

"Today we are sinners in Christ."

"Amen," we all say.

He pours a swig of clear vinegar onto a small cloth, soaking it, and raises it high. It drips, landing on the hem of his vestments.

"May we be one in Christ's agony and may God forgive our sins!" he proclaims and presses the cloth against a girl's lips. Her face pinches and she stifles a flinch, shivering just a little. I try to remember her name. Daisy, maybe. Daisy.

"Amen," she utters, but the priest shushes her, pressing the cloth back against her lips, bringing her own hand to her mouth to hold it there herself. He moves on to the next girl. And the next. By the time he reaches me I think I'm ready, braced for the sour, but I'm not ready. I'm not ready for the sting against my dry lips and prescription Retin-A-ravaged chin and it feels like we've been here and we've been guilty for weeks. It's been four, maybe five hours.

"Christ suffered," the priest calls out after he finishes with Iris, the last. "And so do you."

"Christ suffered," we all repeat. "And so do I," we say, but I'm the only one who says "I." The rest of the girls say "we."

Half the room glances up at me.

A woman enters, older than my mother by maybe ten, twenty years, and I recognize her from the Thank Yous in the middle of the church service. It's Lee Min. She's incredibly tall and thin, dressed in weirdly youth-trendy jeans and shoes but with a white crew-neck sweatshirt that looks like it was bought from the craft store, a cross bedazzled front and center. The Thank Yous are when all the volunteers who have done something remarkable enough to be noticed get noticed, recognized, publicly proclaimed. It all seems very unscripturely to pat each other on the back like this, but I'm just a teenager so I don't say anything out loud. All the old ladies seem to sit ready in their pews, backs straight, trying to act naturally, trying to act like they're doing anything except crossing their fingers, hoping that they've been enough of a holy servant of the church to be famous that week. Lee Min is almost always recognized, and when she isn't recognized she's up at the altar, wearing chalice bearer vestments (like Iris always does), or ushering, or out-volunteering everyone else anyway.

Lee Min bustles into the circle, clutching a bucket. She holds it out to each girl and uses gestures to indicate we're meant to drop in our vinegar-soaked rags. She doesn't speak. She rushes quickly around the circle, much more quickly than the priest moved, and I feel bad for Daisy, who had the vinegar on her skin for far longer than Iris or I did in our cushy spots at the end of the route. Lee Min doesn't make eye contact with any of us. I wonder if she'll get in the Thank Yous for this.

"I think," Violet says, and she pauses dramatically, her voice syrupy and flawless, her thin hair tied with a ribbon in an inhuman, antigravity ponytail at the top of her head. She seems a weird mixture of childish and mature, sexualized, almost. I wonder how old she is. She tries to sound like she doesn't know what to say, like she hasn't planned this all out in her head. It's how I talk to strangers, so I recognize it in anyone. "I think we should maybe break off into pairs or small groups and find quiet corners to pray together."

"Mmm," murmurs a roomful of hungry, thirsty, guilt-shamed teenage girls wearing matching underwear, matching pinprick dents in our palms and matching vinegar-redness on our lips.

"Come with me," Iris says to me. "Let's go to the back corner, okay?"

We sit behind the pew in the back row, tucked between the wooden seatback and the wall where the flags are. The church's flag, weirdly sovereign-looking. The country flag. The state flag, even. The colors, all together, are beautiful. A rainbow. Nature in a three-pack of flags. Greens and reds and browns and yellows. And blues, so much blue. Each flag is rimmed with a golden fringe. Iris and I sit in silence for a while, somewhere between seconds and hours, and in that time I notice the golden fringe is fraying and basically just yellow yarn with one thin metallic thread woven into it. The church flag is in the best shape. Lee Min takes care of the flags. I think I could do this, take care of the flags, if Lee Min ever stopped. I think that could be my *thing*, the thing I'm Thank You'd for.

Iris pulls at my shoulder and I lean toward her.

"I went to the movies two days ago," Iris whispers. "I feel like he *knows*."

"Oh my god" is all I can think of to say. "What'd you see?"

"What?"

"I mean," I pause. Weighing the risks. What if this is a sting op? What if she's a plant, like the cop trying to pick up hookers? No. She's *like a sister*. "Me too. I saw the horror movie."

"Me too!" she whispers and it's a bit too loud and she clasps a single blue-nailed hand across her mouth, covering a smile. I can still tell she's smiling by the way her eyes are wide, wet, happy, surprised. "I mean, I'm sorry."

I pick up her hands in mine. It feels intimate, like when the priest picked up our hands to drive the nail down into our flesh, like when a boy holds our hands, like when our mothers perch us up on the bathroom countertop to put Band-Aids on our paper cuts. "Don't be sorry," I say. "It's okay. I understand. I don't know if anyone else would."

"Thanks, Claudia," she says. "I needed that."

"Me too," I say. "We're supposed to be praying."

"Okay, do you want to start?"

"No," I say. "You start."

"O God, make speed"—she starts, and I join in—"to save us, Oh Lord, make haste to help us." I open my mouth to start the next part but Iris leans forward again.

"But. You know it wasn't my underwear, right?"

I don't answer right away but maybe it's the way my eyes move, or maybe it's the way I tighten my grip on her tiny hands, my hands like ogre hands compared to Iris's.

"Oh, wow" is all she says.

"What?" I ask. I close my eyes, afraid of judgment. Afraid of losing sister status. Afraid of being ratted out.

"Oh my god!" And she's still whispering so it seems safe to open my eyes. "You?" she asks, a grin across her flaking vinegar lips.

"Shh," I say.

"Did you, um."

"No!" I say. "I mean, I don't know what you're asking."

"Did you... have—?"

"No, no, no," I say.

"Did you go to the movie alone?" And her voice is so low that I know she's on my side. She's making sure nobody hears this. Violet clears her throat from far away, the front of the church, and we lean our heads closer together, our hands clasped together as if in prayer.

"I went with..."

"Oh my god, that boy?"

"Yeah."

"Wow, he's hot," she says.

I shrug.

"What did he do?" she asks.

I look at her, skeptical. I don't know what she wants to hear. I don't know what to confess to. I don't know what to be proud of and what to be ashamed of and what to be afraid of.

"He touched me there," I say.

"Yeah? And then what?"

"Iris!"

She squeezes my hands. "Come on, tell me."

"He pulled my underwear down so he could get a better angle, I guess. I forgot it was off until we were outside."

"Angle? Like, he—" She stops for a second. "He put his finger *inside*?"

"Yeah," I say. "It wasn't that great."

"Really?"

"He's kind of lame."

"Ugh," she says, and she brings our hands close to our faces, leaning in. I wonder what it'd be like to see a movie with Iris, to be that kind of outside friend. I wonder how she'd touch me beneath my underwear. I know she'd do a better job of it.

"I think I'm starting my period," I say. "I really can't afford to ruin another pair of panties."

Iris looks down, between us, at my crotch. "Too late," she says, nodding. I look down and there's a brownish blood spot creeping across the white seat of my dress.

"Fuck," I say, too loud.

"Who was that?" Violet says. "Was that *Claudia?*" and her voice is sharp like a knife.

I stand up. "Sorry," I say. "But." I point.

A chorus of "Oh girl" and "Oh man" and "Oh no" and "Poor thing" and "What should we do?" and "Let's not get ourselves worked up" and "Ooh" and "Ahh" and I can't help but wonder if there's some sort of church magic where, after you spend a set length of time in youth service or achieve a set unit of holiness, your period stops and you don't have to worry about this, because they all seem so taken aback. They all seem so... like it doesn't happen to them.

Iris stands next to me and says quietly, "Ignore them. Probably 75 percent of them have their periods right now too. Everyone's in sync. You just happened to beat anyone to soaking through a tampon today."

Before anyone can provide any useful advice, the doors to the sanctuary swing open again. Iris leans close. "Your secret is safe with me," she says. "Is mine?"

I forgot she had a secret in the first place.

Violet is staring at both of us.

It's Lee Min who walks in, not the priest, and I wonder where the priest is.

"Girls," she says, a slight accent. "You will scatter the remaining nails on the stone floor and lie on top of the bed of nails until nightfall."

Nobody moves.

"Do it now. And you must undress. Down to your underwear. I will come back when it gets dark."

I glance at Violet and she's nodding. Lee Min hesitates, like she's going to say something else or maybe apologize or maybe tell us to run away, but then she just spins on her heels and exits the church.

I am not wearing a bra today. Only one other girl isn't wearing a bra, Violet, but she's skinny, tiny, and has perky breasts and I stare at her as she undresses. My breasts are a bit too big to go braless but I was rushed today. I try not to look at the carnage of my underpants. I think all the other girls try not to look at the carnage of my underpants. I lie down and the nails dig into my naked back and the curve of my butt and Iris reaches over and touches my face. "It's almost over," she says and I don't believe she knows what she's talking about.

It's not dark yet when the priest comes in. It's not Lee Min. It's definitely the priest. I move to cover my nipples but he barks, "Nobody move." I wonder if he's a pervert. I wonder if he took this job not because of some divine calling but because of some hope of finally seeing girls shamed, punished, and undressed.

I open my eyes and I watch him. I look at his crotch, remembering my morning, expecting to see some sort of jutting-out sketch of a boner but there's nothing there. Maybe he is the holiest of us all.

And then I smell the vinegar again.

Clutching a stem of green fern, he dips it into a bowl and scatters drops across our nearly naked figures.

"The sting of sin is stronger than the lies," he says. "Do not claim to hide from God. He who hides his sin contains the biggest sin."

I wonder what would happen to me if I confessed. At what point in the proceedings would the other girls be relieved enough to thank me? At what point would it just be considered a minor transgression, more of a Lenten electricity violation than anything sexual? At what point would I be kicked out of the church? At what point would even Iris not speak to me again? At what point would they give up and we could carry on, coming to church every morning before school and all day Sunday, Iris and I galvanized in our friendship by this shared secret, me with six pairs of underwear instead of seven, the vinegar just a silly memory, just a slight bit of post-traumatic flinching whenever we smell salad dressing.

It's nearly dark when I hear shouting outside and recognize my mother's voice. It's all mumbled but I'm certain it's her. Something about "school" and "daughter" and "This ought to be fucking illegal." Something calmly dealt back to her and then the slamming of car doors. When the priest comes inside again and it's still sort of light and he can still see my breasts, he says, "Nothing to worry about. We have told your parents this is an important lock-in youth event and they'll see you tomorrow." He walks to the front of the church and sits at the altar, looking down over his kingdom. I press my body harder into the floor. I wonder if I could sink through it. How much blood is there now? One day later and I'd've had my period when the boy took me to the movies and I'd've said, *No, no, you can't touch me there right now*, and none of this would have happened. I close my eyes and with the pain in my back I envision the priest lifting up his robes and masturbating over our supine bodies, his erection something like a textbook illustration because that's all I've seen. Instead he just sits there until we're shrouded in darkness and Lee Min comes back in. It smells like fresh bread.

"Get dressed," she says. "Eat."

And then, "Claudia, you may come with me."

I panic but I see she has a towel and a clean, tightly folded pair of underwear. I think of the pair squandered on the movie theater floor to the boy who wasn't even any good. I think: This is my chance.

"I'll save you some bread," Iris says and that's when I look past the towel and panties and see Lee Min's tray, and I realize the only food we'll be getting today is plain bread, and the vinegar seeped between our thirsty lips.

Lee Min doesn't talk in the bathroom, but she also doesn't leave me alone. She faces me, clutching a candle, but stares straight ahead in that way that makes you feel like someone's looking over the top of your head, past you, to something else, something better. I don't know if it's politeness, but it's easy, always, to assume there's something else, something better than me.

I dry up, clean up, put the new underwear on, pull on my stained dress, and right as I'm wondering if they'll ask for this pair back someday—or if they'll do some sort of panty accounting, and I'm picturing them coming to my house, tugging open my dresser drawer, picturing the way it tilts precariously down if you pull it out too far and how they won't know that because they're not used to it, and the carefully folded panties in the drawer will slide forward and it won't look as tidy and I wonder if that will affect their judgment—right then I hear the priest's voice, loud, saying something like "Are you sure?" and I hear Violet's voice, frantic, saying something like "I'd never lie to you" and I wonder if her perky breasts are still bare, and then my heart breaks and I feel my stomach jump up to the ceiling because I hear Iris, clearly but a little choked, saying, "No, no. I swear. I do not know anything. I do not know. God as my witness."

"She's lying. It's either her," Violet pauses. I realize I'm frozen in place and when I look at Lee Min she's also frozen. Stunned.

I wonder how much she has figured out and how much is just her reaction to conflict. I wonder if she'll get a Thank You for this part, the part with the bloodied, naked girl in the bathroom. "It's either Iris or it's Claudia."

"Oh god," I hear Iris say and the saddest part of it is that I know this is a genuine plea. Iris fully believes in the judgment of God. She believes in this church, she believes in this liturgy, these rituals, in a way that puts me to shame. Iris doesn't deserve the likes of me. Iris should have picked someone better to be like a sister.

Lee Min is technically between me and the bathroom door but I think I can make a run for it. She doesn't move when I lunge for the door. She doesn't move when I swerve around her. She's still, stock-still, and she's probably just letting me go to avoid trouble, or to avoid implicating herself, or probably just to avoid touching the period blood. I'm out of the bathroom and in the hallway adjacent to the church. The sanctuary is right there. The door to outside is so close. The glow of the municipal streetlights shoves its way through the crack at the bottom of the door.

"Claudia," the priest says from behind me. "Claudia."

I step forward, away from him, toward the door.

"You wear your guilt like a garment," he says.

I keep moving.

"Iris will suffer for this," he says, slowly.

I stop.

When I eventually turn around, the priest could easily have smoke coming out of his eyes, he's so mad. Mad like angry, mad like fire, mad like a madman. This place is run by a fucking madman, I finally let myself think. *This place is run by a fucking madman*, I might have said out loud.

Iris is sobbing. She's a mess. She shakes her head at me, and I stare at her because it's easier than looking at the madman.

"No," she's saying, "no, no, no, no."

"Iris," I say.

The priest steps back and I know he's not giving up. He's taking stock. He's too smart for us. Iris looks at him, and it's like a cartoon, the way she changes from frantic to calm in a split second.

"You should go," she says. She glances to the priest and to all the other girls back in their dresses, standing with their dainty arms folded across their dainty stomachs or clutching the girl next to them, and then she looks me dead in the eyes. "Leave us alone."

"Iris," I say.

"You don't belong here," she says.

I take a step back. And I know with great certainty, the kind of certainty all of us hold for the judgment of God, that Iris will be there for me, on the outside. Iris will be waiting for me. I am not losing Iris. I am gaining Iris. Iris will be mine in a real way, not the way that drives nails into our palms and sponges vinegar onto our lips.

I laugh. There's still period blood everywhere. Now I'm the mad one; I'm the one on fire. I wish I could think of something profound to say, something cutting, something mean, but I just want to run away. I move backward, sort of running, sort of stumbling, looking over my shoulder, and it's like that scene in the horror movie, the one when the boy put his hand between my legs and left my unders cast aside on a grimy theater floor. The characters see the dogs, the carnage, and retreat, manic, insane, scared out of their fucking minds, half wanting to get away from the dogs and half wondering if what got the dogs is still out there and maybe they're running toward it.

In my white dress and my holy underwear, I run.

LESLEY NNEKA ARIMAH was born in the UK and grew up in Nigeria and wherever else her father was stationed for work. Her stories have been honored with a National Magazine Award, a Commonwealth Short Story Prize, and an O. Henry Prize. Her work has appeared in the *New Yorker*, *Harper's Magazine*, and *Granta*, and she has received support from the Elizabeth George Foundation, United States Artists, and MacDowell. She was selected for the National Book Foundation's 5 Under 35 program, and her debut collection, *What It Means When a Man Falls from the Sky*, won the 2017 Kirkus Prize and the 2018 New York Public Library Young Lions Fiction Award, and was selected for the *PBS News Hour–New York Times* Now Read This Book Club, among other honors. She lives in Minneapolis and is working on a novel about you.

T. C. BOYLE is the author of thirty-one books of fiction, including, most recently, the novel *Blue Skies*. "The Apartment" was his seventh story for *McSweeney's Quarterly*, and it was included in his 2022 story collection, *I Walk Between the Raindrops*, along with stories from the *New Yorker* and *Esquire*.

ADRIENNE CELT is the author of the novels *End of the World House*, *Invitation to a Bonfire*, and *The Daughters*, which won the 2015 PEN Southwest Book Award for Fiction and was named a Best Book of the Year by NPR, as well as a collection of comics, *Apocalypse How?: An Existential Bestiary*. Her writing has been recognized by an O. Henry Prize, the Glenna Luschei *Prairie Schooner* Award, and residencies at Jentel, Ragdale, and the Willapa Bay AiR. She's published fiction in *Esquire*, *Zyzzyva*, *Ecotone*, the *Kenyon Review*, *Prairie Schooner*, and *Electric Literature*, among other places, and her comics and essays can be found in *Catapult*, *Vol. 1*

Brooklyn, the *Rumpus*, the *Tin House Open Bar*, the *Millions*, and elsewhere. She lives in Tucson, Arizona.

LYDIA DAVIS is the author of two essay collections, one novel, and seven story collections, including *Varieties of Disturbance*, a finalist for the 2007 National Book Award. Davis is also the acclaimed translator of *Swann's Way* and *Madame Bovary*, both awarded the French-American Foundation Translation Prize, and of many other works of literature. She has been named both a Chevalier and an Officier of the Order of Arts and Letters by the French government, and in 2020 she received the PEN/Malamud Award for Excellence in the Short Story.

JULIA DIXON EVANS is the author of the novel *How to Set Yourself on Fire*, published in 2018. Her short fiction and essays have been in *Hobart*, *Paper Darts*, *Barrelhouse*, *Literary Hub*, *Pithead Chapel*, and elsewhere, and she was a winner of the 2019 National Magazine Award for Fiction. As a journalist, she writes the culture report for *Voice of San Diego*, and has contributed to *San Diego CityBeat*, the *A/V Club*, and other places. She is the founder and host of *Last Exit*, an online journal, workshop, and reading series dedicated to building literary community in San Diego.

ADACHIOMA EZEANO is a 2021 O. Henry Prize recipient. She is an alumna of the Purple Hibiscus Writing Workshop. Her work has appeared in *Guernica*, *FlashBack Fiction*, *Best Small Fictions 2020*, and *The Best Short Stories 2021*.

EMMA HOOPER is the author of the internationally bestselling and award-winning novels *Etta and Otto and Russell and James*, *Our*

Homesick Songs, and *We Should Not Be Afraid of the Sky*. She's also a musician who writes songs about dinosaurs, and a Canadian who once broke her toe in an overzealous cross-country skiing incident.

ESKOR DAVID JOHNSON is a writer from Trinidad and Tobago and the United States. His writing has appeared in *BOMB* and appears at length in his debut novel, *Pay As You Go*. He lives in New York City.

MIMI LOK is the author of *Last of Her Name*, winner of the PEN/ Robert W. Bingham Prize for Debut Short Story Collection, a Smithsonian American Ingenuity Award, and a California Book Award Silver Medal, and a finalist for the Northern California Book Award and a Community of Literary Magazines and Presses Firecracker Award. Her work can be found in the *Believer*, *Electric Literature*, *Lucky Peach*, *Hyphen*, the *South China Morning Post*, and elsewhere. She's the recipient of fellowships from MacDowell, the Hambidge Center, Plympton, and the Anderson Center

MEGAN MCDOWELL is the recipient of a 2020 Award in Literature from the American Academy of Arts and Letters, among other awards, and her books have been short- and long-listed four times for the International Booker Prize. Her translations have appeared in publications including the *New Yorker*, the *Paris Review*, the *Atlantic*, and *Harper's Magazine*. She lives in Santiago, Chile.

KEVIN MOFFETT is the author of two story collections, a narrative app for mobile devices, and a pair of scripted podcasts, most recently *The Final Chapters of Richard Brown Winters* from Gimlet Media.

MARIA REVA writes fiction and opera libretti. She is the author of *Good Citizens Need Not Fear*, set in an apartment block in Ukraine. In November 2022, she was included on the Russian Ministry of Foreign Affairs' list of sanctioned Canadian citizens who are forbidden from entering Russia. Maria's writing has appeared in the *Atlantic*, the *Wall Street Journal*, *Granta*, *The Best American Short Stories*, and elsewhere. She won a National Magazine Award in 2019 and was a finalist for the 2020 Atwood Gibson Writers' Trust Fiction Prize.

SAMANTA SCHWEBLIN is the author of the novel *Fever Dream*, which was a finalist for the International Booker Prize. Her second novel, *Little Eyes*, and the story collection *Mouthful of Birds* were long-listed for the same prize. Her books have been translated into thirty-five languages, and her work has appeared in English in the *New Yorker* and *Harper's Magazine*. Originally from Buenos Aires, she lives in Berlin.

BRYAN WASHINGTON is the author of *Family Meal*, *Memorial*, and *Lot*. He is an American writer from Houston.

C PAM ZHANG is the author of *How Much of These Hills Is Gold* and *Land of Milk and Honey.* She is the winner of the Academy of Arts and Letters Rosenthal Family Foundation Award and the Asian/Pacific American Award for Literature, a Booker Prize nominee, and a finalist for numerous other prizes, including the PEN/Hemingway Award and the Center for Fiction First Novel Prize. Zhang's writing appears in *The Best American Short Stories*, the *Cut*, the *New Yorker*, and the *New York Times*. She is a National Book Foundation 5 Under 35 program honoree and a current New York Public Library Cullman Center Fellow.

ALSO AVAILABLE *from* McSWEENEY'S

ART AND COMICS

BOOKS FOR CHILDREN

HUMOR

COLLINS LIBRARY

ALL THIS AND MORE AT

STORE.MCSWEENEYS.NET

Founded in 1998, McSweeney's is an independent publisher based in San Francisco. McSweeney's exists to champion ambitious and inspired new writing, and to challenge conventional expectations about where it's found, how it looks, and who participates. We're here to discover things we love, help them find their most resplendent form, and place them into the hands of curious, engaged readers.

THERE ARE SEVERAL WAYS TO SUPPORT MCSWEENEY'S:

Support Us on Patreon
visit *www.patreon.com/mcsweeneysinternettendency*

Subscribe & Shop
visit *store.mcsweeneys.net*

Volunteer & Intern
email *custservice@mcsweeneys.net*

Sponsor Books & *Quarterlies*
email *amanda@mcsweeneys.net*

To learn more, please visit *www.mcsweeneys.net/donate* or contact Executive Director Amanda Uhle at *amanda@mcsweeneys.net* or 415.642.5609.

McSweeney's Literary Arts Fund is a nonprofit organization as described by IRS 501(c)(3). Your support is invaluable to us.